KANT, CRITIQUE AND POLITICS

'*Kant, Critique and Politics* not only shows the abiding relevance of Kant's critical philosophy for contemporary debates in social and political theory, international relations and feminist theory; it also challenges the view that his is a "foundationalist" argument. It makes an illuminating contribution to contemporary debate as well as to the understanding of the critical project.'

Howard Caygill, author of *A Kant Dictionary*,
University of East Anglia

'Hutchings lucidly reveals the paradoxes which Kant's critical philosophy was unable to resolve in its endeavour both to limit and to authorize reason. She then goes on, through a series of original and perceptive readings of recent thinkers – Habermas, Arendt, Foucault, Lyotard, international relations and feminist theorists – to show how these Kantian aporias reassert themselves in modernity's tireless attempts at avoiding either relativism or foundationalism.'

Diana Coole, Queen Mary and Westfield College,
University of London

Kimberly Hutchings re-evaluates Kant's work in terms of its significance for the writings of Habermas, Arendt, Lyotard and Foucault. This, however, is not an exercise in the history of ideas; through her clear presentation of Kant's critical philosophy, Hutchings reveals that the critique is in fact a complex and highly ambiguous *political* practice.

Hutchings's reading traces a common Kantian heritage in theories thought to represent the different poles of the modernist–postmodernist debate and sheds new light on the Kantian influence in political philosophy, international relations theory and feminist theory.

Kimberly Hutchings is Lecturer in Political Theory at the University of Edinburgh.

KANT, CRITIQUE AND POLITICS

Kimberly Hutchings

London and New York

First published 1996
by Routledge
11 New Fetter Lane, London EC4P 4EE

Simultaneously published in the USA and Canada
by Routledge
29 West 35th Street, New York, NY 10001

Typeset in Baskerville by
Pure Tech India Ltd.
Printed and bound in Great Britain by
TJ Press (Padstow) Ltd, Padstow Cornwall

British Library Cataloguing in Publication Data
A catalogue record for this book is available from the British Library.

Library of Congress Cataloguing in Publication Data
A catalogue record for this book has been requested.

ISBN 0-415-10507-2 (hbk)
ISBN 0-415-10508-0 (pbk)

This book is dedicated to
Pat and John Hutchings
with all my love and thanks

CONTENTS

PREFACE AND
ACKNOWLEDGEMENTS

Anyone writing a new book on Kant, let alone Habermas, Arendt, Foucault and Lyotard, needs to justify the production of yet another mass of words on such a well researched subject. In traditional Kantian fashion, I find myself striving for some authoritative ground on which to vindicate my efforts. However, this striving, like Kant's striving to authorize critique, is ultimately unsuccessful. All I can do is to offer certain reasons for why I have written this book and for why you may want to read it.

Foremost among my reasons for writing this book is a fascination with the way in which Kant continues to haunt the options of contemporary social and political theory, even when these options seem antithetical to one another. In investigating Kantian critique as a paradoxical political practice rather than as failed or successful metaphysics, I have tried to establish why the legacy of Kant seems so inescapable. A second reason for writing this particular book is to put the recent revival of interest in Kant's political thought, particularly his thought on judgement, into context. Again, I have tried to demonstrate that the importance of Kant's political thought lies not in its claims about the state or history, but in the claims it makes for the political significance of his philosophical practice. A third reason for writing the book is to illuminate the thought of Habermas, Arendt, Foucault and Lyotard by systematically examining their use of Kant. The importance of Kant for all four thinkers is well attested by both the thinkers themselves and existing secondary literature. What I have attempted to do is to explain how such very different theorists are able to share a common philosophical legacy. My fourth reason for writing the book is that the implications of Kant's critical practice are very much apparent in attempts to formulate critical political theory in the contexts of international

relations and feminist theory. By situating these debates in relation
to the Kantian inheritance, I try to elucidate both the positive and
negative implications of the paradoxical politics of critique for
those debates. Finally, I wrote this book because the practice of
Kantian critique has at its centre the radical impossibility of tran-
scending the limits on which critique is premised, and I find this
radical impossibility still at work in the thought of Habermas,
Arendt, Foucault and Lyotard. I cannot answer the question as to
why, when Kant has been dead nearly two hundred years, his work
still receives an echo in today's philosophical imagination, but I
can at least raise that question. If that is all that this book succeeds
in doing, then that is all the vindication which I need for having
written it.

It is impossible to render all the necessary thanks to people who
have helped and supported me personally and academically over the
time during which this book was conceived and written. I would,
however, like to single out certain people to whom I owe a
particularly important debt. I would like to thank Gillian Rose both
for the philosophical inspiration she provides and the support and
encouragement she has given me over the years. Many thanks are
due to Andrew Thacker for reading and commenting on the whole
of the text, and also to Howard Caygill and Moya Lloyd for looking
at certain sections. The following people have helped and encouraged me in my philosophical work: thanks to Keith Ansell-Pearson,
Alan Apperley, Christine Battersby, Jay Bernstein and Kevin Magill.
Thanks are due to the University of Wolverhampton for granting me
a partial sabbatical in 1993 to work on the book. I also owe thanks
to Steve Gill for introducing me to the world of international
relations theory, and to the members of the BISA seminar on international relations theory, the 'Gender and International Relations'
group and the Society for Women in Philosophy, who have provided
the forum for discussion of some of the material that went into this
book. Earlier versions of material for Chapters 7 and 8 have been
published as articles and I would like to thank the readers and
editors involved for their help; Richard Little, Kathleen Lennon
and Margaret Whitford (Hutchings, 1992; 1994). Needless to say,
any errors remaining in these chapters or any other section of the
text remain solely my responsibility. For their friendship, particularly
during the difficult months in which this book was finished, I
would like to thank Marci Green, Bernadette Joslin, Mary Joyce,
Margaret Ponsonby, Susan Pryse-Davies and Jean Scott. For his

proofreading services on the manuscript and his friendship, I would like to thank Mike Cunningham. Last, but by no means least, I would like to repeat my thanks to my parents, to whom this book is dedicated.

INTRODUCTION

The argument of this book is that Kantian critique constitutes a significant resource in the formation of the political thought of Habermas, Arendt, Foucault and Lyotard, and therefore in contemporary social and political theory which makes use of these thinkers. Central to this argument is the claim that Kantian critique is a rather different kind of resource for political thinking than is assumed by those who would place Kant beneath the banner of liberalism.[1] According to this tradition of interpretation, Kant offers certain resolutions to the problems of both the authority of the philosopher's judgement of the state and the nature of the just state. According to the reading of Kant I will be giving, the importance of Kant's critique for contemporary attempts to theorize politics lies precisely in the ways in which Kant fails to resolve these problems. Kantian critique is premised on both the limitation of reason and the assumption of the capacity of reason to transcend that limitation in the process of critique. From the beginning, therefore, critique is an impossible task. The philosophical richness of critique lies in the ways in which it is an exploration of its own impossibility. In an effort to deduce the legitimate scope of theoretical reason, practical reason and judgement, the Kantian critic takes on the roles of legislator, warmonger and judge, but each time the authority of critique appears to be grounded it is always undermined. The alternatives of dogmatism and speculation which critique was intended to transcend continually threaten the work of the critic.

The legacy of Kantianism that I find in the work of Habermas, Arendt, Foucault and Lyotard is the legacy of a critique which perpetually struggles and perpetually fails, not the legacy of a confident authority. This is not to say, however, that all of the thinkers interpret or use Kant in the same way. In Habermas's case,

1

he appropriates the ambition of Kant's critique as well as a Kantian conception of the divisions and limitations of reason, with the result that he (Habermas) repeats the different ways in which Kant attempted to ground critique. The resources of Habermas's critical theory mirror those of Kantian critique almost exactly, both in terms of the roles that the critic plays and the kinds of verdicts on political life that he delivers. Arendt, Foucault and Lyotard are more selective than Habermas in the uses they make of Kantian critique. All three thinkers reject the ambition of critique to give an authoritative grounding for judgement. However, all three thinkers also find an alternative inspiration for their philosophical practice in Kant's concept of reflective judgement. In Arendt's case her use of Kant leads to an account of her political philosophy as poised between authority over and irrelevance to the realm of political action. In Foucault's case his use of Kant sustains the idea of 'critical ontology' as a practice shifting between historical location and an orientation towards self-legislation. In Lyotard's case his use of Kant underwrites his conception of philosophy as travelling between the islands of the 'archipelago' of 'regimes of phrases' or 'genres of discourse'.

The four thinkers, although they are all critics of Kant, are not equally self-conscious when it comes to the implications of using Kant in their theorizing. Both Habermas and Arendt use Kant as an authority whose work will help to establish the possibility of the kind of critical theory or political philosophy they are trying to construct. The result of this is that the tensions inherent in Kant's critical thought are reflected in Habermas's and Arendt's work without being problematized. This means that Habermas's and Arendt's critical practice seems to veer between, rather than transcend, its precritical alternatives. For Habermas these are the alternatives of the positing of unsustainable transcendental grounds for judgement on the one hand, and the 'standardlessness of mere historical understanding' on the other. For Arendt these are the alternatives of legislating for political action in advance on the one hand, and the abandonment of judgement on the other. Both Foucault and Lyotard are more self-consciously aware of the fragility of each of Kant's attempts to ground the authority of judgement. In Foucault's case, however, this awareness helps towards an account of critique as work on the limits of existence which persistently refuses, even as it allows, the orientation of judgement towards the idea of self-legislation. In Lyotard's case this awareness paradoxically takes him closer to Habermas and Arendt than to Foucault. Lyotard identifies the radical impossibility of grounding judgement with the sovereign legislation of pure practical reason, and therefore ends up following the path of Arendt and Habermas in a constant oscillation between the possibility and impossibility of critique.

In tracing the importance of Kant's work in the theorizing of Habermas, Arendt, Foucault and Lyotard I am not claiming that all these thinkers are saying the same thing. However, in identifying each of these critics as working with a conception of critique which is Kantian, I am claiming that their critical work shares certain characteristics. I have called these characteristics the 'politics of critique'. As I will demonstrate in my analysis of the work of Kant and the later theorists, the politics of critique has two dimensions, both of which have consequences for contemporary social and political theory which utilizes that work. The first dimension is what might be termed an in-built tendency to failure or collapse; the second dimension involves the ways in which critique resists collapse and remains critical. The first dimension is exemplified in the fact that the critical discourses I consider, from Kant's onwards, can all be read as lapsing back into precritical alternatives. In the work of Kant, Habermas and Arendt, in particular, critique seems in constant danger of reverting either to an authoritarian dogmatism, in which the philosopher holds the key to judgement, or to a radical scepticism in which judgement becomes impossible. However, this tendency is also apparent in the ways in which Foucault and Lyotard, in finding a way between philosophical authoritarianism and pure description, at times seem to fall back into one or other of those moments in their account of their own practice. It is my argument in this book that to read any of these thinkers as instantiating one or other of their precritical alternatives (these alternatives are not the same in each case, although they all relate back to the dogmatism/scepticism choice which Kant refuses) is to fail to do justice to the complexity of the politics of critique. Even in the work of Kant and Habermas, who are most easily read as authoritative, legislative critics, the dynamics of critique are always as much about putting the authority of critique into question as about grounding and exercising that authority.

The tendency of critique to be haunted by its precritical alternatives encourages a reading of critical thinkers as authorities or as failures. In the last two chapters of this book, I will be arguing that it is the latter kind of reading that dominates attempts to account for critical theory in the contexts of international relations theory and feminist theory. The result of this is that the battles of reason to which Kantian critique was designed to bring the 'peace of a legal order' are fought again. This time, however, 'modernist' critics are set against 'postmodernist' critics; with the former charging the latter with the abandonment of epistemological and normative standards of judgement (scepticism), and the latter charging the former with setting up an unsustainable, colonizing authority (dogmatism).[2] This kind of polarization of critique results in accounts of critical practice in which critique becomes identified with one or other of the roles the critic plays, and a neglect of the tensions within the work of each critic. A 'legislative' mode of critique, primarily associated with the work of Habermas and sometimes Arendt, is set against a 'strategic' or 'aesthetic' mode of critique, associated with the work of Foucault, Lyotard and also sometimes Arendt;[3] whereas I would argue that what is characteristic of the practice of critique in the case of all of the thinkers is the way in which the critics move between the resources of legislation, strategy and judgement.

The idea of critical practice as moving between different resolutions to the question of what being critical means brings me to the second dimension which, I argue, characterizes the politics of critique. That is, the ways in which critique is able to be sustained without a lapse back into the precritical alternatives it is designed to avoid. It is difficult to capture the nature of this dimension, since it amounts to a kind of constant oscillation between the pursuit of an authoritative ground for judgement and the recognition of the impossibility of that pursuit. This paradox is at the heart of a critique which is positioned, as Kant's critique is positioned, on the border between nature and freedom. It is also at the heart, I would argue, of any critique which seeks to work 'in-between', whether this is in between *system* and *lifeworld*, *vita activa* and *vita contemplativa*, *freedom* and *power* or *genres of discourse*. In the examination of the thinkers which is the principal focus of this text, I am not concerned with arguing for or against them but with trying to grasp the implications of their theoretical practice. In my conclusion I will argue that whereas the dangers of critique are apparent in the tendency to lapse back into precritical alternatives, the positive possibilities of critique are apparent in the ways in which it constantly both asserts and subverts it own authority. However, whether critique is read negatively or positively it always returns the critic to the same difficulty, which is that the practice of critique cannot be accounted for within the resources of critique. Critics working with the Kantian conception of critique are always attempting the impossible.

The above summary of the argument of this book leaves two questions unanswered. First, why do I refer to the practice of critique as *political*? Second, what has all this to do with the substantive concerns of political theory in terms of understanding, judging and changing political actualities? The choice of the word *politics* to describe the practice of critique follows the vocabulary employed by Kant, Habermas, Arendt, Foucault and Lyotard themselves. Within Kant's work the nature and purpose of critique is described in the essentially political terms of legislation, government and judgement or, alternatively, of warmongering and peacemaking. The other critical thinkers considered in this text also make analogies between their theoretical practice and particular kinds of political activity, from legislating to strategy and judgement. However, the political significance of critique is not just a matter of the metaphors used to describe it. For each of the principal thinkers considered in this book, their philosophical practice has important political implications. In Kant's case, the philosopher has a capacity to judge which is unavailable to kings and which ought to guide the decisions of kings. In Habermas's case, the philosopher is able to distinguish between the logic and dynamics of historical development and thus both recognize and preserve the possibility of progress in history. In Arendt's case, the philosopher becomes identified with the archetypal political judge. In Foucault's case, the practice of genuine philosophy, which he terms 'critical ontology', is an example of the work of freedom in a way analogous to radical political movements. In Lyotard's case, philosophy is identified with both art and politics as a genre of discourse which has no rules given in advance. In all of these cases, therefore, the ways of theorizing involved are centrally bound up with both the ways in which politics is conceived and the ways in which actual political relations will be understood and judged.[4] My choice of the word *politics* to describe the dynamics of the practice of critical theorizing therefore reflects both the political status each theorist accords to his or her own practice and its substantive implications, even though my main concern is not the substantive political claims of any of the theorists investigated here.

The argument of this book is inevitably partial in several significant ways. This is evident, in particular, in both the selection of post-Kantian theorists for discussion and in the readings of the theorists that are discussed. In tracing the influence of Kant's thought on current theory I have deliberately neglected the important role played by Kant in the revival of liberal political theory since the work of Rawls. The reason for this is that I am interested in the Kantian legacy within social and political theory that identifies itself as explicitly critical of the liberal mainstream in both theory and practice. Rawls draws upon Kant's moral philosophy to help to underpin a particular vision of the just society. In doing this, Rawls neither acknowledges. the radical ambiguities of Kant's attempts to legitimate the claims of reason in theory and practice, nor seriously challenges the presumptions of liberal social democracy; in this book I am concentrating on theorists who aim to do both of these things. Given this, however, it is obvious that my selection of thinkers is not only partial because it omits consideration of Kantian liberalism.[5] I have also omitted consideration of a variety of non-liberal thinkers who have engaged with the politics of Kantian theory from Hegel and Marx to Marcuse, Adorno and Merleau-Ponty amongst others. My choice of theorists is not dictated by the idea that Habermas, Arendt, Foucault or Lyotard are more indebted to Kant than any others. It is, however, influenced by the ways in which the names of these thinkers recur in debates about the possibility of critical theory in the contexts of international relations and feminist theory; and, in particular, by the ways in which, within these contexts, a theoretical choice between 'legislative' critique (Habermas, Arendt) and 'strategic' or 'aesthetic' critique (Arendt, Foucault, Lyotard) surfaces repeatedly.

My exposition and analysis of the work of Habermas, Arendt, Foucault and Lyotard is mediated through the reading of Kant presented in the first two chapters and highlights the significance of Kant at the expense of other formative influences on the work of these thinkers. This lays my own argument open to the charge of circularity and also to the charge of fetishizing the philosophical tradition in assuming the decisive importance of the philosophical origins of critique. My response to the first charge would be that it is the case that my argument is circular in the sense that in selecting a standpoint (Kant's critique), in the light of which to interrogate later critical theorists, I am inevitably influencing the nature of my conclusions in advance. However, I would argue that any attempt to examine the practice of critique in contemporary critical theory is going to exhibit a similar circularity, given that no 'innocent' (in the sense of unmediated by preconceptions) interpretation of what critique means is possible. There are other ways of understanding critique than mine. The point of my particular tracing of critical practice back to Kant is not so much to prove the connection (which is amply acknowledged by all the theorists concerned anyway), but to gain insight into the kind of theoretical practice in which the critics are engaged.[6] The second charge seems to me to be more important than the first. All of the critical thinkers I consider, including Kant, are also political activists and campaigners, whose political views are formulated in response to the events of their time.[7] In focusing on the Kantian heritage at work in the thought of these critical thinkers, I appear to be endorsing an abstraction of critique from politics which is not true to the origins and aims of their thought. My answer to this charge is twofold. First, I would stress that my concern is with the ways in which these thinkers account for their critique philosophically, an account which does not preclude a historical or political accounting. Second, I would return to the points made above as to the political nature and significance of critique. The use of Kantian critique by these theorists is not unthinkingly determined by philosophical tradition, rather it reflects the deep link between philosophical and political conditions and problems.[8]

The eight chapters of this book are structured in three parts: the first part comprises the first two chapters, which focus on Kant; the second part encompasses Chapters 3 to 6 on the four critical theorists; and the third part, Chapters 7 and 8, is on international relations theory and feminist theory. The first two chapters examine Kant's critical philosophy in both his explicitly non-political and his political writings. Traditional readings of Kant have not focused on the political significance of his work. The three famous critical texts on theoretical reason, practical reason and judgement seem only tangentially concerned with politics. The explicitly political writings are to be found in late and comparatively obscure texts and they have not been accorded an important place in the canon of western political theory. However, in recent years this orthodoxy has been increasingly brought into question. The reissuing of an augmented edition of Hans Reiss's collection of Kant's political writings, in the Cambridge series of texts in the history of political thought in 1991, confirms the growth of interest in Kant's politics. There has been a flourishing of secondary literature on Kant as a political philosopher; and Rawls's use of Kant has paved the way for Kant's work to become one of the most important reference points in debates between liberals and communitarians. Moreover, there has been a revision of the assessment as to the importance of politics in the major critical works. Commentators such as O'Neill claim that the

Critique of Pure Reason is an essentially political text; and a growing number of theorists, including Arendt and Lyotard, argue that Kant's real political philosophy is to be found in the *Critique of Judgment*.[9] In the first chapter, my aim is to examine the nature of Kant's critical philosophy in general and to elucidate the politics of critique inherent within it. I argue that the politics of critique are essentially paradoxical and antinomic. Kant's attempts to establish the limits of reason's legislation in theory and practice are continually frustrated by the presumptions of critique; and the critic's judgement swings between the assumption of absolute authority and despair at its own incapacity. The concept of reflective judgement, which is introduced to mediate between the realms of the understanding and reason, seems to offer an alternative to judgement grounded in an incomprehensible law. However, I argue that the tensions between the necessity and impossibility of theoretical and moral judgement are repeated in the exposition of the aesthetic judgement of taste. In the second chapter it is argued that the politics of critique is reflected in Kant's theorization of politics. This is evident in the three aspects of Kant's political thought which I identify as a theory of right, a philosophy of history and a political philosophy of judgement. Each of these aspects of Kant's political thought needs the others to fulfil the requirement that the gap between empirical and transcendental worlds should be bridged; each in turn fails to fulfil these requirements. What emerges from the first two chapters is the conclusion that the implications of Kant's politics of critique and his critique of politics are not monolithic but plural, paradoxical and mutually undermining. The critic has the key to authoritative judgement on the one hand, and is the unwitting servant of providence on the other; political life is about the conscious fulfilment of the demands of practical reason through a principle of right within the state on the one hand, and a Hobbesian state of nature on the other.

In the middle section of the book, the way that the volatile legacy of the politics of critique is at work in the thought of Habermas, Arendt, Foucault and Lyotard will be examined.[10] All of these thinkers are, in different ways, critics both of their time and of the dominant philosophical traditions through which modern times have been comprehended and judged. All of these thinkers make use of Kant's critical thought in their attempts to account for and empower their own critique. All of these thinkers are also critical of Kant and either seek to improve on Kant (Habermas), or draw on only certain aspects of his critical thought (Arendt, Foucault, Lyotard). The focus of these chapters is primarily on the politics of the theory of the four thinkers and the way in which it continues to reflect Kantian paradoxes and antinomies. However, it will also be suggested that the kind of critique of contemporary social and political actualities inherent in the critical discourse of each thinker also returns us to the options of Kant's political philosophy. The critical theorists shift between a theoretical politics of constitutional legislation and one of strategy and judgement. Conceptions of the political shift between the juridical and the aesthetic and between the necessity and impossibility of progress.

The final section of the book pursues the Kantian legacy in the context of two specific areas of critical political theorizing. The argument here attempts to flesh out the conclusions of the earlier sections by demonstrating the politics at work in the debates through which the possibilities of critical theorizing are being constructed in international relations and feminist theory. I will be arguing that debates within these two areas of political theory demonstrate very clearly both the dangers and the positive possibilities of the Kantian legacy: dangers in the sense that the tendency to embrace one or other of the antinomic poles of critique is ever present – the wars of reason are always there to be fought again; positive possibilities in the sense that this polarization directs attention to the self-subverting nature of critique and the way it is premised on the unanswerability of its own questions. In my conclusion I reflect on how the politics of critique at work in these areas of critical political theory suggests both what needs to be avoided and what needs to characterize a critical practice that can sustain itself as critical. This in turn suggests what the implications of a critical political theory for the under-standing and judgement of political actualities might be. At the heart of these implications lies the radical impossibility of critique itself and of the political ideals with which it presents us.

1

PHILOSOPHY AS CRITIQUE

INTRODUCTION

The object of this book is to explore a series of attempts to articulate critical social and political theory and to understand the dangers and difficulties inherent in these attempts. Central to the argument of this book is the claim that the critical dimension of the work of Habermas's *critical theorist*, Arendt's *political judge*, Foucault's *specific intellectual* and Lyotard's *critical nightwatchman* is in each case shaped by an inheritance from the original philosophical critic, Kant. All of these thinkers explicitly draw on aspects of Kant's critical philosophy in their work. All of them also repudiate, ignore or denigrate other aspects of Kantian critique. It is as if Kant's critique offers a range of political possibilities from which a selection can be made by contemporary critics. This range of political possibilities is not confined to Kant's explicit pronouncements on politics but is also implicit in his overtly non-political work on theoretical reason, practical reason and judgement. In this chapter my aim is to offer a reading of Kant's critical philosophy focusing on the politics implicit in the practice of critique in the three major critical texts. In the following chapter the ways in which the implicit politics of critique cash out in the explicit critique of politics in Kant's writings on right and history will be examined. These two chapters are designed to clarify the nature of the resources of Kantian critique on which the later theorists are drawing.

It is obviously impossible to do full justice to Kant's principal critical writings in the course of a single chapter. What is offered in the first two sections of this chapter is the tracing of aspects of Kant's arguments in the *Critique of Pure Reason*, *Critique of Practical Reason*, and the *Critique of Judgment* which demonstrate the political logic of the critical philosophy. I will argue that this philosophy is characterized by a pattern in which the presuppositions of critique continually frustrate and complicate attempts both to deduce the legitimacy of cognitive, moral and aesthetic claims and to realize those claims within the world. The practice of critique thus comes to veer between the political options of rigid order or absolute anarchy, with the critical philosopher embracing in turn the roles of legislator and warmonger in a never-ending, but always unavailing, effort to achieve a peaceful resolution to the conflicts of reason. In the final part of this chapter, I go on to orient my own elucidation of critique in relation to two contemporary readings of the politics of Kantian critique in the work of Onora O'Neill and Howard Caygill respectively. In conclusion, following on from the discussion of O'Neill and Caygill, I suggest that Kant's conception of critique leaves us with a highly politicized philosophical practice which is both volatile and paradoxical. At the same time as opening up the questions of what we may know, what we ought to do and what we may hope for, the Kantian critic is also rendering those questions unanswerable. The practice of critique is not safe; it swings between the ideal and the real, between liberal and authoritarian moments, between limitation and legislation and between subversion and submission.

LIMITATION AND LEGISLATION

The critique of reason is Kant's response to the twin dangers which, he argues in the Prefaces to the first and second editions of the *Critique of Pure Reason*, confronted the metaphysics of his time. These are the dangers of unfounded dogmatism on the one hand and rampant scepticism on the other. According to Kant, the philosophy of his time offered two equally unacceptable alternatives. The rationalism of thinkers such as Leibniz and Wolff made speculative claims about knowledge which could not be substantiated. The empiricism of thinkers such as Hume seemed to undermine any claims to knowledge at all. Scandalously, the history of reason has brought the Queen of the Sciences into disrepute, and reason itself must therefore, as it were, bring itself into question (A: viii–ix).[1] This is something that has never been done before and the method and tools of critique are unfamiliar, taking the form of a tribunal of pure reason in which pure reason is both on trial and judging. Two things, however, are clear from the beginning of the *Critique of Pure Reason*: first, pure reason in human beings is limited and the process of critique will establish its boundaries; second, if metaphysics is to be put on the road to science, it must follow the model of mathematics and physics and dictate to nature rather than have nature dictate to it (B: xii–xiv). The critical project therefore combines moments of both limitation and legislation. In establishing what pure reason cannot accomplish, its legitimate possessions are identified and protected.

In the 'Introduction' to the *Critique of Pure Reason*, Kant separates the cognitive judgements of the understanding into two kinds: analytic and synthetic (A: 6; B: 10). Analytic judgements are those founded on the identity of subject and predicate, their explication yields no new knowledge. Synthetic judgements are founded on difference, the predicate is not already included within the subject, and therefore they yield knowledge. Kant explains the distinction using the example of a body. The claim that a body is extended, i.e. occupies space, is an analytic claim according to Kant, because it is part of the concept of bodies that they are entities in space. The claim that a body is heavy, in contrast, is a synthetic claim, since there is nothing in the concept of body that indicates specific weight. A priori knowledge is knowledge that is necessary and universal, entirely independent of experience. Kant claims that the model sciences of mathematics and physics are both distinguished by the possession of synthetic judgements a priori as principles, and argues that, if metaphysics is to be a science, it must also involve such principles. The critique of pure reason is launched as the quest to deduce the possibility of judgements of reason which combine the synthetic and the a priori (B: 19). In order to answer the question of the possiblity of synthetic judgements a priori, Kant differentiates three human faculties: intuition (the faculty of sense); under-standing (the faculty of concepts); and reason (the faculty of the unconditioned). These are examined in the 'Transcendental Aes-thetic', 'Transcendental Analytic' and 'Transcendental Dialectic' respectively.

The arguments of the transcendental aesthetic and analytic are well known and it is unnecessary to rehearse them in detail here.[2] However, there are some aspects of the argument that are crucial for a grasp of the nature of Kantian critique in general to which I would like to draw attention. One such aspect is the famous distinction between phenomena and noumena that emerges from the argument in the 'Transcendental Aesthetic'. Kant argues that intuition of objects of sense perception is only possible under the forms of space and time, the pure a priori forms of intuition. Appearances always obey the conditions of space and time and are not things-in-themselves (A: 41–49; B: 59–73). This argument supports the twin assumptions of critique, that reason is limited (in the sense that it cannot know things as they are in themselves), but that metaphysical science is still possible (in the sense that reason can become aware of the nature of its limits). In parallel with the distinction between appearances and things-in-themselves Kant draws a distinction between two kinds of cognition: finite cognition, which only knows things as appearances; and infinite, divine intellection, which knows things not just as they appear but as they are (B: 71–72). The nature of Kant's distinction between phenomena and noumena is never wholly clear; at times it seems that the idea of the thing-in-itself is a hypothetical limiting concept; at other points the thing-in-itself is referred to as if it were a concrete entity forever beyond our grasp. However, the importance of the phenomena/noumena distinction lies in the way in which it testifies to the dependence of critique on both limitation and transcendence. The thing-in-itself confirms both the power and the weakness of pure reason. Reason's power can be seen in the way in which appearance is regulated by the understanding. Reason's weakness can be seen in the way in which the thing-in-itself remains forever beyond the reach of cognition; we cannot know whether it exists or not.

The establishment of the two forms of intuition a priori gives Kant one of the two factors he requires for the solution of the general problem of transcendental philosophy; that is, an a priori predicate with which a concept may be combined without reference to actual experience. In addition to this, however, he needs to establish pure concepts of the understanding which apply to the objects in intuition synthetically a priori. These concepts have to be more than simply identified and tabulated, they have to be deduced, i.e. their *right* to apply to intuition and thus to become lawgivers of nature has to be established (A: 84–86; B: 116–118). These pure concepts of the understanding are termed 'categories'. Kant offers two different deductions of the categories in the first and second editions of the *Critique of Pure Reason*; they differ in significant respects, but their purpose is the same. In both of the deductions Kant is explicating the unifying and legislative force of the understanding in cognizing the phenomenal world. In the first deduction (A: 95–130) Kant begins by outlining three subjective sources involved in the foundation of possible experience: 'apprehension of representations in intuition'; 'reproduction of representations in imagination'; and 're-cognition of representations in concepts'. This third source, grounded in a pure productive synthesis of imagination, assumes a key import-ance as the necessary unity of apperception.

> Appearances in experience must stand under the conditions of the necessary unity of apperception, just as in mere intuition they must be subject to the formal conditions of space and time. Only thus can knowledge be possible at all.
>
> (A: 110)

The second deduction (B: 129–169) concentrates from the start on the unity of apperception, which is defined as a kind of originative unifying synthesis underlying all other unities (B: 131). The tran-scendental unity of apperception is the moment of the 'I think', not the self-knowledge of 'I' as phenomenon, but the original, unified, abstract being of the understanding (B: 155–156). A parallel is drawn between the role of space and time in intuition, and that of the unity of apperception in cognition. As with time and space, the work of the unity of apperception is said to be necessitated by the finite nature of human thought (B: 138–139). Thus the unity of appercep-tion is defined as the condition of the possibility of all coherent experience. At the completion of this second deduction, Kant has clarified the nature and ground of the second factor which makes synthetic judgement a priori possible. The transcendental unity of apperception is the form of the understanding in its relation to the original a priori forms of intuition, space and time; together they enable the synthetic a priori cognition of appearances. Moreover, each factor is powerless without the other (B: 147–148).

After the deduction of the categories Kant goes on to explain further the process of cognitive judgement and how the rules of the understanding are bound to experience through the schemata and the table of the principles of judgement, determinate and regulative (A: 130–292; B: 169–349). The table of the principles of judgement valid only in relation to possible experience is divided into the mathematical 'axioms of intuition' and 'anticipations of perception', and the dynamical 'analogies of experience' and 'postulates of empirical thought' (A: 161; B: 200). The mathematical principles involve the necessary determinations of pure and empirical intuition in terms of quantity and quality. The analogies of experience and postulates of empirical thought, which deal with the necessary connection of perceptions and with their modal status are, however, regulative as opposed to constitutive principles, which do not determine the object of experience, but merely assist in the experience of it (A: 179; B: 221–222).

Throughout the critical philosophy, critique has a dual task, both to deduce the legitimacy of the claims of reason and to apply those claims in the appropriate realm. In the context of theoretical reason, the deduction of the categories and the examination of the principles of judgement appears to complete the task of critique. Having concluded his survey of the principles of judgement, Kant claims that the 'land of truth' has been fully explored and the entitlements of pure reason have been fully established (A: 235–236; B: 294–295). The critique, however, does not come to an end with the confirmation of its realm of operation in the cognition of phenomena. Instead, reason continues to push beyond the ground of the principles of judgement through the dynamic of two of those sets of principles themselves, that is, the analogies of experience and postulates of empirical thought. The problem raised for reason by these principles is that they appear to imply concepts which are themselves unintelligible in relation to experience. For example, the second analogy of experience is the rule of causal succession. In the case of causal succession, the series of conditioned moments becomes caught in an infinite regression, which can only find its origin in the unconditioned, a concept without application to the realm of sensible intuition. It appears that there is a higher unity above and beyond that of the understanding and towards which the understanding is oriented.

> Just as the understanding unifies the manifold in the object by means of concepts, so reason unifies the manifold of concepts by means of ideas, positing a certain collective unity as the goal of the activities of the understanding, which otherwise are concerned solely with distributive unity.
>
> (A: 644; B: 672)

Just as the 'Transcendental Aesthetic' introduces the notion of the thing-in-itself, which is both necessary for the possibility of metaphysics and unknowable within it, so the 'Transcendental Dialectic' introduces ideas of reason which are either necessary for cognition or implied by it and yet are unknowable within it. In both cases reason's ambition is to know the grounds of its own legislation. However, in seeking to know this Kant demonstrates that reason tries to cross the boundary between finite and infinite and, as a consequence, falls into antinomy. Contradictory claims seem to be implied by the principles of judgement. Returning to the example of causal succession given above, equally good arguments can be given to support the idea of infinite regression lying behind each causal claim and to support the idea of a first cause as the originating point for every causal chain. The understanding is forced to be content with accepting the regulative necessity of the ideas of reason, whilst being wholly unable to establish their truth.

> Here the contention is not that its own assertions may not, perhaps, be false, but only that no one can assert the opposite with apodeictic certainty, or even, indeed, with a greater degree of likelihood. We do not here hold our possessions upon sufferance; for although our title to them may not be satisfactory, it is quite certain that no one can ever be in a position to prove the illegality of the title.
>
> (A: 740; B: 768)

Ideas of reason are concepts which transcend the possibility of experience themselves, whilst at the same time helping to make experience possible. Ideas provide the rules which are implicit in the process of cognition, but as they cannot be known they must always be treated hypothetically 'as if' they could be known. If ideas are treated as principles of judgement, the result is a series of sophistications and illusions which Kant discusses in the paralogisms and antinomies of reason (A: 341–567; B: 406–595). Ideas provide rules to regulate the understanding, but they also imply ideals or rational archetypes which are the goals towards which cognition is necessarily oriented, the ideals of God, freedom and immortality. These ideals do not themselves condition theoretical reason, but are nevertheless implied by it. Like the concept of the thing-in-itself, the ideals of reason mark the boundaries of the legislation of pure theoretical reason and therefore testify both to its power and to its limitation.

The *Critique of Pure Reason* ends with a section e led the 'Transcendental Doctrine of Method'. In this section Kant eviews, on the basis of the arguments of the previous three sectio ;, what reason can and cannot do, returning to the dilemmas of metaphysics with which he began. It is in this section of the text that Kant has most to say about what the critique of reason means, in contrast to either dogmatic or sceptical assertions of reason. In relation to theoretical reason, critique is claimed to involve a process of constant self-criticism and openness to debate (A: 738–739; B: 766–767); as well as a shift from a state of war in metaphysics to a legal order

(A: 751–752; B: 779–780). Kant explicitly compares the latter to the necessary move from a Hobbesian state of nature to a political state. Thus critique legitimates and encourages freedom of speech, while arguing that only certain speech is legitimate. Dogmatic and sceptical philosophers are speaking illegitimately of what cannot be known.

> The critique on the other hand, arriving at all its decisions in the light of fundamental principles of its own institution, the authority of which no one can question, secures to us the peace of a legal order, in which our disputes have to be conducted solely by the recognized methods of legal action. In the former state, the disputes are ended by a victory to which both sides lay claim, and which is generally followed by a temporary armistice, arranged by some mediating authority; in the latter, by a judicial sentence which, as it strikes at the very root of the conflicts, effectively secures an eternal peace.
>
> (A: 751–752; B: 779–780)

The argument of the *Critique of Pure Reason* begins and ends with the same 'judicial sentence', confining the rights of theoretical reason to the world of appearance and the cognition of phenomena. This sentence has some peculiar characteristics, however, in particular in its dependence on the use of limiting regulative ideas which suggest a world beyond the bounds of finite reason yet necessary for its legislative power. Critique is put forward not so much as providing a resolution for the disputes of reason, but as authoritatively establishing the mode within which such disputes may be conducted. However, the critical tribunal operates according to a paradoxical logic in which judgement is simultaneously absolutely legitimate and also impossible to legitimize. The eternal peace secured by the judicial sentence of the critical tribunal is neither restful nor secure. Rather it is a condition of perpetual striving in which reason continually overreaches itself even as it accepts its limitations. In the process of critique in the realm of theoretical cognition, reason combines within itself legislative, executive and judicial powers, but the internal politics of reason are neither those of a constitutional monarchy (republican in Kant's sense) nor of an absolute sovereign power. The domestic order of the realm of the understanding is both dependent on and threatened by what lies beyond its legislative boundaries. What is originally presented as the achievement of security and peace becomes increasingly destabilized as critique proceeds.

FROM THEORY TO PRACTICE AND HOPE

At the end of the *Critique of Pure Reason* Kant poses three questions to which critical philosophy must provide the answers: What can I know? What ought I to do? What can I hope for? (A: 805; B: 833). Although the critique of theoretical reason is clearly directed towards answering the first of these questions, the introduction of the ideas and ideals of reason as underlying and implied by the principles of judgement necessarily connects the answer to the first question with the answers to the latter two. The ideals of God, freedom and immortality are goals towards which theoretical reason is oriented. They are implied by the rules that regulate the principles of judgement in the realm of the understanding but they have no direct legislation within that theoretical realm. The true significance of these ideals, Kant argues, is not theoretical but practical. Practical in the sense that reason here is doing more than establishing what can be known about the world, it is seeking to influence the world directly.

> Laws of this latter type, pure practical laws, whose end is given through reason completely a priori, and which are prescribed to us not in an empirically conditioned but in an absolute manner, would be products of pure reason. Such are the moral laws; and these alone, therefore, belong to the practical employment of reason, and allow for a canon.
>
> (A: 800; B: 828)

In the shift to practical reason critique moves from the question of how cognitive synthetic judgements are possible a priori to the question of the possibility of the moral law. This means that critique is now operating in relation to a realm of reason which is beyond the reach of the understanding and therefore essentially unknowable. Kant responds to the question of the possibility of the moral law in the *Grounding for the Metaphysics of Morals* and in the *Critique of Practical Reason*. In the treatment of practical reason, critique echoes the distinction introduced in the realm of theoretical reason between divine intellection and limited human cognition. Kant argues that there are two principles of causality: the principle of transcendental freedom in which pure reason, in the shape of the moral law, is the motivating force; and the principle of natural causation. Human beings, owing to their possession of free will, may be motivated by either principle; they may act autonomously or heteronomously.

Because human will, unlike holy will, is open to sensuous influences, the moral law necessarily takes the form of an imperative, which strives to countermand such influences; this is termed a 'categorical' imperative. The critique of practical reason thus necessitates the deduction of the possibility of a categorical imperative.

> Thus the question as to how a categorical imperative is possible can be answered to the extent that there can be supplied the sole presupposition under which such an imperative is alone possible – namely, the idea of freedom. The necessity of this presupposition is discernible, and this much is sufficient for the practical use of reason, i.e., for being convinced of the validity of this imperative, and hence also of the moral law; but how this presupposition itself is possible can never be discerned by any human reason.
>
> (IV: 461; 60)

Owing to the limitation of human reason, critique is unable to ground the idea of transcendental freedom which makes moral legislation possible. Instead, the ideas of freedom and the moral law are argued to be mutually supporting and apodeictically certain. In the formulations of the categorical imperative discussed in the *Grounding for the Metaphysics of Morals* pure practical reason emerges as both the motivation for moral action and as the goal implicit in such action, the ideal of a kingdom of ends (IV: 143; 39–40). The *Critique of Pure Reason* involved not only the deduction of the legitimacy of the concepts of the understanding, but also the explanation of how those concepts could be bound to experience. Likewise, the question of how the categorical imperative is possible involves not only its transcendental justification in ideas of reason, it also involves the explanation of how those ideas of reason apply directly to the world of sensuous determination, the phenomenal world of experience. The application of the moral law to the phenomenal realm is accomplished via the processes of hypothetical universalization implicit in the first two formulations of the categorical imperative in the *Grounding for the Metaphysics of Morals*:

> Act only according to that maxim whereby you can at the same time will that it should become a universal law.

> Act as if the maxim of your action were to become through your will a universal law of nature.
>
> (IV: 421; 30)

In the *Critique of Pure Reason* it was clear that the ideas of reason had no constitutive application to experience. The possibility of moral judgement, however, is protected by the use of a *hypothetical* as opposed to an *actual* identification of noumenal and phenomenal realms. The actor must judge *as if* under the conditions of a supersensible nature, governed by practical reason, and then decide if the maxim of the action is universalizable and act accordingly (V: 63–71; 65–74). The uneasiness of the relation of human action to the moral law, whether as motivating force or the ideal goal of a kingdom of ends is well demonstrated in Kant's doctrine of virtue, which forms the second part of *The Metaphysics of Morals*. In this text Kant explores the consequences of the tension between moral obligation and sensuous being and tries to work out how the two can remain essentially unrelated and yet be related within the context of human ethical action. The two most important factors in this endeavour are the notions of 'conscience' and 'perpetual progress'. The former is, according to Kant, one of the natural moral dispositions within the judging subject which enable the moral law to gain a hearing (VI: 399; 200–201). In conscience, man is his own innate judge, the representative of the moral law, before whom his baser self may be arraigned. In this sense the moral law does exist in the sensuous realm as a sense of obligation and striving.

> It is man's duty to *strive* for this perfection, but not to *reach* it (in this life), and his compliance with this duty can, accordingly, consist only in continual progress.
>
> (VI: 446; 241)

As is clear from the quotation above, however, the moral law can never fully exist in the phenomenal realm other than as an obligation and a striving, a ground that cannot be understood, only obeyed, and an end that can never be reached. The critique of practical reason makes the division between real and ideal more emphatic than in the critique of theoretical reason. And yet, paradoxically, the tendency of theoretical reason to step beyond its limits, in the context of the critique of practical reason, becomes a demand that those limits must be overstepped and the gulf between nature and reason be bridged.

In the critique of theoretical reason the power of reason to regulate the understanding problematized the status of the laws governing experience and knowledge. Ruling the island of truth was dependent on navigating the surrounding speculative seas, yet that navigation was itself dependent on the sovereign security of the island of truth. The problem of how reason can know what it cannot know was resolved by reference to distinctions between noumenal and phenomenal worlds and constitutive as opposed to regulative rules. Nevertheless the legislation, government and judgement of reason that follows from critique is full of tension and liable to failure. Critique fulfils a dual role, both of tracing the boundaries of the island of truth and of policing reason's tendency to mistake the extent of its territory. However, when it comes to the critique of practical reason, the role of critique is less to police the limits of reason's realm than to explain how those limits may be transcended so that reason may directly constitute the world. The ideas and ideals of reason that both underlie and orient theoretical understanding acquire a foundational primacy in the form of the moral law. Unfortunately the power of practical reason runs up against the presupposition of critique that human beings are inherently limited, neither capable of knowledge of things in themselves nor of a purely good will. Therefore the critique of practical reason becomes an endless quest to overcome the gulf between human and divine on which it is itself premised. Nature and freedom are divided yet the categorical imperative demands the bridging of this divide. In order to bring this resolution about, critique has recourse once more to the resource of the *as-if* identification of real and ideal. But whereas in the critique of theoretical reason the invocation of hypothesis destabilizes the aims of the critic, in the critique of practical reason it simply confirms the impossibility of the critic's task. The greater power of practical reason is commensurate with its greater failure; it is at once an absolute authority and an empty one.

In the *Critique of Judgment* Kant explicitly addresses problems raised by his exploration of the realms of the understanding and reason in the first two critiques. He does this by focusing on the faculty of judgement as a faculty with its own a priori principles to be deduced complementary to the categories of the understanding and the idea of transcendental freedom or the moral law. Judgement in both of the first two critiques is constituted as the problem for which the transcendental critic seeks a solution. However, neither the first nor the second critique resolves the problem of how either cognitive or moral judgements are possible without raising a host of further questions and invoking a series of distinctions and divisions which appear to disable judgement even as the conditions of its possibility are laid bare. The *Critique of Judgment* therefore is introduced as a mediation between the powers of reason and the domains of theory and practice which they legislate and govern.

And yet the family of our higher cognitive powers also includes a mediating link between understanding and reason. This is *judgment*, about which we have cause to suppose, by analogy, that it too may contain a priori, if not legislation of its own, then at least a principle of its own, perhaps a merely subjective one, by which to search for laws. Even though such a principle would lack a realm of objects as its own domain, it might still have some territory; and this territory might be of such a character that none but this very principle might hold in it.

(V: 177; 16)

Kant distinguishes between two kinds of judgement, determinate and reflective. The former involves the subsumption of particular instances under a general rule. The latter involves judgement of a particular in which the rule is not already given and must be sought. According to Kant, examination of determinate judgement will not yield the principle peculiar to the faculty of judgement, since in such cases judgement is directly dependent on the understanding and the power of theoretical reason. In the case of reflective judgement, however, judgement does not rely on anything outside itself to provide a principle of judgement but, as it were, legislates for itself. It is therefore the critique of reflective judgement with which the two parts of the *Critique of Judgment* are concerned. The first part deals with a critique of aesthetic judgement, the second with a critique of teleological judgement. The latter critique investigates the imputation of objective ends to natural processes as an aid in the understanding of nature. As such, according to Kant's introduction to both critiques, it is a branch of the critique of theoretical reason and is not in itself a special power of judgement without reference to concepts in the sense in which Kant claims aesthetic judgement is.[3] It is therefore the critique of aesthetic judgement through which Kant aims to elucidate the principle peculiar to the faculty of judgement as such. In the *Critique of Pure Reason* the elucidation of the conditions of theoretical judgement depends on the answer to the question of how synthetic judgements are possible a priori. In the critique of aesthetic judgement the principle of the faculty of judgement as such can be located through answering the question of how aesthetic judgements of taste are possible a priori. Only in the case of such judgements does the feeling of pleasure and

23

displeasure operate independently of theoretical and practical interest (V: 196–197; 37).

In his critique of aesthetic judgement, Kant examines two kinds of judgement, judgements of the beautiful and of the sublime. He begins with the estimation of beauty in an object. The sole determinate of the judgement of beauty in an object is the subjective feeling of pleasure or displeasure in that object, unaccompanied by any interest. At the same time as being completely subjective, the judgement of beauty lays claim to an objective validity, commanding the agreement of all others. The judgement of beauty is universally communicable, yet, Kant makes clear, it cannot be objectively grounded, since there is no concept of the understanding under which our intuition of the object is being subsumed. The exposition of the judgement of beauty therefore comes back to its two key elements, the feeling of pleasure and its universal communicability. The pleasure, Kant argues, comes not directly from the object itself, but from the subjective harmony or accord in the play of the cognitive faculties which attends the representation of the object. The subjective basis of the judgement is thus commonly present in all human beings, and in making such a judgement one is implicitly claiming that it exemplifies a feeling that is available to everyone (V: 239–240; 89–90). In contrast to his accounts of theoretical and practical judgement, Kant links the subjective basis of judgement to an empirical history of human community. At he same time, he is clear that the judgement of beauty does not gain its authority from empirical location or interest (V: 296–298; 163–165).

The process involved in the estimation of the sublime is different from that involved in the judgement of beauty. Here, rather than a general and happy accordance of imagination with understanding, there is a violent assault on the cognitive faculties which are incapable of either representing or knowing the ideas to which certain perceptions of nature give rise. In the estimation of beauty in an object, we are at ease with our limitations, since the object seems almost to adapt itself to our powers of judgement. In the judgement of the sublime we are reminded of the demand that we exceed those limitations. The universal validity of judgements of the sublime derives from the imputation of a universally present moral feeling, the presence of which is derived from presumptions required by pure practical reason (V: 265; 125). Kant does not consider that a separate deduction of the possibility of the aesthetic judgement of the sublime is necessary, since although the judgement of the sublime is grounded in feeling, it has its necessity in reason (V: 208; 142–3). In the case of judgements of beauty, however, a deduction is necessary because judgements of beauty cannot be subsumed by either the understanding or reason; they have their own unique ground.

> Now, as far as the formal rules of judging [as such] are concerned, apart from any matter (whether sensation or concept), the power of judgment can be directed only to the subjective conditions for our employment of the power of judgment as such (where it is confined neither to the particular kind of sense involved not to a[ny] particular concept of the understanding), and hence can be directed only to that subjective [condition] which we may presuppose in all people (as required for possible cognition as such). It follows that we must be entitled to assume a priori that a presentation's harmony with these conditions of the power of judgment is valid for everyone.
>
> (V: 290; 155)

The a priori necessity of judgements of taste is seen to derive from the conditions of possibility of all judgement and therefore of all experience and knowledge. These conditions are the power of the imagination in its free synthesis of intuitions and of the understanding in its lawful subsumption of intuitions under concepts. In the judgement of beauty, what can be neither theoretically cognized nor practically realized, the 'supersensible substrate of humanity' (V: 340; 213), is subjectively felt and generally communicated as a specific kind of pleasure. The autonomy and authority of this kind of judgement, however, remains somewhat mysterious. It is an authority linked with the supersensible, which is the basis of freedom, and which in some sense underlies the human *sensus communis*. It is also an authority tied to a concept of purposiveness, in which empirical presentations are in tune with the free play of cognitive faculties, and in which aesthetic ideas individually exhibit or symbolize the highest goals of reason within the imagination (V: 313–314; 182). It seems that aesthetic judgement mediates between the domains of nature and freedom (understanding and reason) because it invokes the possibility of harmony between both humanity and nature and between humanity and freedom. This possibility is not a directly practical one, however, since the principle peculiar to judgement is purely subjective, it legislates only for itself, unlike understanding and reason. Nevertheless, Kant suggests that the possibility of the judgement of beauty provides us with hope for the bridging of the gap between nature and freedom, since in such judgements and in works of art that give rise to such judgements, the gap is experienced aesthetically as closed. The beautiful stands as a symbol of morality, though it cannot be identified with morality itself. The outcome of the critique of judgement is neither that the possibility of such judgement is made clear nor that the divisions between the faculties and their domains is successfully mediated. Instead the critique of judgement confirms the mysterious origins of reason's authority and the ways in which it is limited both theoretically and practically. What it also confirms, however, is the commitment of critique to overcoming its own presuppositions, even if only through the medium of hope in the judgement of the philosopher.

In the case of each of the critiques, of theoretical and practical reason and of judgement, the aim of the critique is to trace both the limits and the possibilities of the specific faculties in question. The peculiarity of the first critique lies in the way in which critique necessarily pushes beyond the limits it is itself concerned to trace. Although theoretical cognition is bound to the world of appearances, nevertheless it postulates and depends on an intelligible realm outside the scope of its own legislation. Having pushed beyond its limits, pure theoretical reason then gives itself a sovereignty as practical reason which it cannot comprehend. Thus the attempt to inaugurate the critique of reason in its practical aspect is declared in advance to be impossible. The argument of the *Critique of Practical Reason* becomes little more than the confirmation of the legislation of an unknowable power of transcendental freedom in the moral law. Critique becomes bogged down in explaining how intelligible and sensible worlds can be made to meet without ever meeting, the *as-if* identities of actual and possible worlds. The *Critique of Aesthetic Judgment* confirms both the unknowability and power of the supersensible and exhibits the struggles of critique to mediate between nature and freedom – a mediation which is both required by reason and impossible to achieve, although its achievement can be hoped for. In summary, the idea of critique emerges as inherently paradoxical.

The exercise of critique is necessarily an exercise of theoretical reason, an attempt to grasp the principles of knowledge, morality and judgement. Yet as an exercise of theoretical reason, critique is dependent on practical reason, in the form of the ideas of reason that regulate cognition and cannot be grasped by it, and the equally elusive ideals of reason towards which cognition is oriented. At the same time, critique as theoretical reason continually strives to move beyond the boundaries of cognition to the intelligible realm in which it is grounded but cannot do so. Caught up in the tangles of its own incapacity, theoretical reason in the critic, the philosopher Kant, is obliged to invoke either supersensible grounds and goals of reason's authority or hypothetical identifications of nature and freedom or principles of hope derived from the possibility of aesthetic judgement in order to explain and legitimate the possibility of critique itself. The critiques of the faculties are always also a critique of critique itself in the sense of displaying how critique can be legitimated and the extent of its powers.

THE POLITICS OF CRITIQUE

The idea that Kant's critical philosophy is inherently political is not common to the majority of interpretations of any of the three critiques discussed above. The tradition of discussing the first two sections of the *Critique of Pure Reason*, the 'Aesthetic' and the 'Analytic', as philosophically significant and marginalizing the rest in the work of English language commentators such as Strawson, has encouraged the study of the theoretical and practical aspects of Kant's philosophy as separate and, to some extent, self-contained (Strawson, 1966). This dismembering of Kant's critical philosophy helps to draw attention away from the juridical and legislative language shared by all of the critiques and the possible political significance of the critical philosophy as a whole. It is significant that commentators who do claim a political dimension to the project of critique tend to take a holistic view of the critical project and to take seriously Kant's claim as to the primacy of practical reason over theoretical. It is also significant that those claiming that there is a politics of critique in Kant's work disagree about the nature of that politics.

> Both Kant's metaphysics and his jurisprudence are theories of property. Both knowing and having are ways of appropriating or securing the right to the use of a thing, be it a concept or an object in the world.
>
> (Shell, 1980: 179)

Susan Meld Shell offers a reading of Kant's critical philosophy as essentially a theory of property, an attempt to ground legitimate possession in relation to concepts as well as objects. At the centre of Shell's reading of critique is a concept of the power of reason to accomplish in practice what it accomplishes only phenomenally in theory, i.e. to constitute the world. In this conception the politics of critique is authoritarian and dictatorial. A very different reading of the politics of critique is to be found in Hans Saner's work, in which the thrust of both precritical and critical writings is deemed to be that of metaphysical peacemaking. For Saner, the critical philosophy is about taking metaphysics from a state of war to one of legitimate conflict.

> The trial of reason is its own self-imposed infinite task of self-enlightenment and self-purification. The peace of reason is thus not a state of trustful rest but one of vigilance and self-examination.
>
> (Saner, 1973: 256)

According to Saner, in the case of theoretical reason, the constant struggle is with reason's in-built tendency to transcend its proper realm and hence relapse into the state of warring dogmas. In the case of practical reason, the struggle is between the objective imperative of the moral law and subjective impulsion by natural desires and ends. These struggles are established as both infinite and legitimate by the process of critique. In Saner's view, critique appears less as the dictatorial subjugator of nature, more as the constitutional monarch encouraging the process of liberal enlightenment and modestly aware of the limitations of its own powers.

The most sustained recent claim for the essentially political nature of Kant's critical philosophy comes from O'Neill in her book *Constructions of Reason* (1989). In the first section of this book O'Neill puts forward a case for reading Kant's critical *oeuvre* as an anti-rationalist, anti-foundationalist argument intrinsically connected to an austere liberalism (O'Neill, 1989: 4). This reading is dubbed a 'constructivist' one and poses a challenge to those readers of Kant who argue that in his work critique tends to lapse into metaphysics.[4] O'Neill grounds her argument in an interpretation of the meaning of the priority of practical reason in Kant, which is supported by a reading of the 'Transcendental Doctrine of Method' in the first critique.

> On standard views of the matter, Kant's political writings are at most a corollary of his ethical theory, whose critical grounding is suspect. I hope to unsettle this view by showing that a series of connected political and juridical metaphors constitute the deep structure of the *Critique of Pure Reason*.
>
> (O'Neill, 1989: 4)

The first point that O'Neill makes in her reading of the first critique is that the method of critique is not established in advance at the beginning of the text. Instead it is hinted at in the statement of the problem that critique is supposed to be addressing – the vindication of reason's claims. In contrast to Descartes, O'Neill claims, Kant sees the problem of vindicating reason as a shared one and gestures towards the idea of the critique of reason as both reflexive and political, a common self-questioning. It is not until the end of the text that the method of critique is properly outlined, a fact that O'Neill argues is in itself evidence of the non-algorithmic nature of critique, which cannot prescribe rules prior to its own self-reflection (O'Neill, 1989: 18). The first chapter of the 'Doctrine of Method' is entitled 'The Discipline of Pure Reason'. In this chapter Kant reflects back on what has been learned in the process of critique and explores the self-discipline of reason that follows from critique. This section is crucial for O'Neill's claims as to the practical and political nature of Kant's task (O'Neill, 1989: 11–17).

Kant calls the discipline of pure reason a 'negative legislation', 'a system of precautions and self-examination'; in other words, it is the recognition of reason's limitations. In the first section on discipline, Kant spends considerable time rejecting an analogy between mathematics and philosophy. Unlike the geometrician, the metaphysician is unable to deduce a stable and demonstrable system from axioms given in advance. The dogmatic use of reason in philosophy results rather in flimsy and illusory houses of cards. O'Neill argues that this is further confirmation of the fact that there are no algorithms of reason and no transcendental foundation for it. This then makes the vindication of reason without foundation necessary, and clues to what such a vindication means are to be found, according to O'Neill, in the later sections on the discipline of reason.

> For reason has no dictatorial authority; its verdict is always simply the agreement of free citizens, of whom each one must be permitted to express, without let or hindrance, his objections or even his veto.
>
> (A: 738; B: 766; O'Neill, 1989: 15)

Kant moves from a discussion of the dogmatic use of reason and its pitfalls in metaphysics to the polemical use of reason and it is in this section that O'Neill finds the key to the method of a non-foundational vindication of reason. Reason is vindicated not by dogmatic fiat but by the conditions of its possibility which are

29

the product of debate and free agreement. Here O'Neill finds a strict analogy between the grounding of cognitive and political orders.

> The reason why Kant is drawn to explicate the authority of reason in political metaphors is surely that he sees the problems of cognitive and political order as arising in one and the same context. In either case we have a plurality of agents or voices (perhaps potential agents or voices) and no transcendent or preestablished authority. Authority has in either case to be constructed.
>
> (O'Neill, 1989: 16)

As long as reason is deployed dogmatically, and the choice is between the authoritarianism of rationalism and the anarchy of scepticism, reason is in a state of war and contradiction. Only reconciliation between the two sides can end this state of war and this can only be built on terms to which both sides can agree; otherwise, thinking and communication become impossible. The terms are the terms which critique has explored and which enable reason to rise above the warring factions. This is not to be accomplished by resolving the dilemmas of rationalism and scepticism, but by opening up the acknowledgement of reason's inability to answer certain questions to debate and criticism and by gradually building a consensus around the claim that reason must rely on ideas it cannot know.

The political and juridical metaphors that O'Neill draws attention to and that pervade the whole of the *Critique of Pure Reason*, but particularly its opening and closing sections, are those of *tribunal*, *debate* and *community*. In examining these metaphors as they are at work in the 'Doctrine of Method', O'Neill finds support for her explanation of the priority of practical reason and the centrality of politics in Kantian critique (O'Neill, 1989: 17–27). The idea of the tribunal of reason, according to O'Neill, is another indication of the absence of an algorithm of reason or any alien authority which in some sense legislates for it. Critique is a matter of judgement and deliberation, not a following of abstract rules. Also a tribunal involves a plurality of participants, not necessarily in prior agreement and engaged in a common task.

> The central point that Kant makes with these analogies is that reason's authority must (since it receives no antecedent or

transcendent vindication) be seen as a practical and collective task, like that of constituting political authority.

(O'Neill, 1989: 18)

The image of debate is identified as particularly significant by O'Neill, since it draws attention to the way in which debate is impossible without some shared terms of reference. Engaging in debate carries with it an obligation to reject that which renders debate impossible; it involves the creation of conditions in which a world can be shared.

> Once more we are led back to the pivotal role of the Categorical Imperative in the politics of reason. What is to be vindicated is not reason, considered in abstraction from any particular reasoners, but the reasoning of those who like ourselves have no preinscribed modes of coordination, and find that their native endowment provides neither algorithm nor instinct for acting or for thinking. What can such beings do? There is no maxim of reasoning whose antecedent authority can compel them: and yet they cannot share a world in which there is no cognitive order.
>
> (O'Neill, 1989: 23)

The very minimum that the participants in debate can do is refrain from adopting principles that the other participants cannot adopt. This, for O'Neill, is what the categorical imperative means; it is a negative, practical instruction which explains both how reason grounds its own authority and how this is necessarily a practical grounding. It also explains the importance of community and the idea of common sense in Kant's work:

> Reasoned thinking is governed not by transcendent standards but by the effort to orient one's thinking in ways that do not preclude its accessibility to others.
>
> (O'Neill, 1989: 26)

The main focus of O'Neill's text is not on the first critique but on Kant's moral philosophy. Using the constructivist reading of Kant and the relation between practice and theory it establishes, O'Neill goes on to argue that Kant's moral thought is not necessarily either rigidly prescriptive or emptily formal, which are the two traditional, and she claims incompatible, allegations against Kant. The argument continually hinges on the claim that critique is about establishing in

31

practice the conditions of possibility of both cognition and action in a shared world. This means that critique is only ever a setting of parameters to thought and action, it does not provide precise prescriptions and it relies on continual public examination of its assumptions. In this context, the distinction between sensible and intelligible worlds is read simply as a way of specifying the conditions necessary for cognition and action respectively. The categorical imperative, according to O'Neill, can do some work in drawing the lines beyond which toleration is possible, but it is only ever a starting point for moral judgement, and does not exert an absolute authority over it.

O'Neill offers a closely argued reading of the politics of critique, one which in some ways corresponds to Saner's vision of the metaphysical peacemaker, but also pays careful attention to the founding of the authority of reason. The politics of critique on this reading are non-authoritarian, a kind of disciplined liberalism which counters the priority of freedom with the necessity of coexisting with other freedoms at the very foundation of human cognition and action. Although there is acknowledged to be an element of continual struggle in the critical project, painful diremptions and inconsistencies are not apparent at the heart of critique. Instead it appears as open, public and constructive.

The key to O'Neill's reading of Kant is her reading of the 'Transcendental Doctrine of Method'. I would like to suggest that if we look back at this text we find a more complex and contradictory politics at work than O'Neill identifies. Further, if we take seriously the arguments of the first three sections of the first critique, the 'Aesthetic', the 'Analytic' and the 'Dialectic', and above all the *positive* significance accorded to the principle of transcendental freedom in the practical context, it is clear that O'Neill's reading is rendered somewhat one-sided.

> The compulsion by which the constant tendency to disobey certain rules is restrained and finally extirpated, we entitle discipline.
>
> (A: 709; B: 737)

The metaphors of obedience and compulsion are as much a part of the discipline of pure reason as images of debate and community. As was noted above, the method of critique is characterized both as free debate and as the passing of 'judicial sentence' by Kant. O'Neill reads the free debate of reason advocated by Kant in the second section of the *Discipline* as indicating reason's constant and public self-examination, yet it could also be likened to the position of the enlightened despot who says, 'Argue as much as you like and about whatever you like, but obey' (VIII: 41; 59). Whether they like it or not, whether they acknowledge it or not, the philosophical polemicists are bound by the limits of reason and will be forced to abide by them; their debate, which fulfils the conditions necessary to make debate possible, has been declared empty in advance by the findings of the first part of the critique. The war is already over. Unfortunately, the peace that critique brings is a fragile one, since with the notions of the thing-in-itself and the ideas and ideals of reason, it seems that hostilities are opened again in the terrain of transcendental claims. These hostilities are kept in check theoretically by the purely negative significance of these transcendental ideas, but they are granted a positive and objective, indeed constitutive, validity in the realm of pure practical reason. The claims that Kant makes for the categorical imperative are much stronger and more positively authoritative than O'Neill allows. By construing the categorical imperative as a negative strategy, O'Neill is able to find its application to experience relatively unproblematic. But for Kant it is a problem, precisely because the dualisms established by the first critique, whatever their ontological status, become logically entrenched in the practical philosophy. Hence the struggle, through the different formulations of the categorical imperative, and through the hypothetical identification of sensible and intelligible worlds, to make the actualization of the commands of practical reason possible. Kant is not consistently self-reflexive in critique. The paradox of reason's limitation and its legislative ambition is never itself vindicated though it provides the ground for the project of critique. The politics of critique revealed in the discipline of reason, therefore, are neither simply authoritarian nor simply liberal; instead they remain paradoxically both.

A different reading of the politics of critique is to be found in Caygill's book *Art of Judgement* (1989). Caygill's focus is mainly on the *Critique of Judgment*, and the two traditions of taste and of aesthetics with which Kant engages in the text. In the course of a detailed argument Caygill suggests that the third critique is both the most profoundly metaphysical and profoundly political of Kant's texts, and that it brings to the surface the political presuppositions and implications of critique more clearly than the other critical writings.

The crisis of metaphysics which forms the pretext of critique can be abstractly understood as the conflict between the dogmatism of rationalist thinkers such as Wolff and the scepticism of empiricist thinkers such as Hume. Caygill, however, enriches the understanding of critique by analysing much more deeply the history of reason out of which critique emerges and of which critique is a part. In particular he examines the alternative accounts of judgement to be found in the empiricist and rationalist traditions, and argues that for both of these traditions judgements of pleasure and of beauty problematize those accounts. In both traditions the judgement of taste or aesthetic judgement exceeds the relations of synthesis and subsumption which are the mark of logical judgement. Such judgements suggest a ground beyond judgement which cannot itself be expressed in the language of judgement. Caygill traces the complexity of the empiricist theory of *taste*, in which the pursuit of self-interested pleasure is mysteriously brought into harmony with the rational will of providence, and goes on to examine the parallel antithetical tradition of aesthetic judgement, in which the particular feeling is subsumed under universal reason. This is more than the exposition of an abstract philosophical debate, however, since Caygill argues that the accounts of judgements of taste and of beauty are identifiable with specific political agendas and possibilities of crisis. The former theory of judgement is tied up with an account of civil society, in which faith in the operations of the hidden hand of civil society disguises the violent direction of production which makes that society possible. The latter tradition, by contrast, reflects the politics of the police state endorsed by dictatorial reason.

> The theory of civil society was haunted by the problem of taste, while the theory of the police state formed the matrix for the emergence of aesthetics. For both of them, beauty was the crisis point of judgement since it exceeded judgement.
>
> (Caygill, 1989: 38)

Caygill argues that, in all of his critical work, Kant is in dialogue with and within this history of reason. This means, according to Caygill, that Kant is also involved in a profoundly political debate, particularly when he comes to focus on aesthetic judgement and the question of the principle peculiar to judgement. In so far as Kant criticizes and transcends the empiricist and rationalist traditions, he is invoking a new dawn for both reason and history.

Both accounts of judgement were considerably overdetermined by differing perspectives on political and religious culture, so when Kant negates them he is also negating the political and cultural freight which they carry. His negation of the accounts of judgement intimates a thinking and a politics beyond judgement.

(Caygill, 1989: 297)

In the reading of Kant's critique of judgement which Caygill goes on to expound, he argues that Kant does not wholly succeed in offering a new account of judgement and of politics which escapes the violence behind the hidden hand or the authoritarian perfectionism of the police state. Instead Kant's treatment of the two forms of aesthetic judgement, the judgements of beauty and the sublime, is seen to present us with two alternative vocabularies of judgement, only the former of which offers a genuine transcendence of, or progress for, the history of reason. In the case of the former, the productive legislation of judgement, with the self-proportioning accord of the faculties that underlies judgement, suggests a politics to some extent reminiscent of O'Neill's reading of Kant which is exemplified by the idea of a self-proportioning constitution, but with a less abstract and more historicized understanding of what this means. In the case of the latter, the judgement of the sublime, we find an authoritarian, legislative politics, in which an anarchic manifold is violently subsumed under centralizing law. These two kinds of politics, however, are not separate and self-contained for they are two sides of the same coin of critique and reflect the tension between the critical and metaphysical moments in Kant's thought. Ultimately Caygill argues that the politics of critique which triumph in Kant do not exceed the terms of the history of reason of which critique is meant to be the culmination. Nevertheless the lapse into authoritarian dualisms is not necessarily the fate of the third critique which can also be read more positively.

Everything depends on the way in which 'realization and restriction' is thought in culture. On the one hand Kant thinks it in terms of the proportioning of activity, the bringing to appearance of natural finality through human projection, and the construction of a world in which human ends find themselves realized in the *summum bonum*. But the proportion underlying this disposition is difficult to represent. And when Kant tries to do so, he translates it into the language of judgement. Instead of recognizing a proportion within human freedom which may be realized and restricted through an ethical life, he sees in it only the spectacle of a lawless manifold which must be subsumed under unity.

(Caygill, 1989: 390)

For Caygill the political possibilities of critique are shaped by a history of reason and a language of judgement which are put into question by the nature of the aesthetic judgement of taste or beauty. In his aesthetic writings, therefore, Kant goes furthest in developing a language beyond judgement and suggesting a politics beyond the terms of civil society and the police state. There is a constant tendency, however, to lapse back into the violent and authoritarian terms of judgement inherent in the history of reason and in the metaphysical ends of critique itself.

> The accord of freedom with conformity to law so crucial in the first part of the *Critique*, where it is thought in terms of a proportioned activity which exceeded the bias of the traditions, is now rendered in terms of their violent unification. Instead of the active proportionality of life there is now the unification of individual freedom under law.

(Caygill, 1989: 391)

Kant's great difficulty, according to Caygill's account, is the articulation of the politics implicit in the judgement of beauty. The implication seems to be that the new politics of critique cannot be fully expressed within the terms of critique. The politics of critique, therefore, are presented as having the persistent tendency to lapse into the violence of a legislation which disguises its own origins. Unlike O'Neill, Caygill reads the implicit politics of critique as radically ambiguous.

O'Neill and Caygill both draw attention to the political significance of Kant's explicitly non-political work. Both also suggest that the political significance of Kant's critical work lies much more in the nature of his critical practice than in his explicit pronouncements on politics. To this extent I would agree with both thinkers; however, it is Caygill who, in my view, is most attuned to the paradoxes of the critical endeavour and whose account comes closer to the complexity and frustrated ambition of the arguments and politics at work in the three main critical texts.

CONCLUSION

In the first two parts of this chapter it was apparent that critique sets itself tasks which it is unable to fulfil. The dual determination of critique in the acknowledgement of reason's limitation and the assertion of its legislative power implies a set of dichotomies and a series of attempts to overcome them. This opens up Kant's texts to opposing interpretations and enables him to be read not only along both liberal and authoritarian lines but also as invoking alternative accounts of reason and history which break out of the juridical vocabulary of critique. Any given reading of the implicit politics of the practice of critique is liable to be subverted and destabilized by the tensions between these different possibilities. In trying to ground the possibility of critique through critique itself Kant becomes caught up in his own net of ways of resolving the problems inherent in the history of reason. The critic legislates, governs and judges on behalf of reason, but always also bears witness to the impossibilities of that legislation, government and judgement, except on the basis of hypothetical *as-if* identifications or hope. In the following chapter I will be examining how the politics of the practice of critique is reflected in Kant's critique of politics and his theories of right, history and judgement respectively.

2

KANT'S CRITICAL POLITICS

INTRODUCTION

Kant's political writings all date from the later part of his career and form part of the critical project as a whole.[1] The only systematic work on politics, the first part of *The Metaphysics of Morals*, was published in 1797, and his famous political essay 'Perpetual Peace: A Philosophical Sketch' in 1795. The other essays, articles and fragments on politics were published between 1784 and Kant's death.[2] As with all of Kant's critical work, in his political writings Kant is in dialogue with a variety of philosophical antecedents. He is also responding to historical events, most notably the American and French Revolutions and the effects of enlightenment and counter-enlightenment policies within the Prussian state. In *The Metaphysics of Morals* the legacies of the natural law tradition and of the work of Hobbes, Locke and Rousseau are all evident. One of the reasons why Kant has rarely been accorded the status of a great political thinker is the extent to which he seems simply to repeat a hotchpotch of ideas from competing traditions rather than saying anything radically new. Very often the arguments of Kant's political critique seem inconsistent and badly thought through in comparison to his other critical work. This impression is confirmed by the distinctive subject matter and approach of Kant's systematic meta-physics of right as opposed to the lesser writings on politics. The first part of *The Metaphysics of Morals* focuses on the question of the legitimacy of states and the nature of the right constitution. The essays on perpetual peace, theory and practice, history and enlight-enment touch on questions of law and right, but are more nearly concerned with history, war, culture and political/moral progress. This variety in Kant's political work coupled with its fragmentary nature has enabled, indeed encouraged, commentators to approach Kant's politics selectively. The result is that Kant has been read as both subversive and authoritarian, moralistic and Machiavellian in his theories of law and history.[3] For Kant himself, his political thought is an extension of his critical philosophy, combining both the critical task of establishing the ground and limits of political right and the metaphysical task of spelling out the implications for the nature of a legitimate state and government. An adequate reading of Kant's politics, therefore, needs to be familiar with the nature of critique as such. I would argue that the many tensions and apparent paradoxes and inconsistencies in Kant's political thought are not accidents or unfortunate lapses to be excused on grounds of old age. Instead they are implied by the presuppositions of critique itself. This will be demonstrated through an examination of three aspects of Kant's political thought which can be analytically distinguished, though not separated from one another. The first aspect is that of right, which is the focus of *The Metaphysics of Morals* Part I and more tangentially of the essays on theory and practice and perpetual peace. The second aspect is that of history and international relations, which is the focus of specific essays on history and the essay on perpetual peace, but which also surfaces in texts such as *Anthropology from a Pragmatic Point of View* and *Critique of Teleological Judgment*. The third aspect is judgement itself, addressed in the political writings on history, theory and practice, and enlightenment, and in both parts of the *Critique of Judgment*. What emerges from this examination is the conclusion that the circle that connects Kant's theory of right with his critique of judgement manifests the same political logic which was found to be implicit in his major critical writings. The politics of the practice of critique are confirmed in the explicit political possibilities sanctioned by critical political theory.

The discussion of Kant's politics proper, however, cannot be begun without first examining Kant's account of the relation of politics to the other realm of practical philosophy, morality. The theory of right is the first part of *The Metaphysics of Morals*, the second part of which outlines a corresponding theory of virtue. The doctrines of virtue and right are both outcomes of the critique of practical reason and are a response to its categorical imperative (VI: 216–217; 44–45). In the Introduction to both parts of *The Metaphysics of Morals*, Kant explains the distinction between right and virtue, legality and morality. This explanation is grounded on the human limitations explored in the

Grounding for the Metaphysics of Morals and the *Critique of Practical Reason*, but is presented more dogmatically and schematically than in either of those texts. Kant distinguishes two senses of will: will in the sense of free will or choice (*Willkür*); and will in the sense of the determining power of practical reason (*Wille*) (VI: 213; 42). The former is a peculiarly human capacity which is capable of being affected, though not determined, by sensuous impulse or of being determined by the categorical imperative itself. If human maxims are not simply in accordance with, but determined by, the categorical imperative, so that both the ground and end of actions are in the moral law, then this is the domain of virtue. If, however, as the *Willkür/Wille* distinction makes possible, human maxims are subjectively grounded then this is the domain of right. Right has to do with the aspects of the moral law that it is permissible to coerce human beings into fulfilling; right actions need not be virtuous.

> The lawgiving which makes an action a duty and also makes this duty the incentive is *ethical*. But that lawgiving which does not include the incentive of duty in the law and so admits an incentive other than the Idea of duty itself is *juridical*. It is clear that in the latter case this incentive that is something other than the Idea of duty must be drawn from *sensibly dependent* determining grounds of choice, inclinations and aversions, and among these, from aversions; for it is a lawgiving that constrains, not an allurement, which invites.
>
> (VI: 219; 46)

The distinction between virtue and right is a consequence of human limitation which necessitates distinct metaphysical doctrines. The doctrine of right, however, seems a paradoxical enterprise from the start. The idea of an *external* fulfilment of the demands of practical reason contradicts the account of morality given by Kant in the *Grounding* and the *Critique of Practical Reason*. As Kant himself frequently asserts, an *external* fulfilment of the ends of reason is not a genuine fulfilment. If the realm of right is one which deals in the manipulation of non-virtuous will then how can it be part of a metaphysics of morals? In a sense, the whole of Kant's political thought is a response to this question. In the doctrine of right, the answer revolves around an argument for the deduction of pure principles of right from practical reason itself, so that the non-virtuous realm of legality is itself legitimated by reference to the moral law. In Kant's philosophy of history another answer is formulated, in which world politics approximates more and more closely to the ideal of a kingdom of ends. In Kant's writings on judgement a third answer is given, in which the philosopher's assessment of the course of history helps to steer the realm of right towards the realm of virtue. As will be demonstrated, all of these answers are problematic in the light of Kant's own presuppositions. The strict division between legal and moral and the idea of a dual determination of human will continually undermine Kant's attempts to draw the two realms together.

RIGHT

The first thing that Kant makes clear in the Introduction to the doctrine of right is that he is not concerned with positive law, but with a priori principles of right. These are the principles on which positive legislation should be founded and are derived from practical reason itself. Right has to do with the external form of relations between human wills, not with the motivation or ends underlying different human choices, except when they contradict the possibility of choice itself. On the basis of this, Kant formulates the universal principle of right as follows:

> Any action is *right* if it can coexist with everyone's freedom in accordance with a universal law, or if on its maxim the freedom of choice of each can coexist with everyone's freedom in accordance with a universal law.
>
> (VI: 230; 56)

The principle of right is not in itself an incentive to action, but it authorizes the possibility of coercion to force human freedom into conformity with it. Thus, Kant argues, a fully reciprocal use of coercion is the mark of strict right, in which there is no trace of virtue: 'Right and authorization to use coercion therefore mean one and the same thing' (VI: 232; 58).

Having presented the universal principle of right, Kant goes on to specify the nature of right. He defines it as the capacity to obligate others to a duty. There are two kinds of right according to Kant: innate right, which is naturally inherent in humanity; and acquired right, which requires a juridical grounding (VI: 237; 63). The only innate right is that already summed up in the universal principle of justice: the right to freedom from constraint in accordance with universal laws. This right requires no deduction. According to Kant,

41

this right is a simple reflection of the internal property of free will inherent in all human beings, a mark of both their moral limitation and moral possibilities. The first part of the doctrine of right, therefore, focuses on acquired right in relation to persons and things, or private right. Kant has defined right as the capacity to obligate others to a duty, a duty to respect choices that do not conflict with universal laws. In the section on private right, the freedom to choose which is the peculiar characteristic of human will is presented as inherently proprietorial. The exercise of freedom which others should have a duty to respect is the exercise of claiming something external as one's own.

> It is therefore an a priori presupposition of practical reason to regard and treat any object of my choice as something that could objectively be mine or yours.
>
> (VI: 246; 69)

It is as users and potential owners of objects of will that wills externally relate to one another. Kant lists three kinds of thing that can be external objects of my will: an external physical object; the choice of another to perform a specific act, for example, the fulfilment of a promise; and the status of another in relation to me, such as a wife, a child or a servant. There are, however, two senses in which the above may be possessed. The first is in the sense of empirical possession in which I literally control or hold the objects of my will. The difficulty with this sense of possession is that it is grounded solely on empirical factors such as strength, which are unreliable and changeable. The capacity to obligate others to respect your rights of possession cannot be universally grounded in contingent empirical factors. The second sense of possession is intelligible possession, in which rights over the objects of your will are grounded in abstraction from all conditions of intuition in accordance with universal laws. For this, a deduction of proprietory right from pure principles is therefore required.

> The question, How is it possible for *something external to be mine or yours*? resolves itself into the question, How is *merely rightful* (intelligible) *possession* possible? and this, in turn, into the third question, How is a *synthetic* a priori proposition of Right possible?
>
> (VI: 249; 71)

In attempting to deduce the possibility of intelligible possession, Kant runs into the same difficulties he encountered in trying to deduce the categorical imperative. Because he is dealing with something in complete abstraction from conditions of intuition, since intelligible possession cannot be bounded by space or time, the principles which ground intelligible possession are beyond the scope of the understanding and cannot be grasped theoretically. Thus, rather than presenting a deduction, Kant argues instead that the idea of intelligible possession is a necessary corollary of the universal principle of right, since only if possession is guaranteed can there be freedom according to universal laws, because freedom is only possible as possession, i.e. power over something or someone else. The kind of guarantee represented by the idea of intelligible possession as grounded in the universal principle of right is not, however, in itself sufficient to guarantee possession in practice. This can only be done when there is a universal and reciprocal recognition of rights to property.

> So it is only a will putting everyone under obligation, hence only a collective general (common) and powerful will, that can provide everyone this assurance. But the condition of being under a general external (i.e. public) lawgiving accompanied with power is the civil condition. So only in a civil condition can something external be mine or yours.
>
> (VI: 256; 77)

Kant argues, therefore, that private right, i.e. legitimate external acquisition, is dependent on the idea of an original universal act of will on the part of all people. This idea of a social contract marks the difference between a state of nature, in which possessions can only be held provisionally, and a civil condition in which possessions can be guaranteed. Kant is very careful, however, to deny that the original common commitment to respect property is a historical event; rather it is a necessary hypothesis if the principle of universal right is to be realized. In the discussion of external acquisition that forms the second chapter of the doctrine of right, constant use is made of the notion of an original common, validating act of will on the part of all people which legitimates private rights to own property and engage in contractual relations (VI: 258–265; 80–85). This idea works in two different ways in Kant's text. On the one hand, it has the status of an idea of reason, hypothetically necessary yet existing in a sphere beyond human understanding. On the other hand, it is part of a pragmatic argument that points out that the concept of intelligible possession is useless in practice, unless it is enforced by a system of public power which can coerce respect for the principles of right. The two ways in which the concept of the common will works reinforce each other: just as it is a demand of practical reason that people unite in a juridical condition, so it is also a consequence of natural self-interest. At the end of the section on private right, it is clear that private right depends on public right, both really and ideally.

> From private Right in the state of nature there proceeds the postulate of public Right: When you cannot avoid living side by side with all others, you ought to proceed to leave the state of nature and proceed with them into a rightful condition, that is a condition of distributive justice.
>
> (VI: 307; 121–122)

The 'rightful condition' that succeeds the state of nature is one in which persons relate juridically to one another; that is, with reference to the idea of a primary common act of will. The *state* is the juridical condition viewed as a whole in relation to its members. Kant's examination of the principles of private right leads on to the examination of the principles to which a state must conform in order to be rightful. In the second part of the doctrine of right, Kant is dealing with the *idea* of the state rather than with actual states, though he is setting up principles by which actual states may be judged. The first point about the idea of the state is that its legislative authority is necessarily grounded in the idea of a common act of will, since this is a necessary hypothesis for all juridical relation (VI: 313–314; 125). It is clear from Kant's argument, however, that this is essentially a logical requirement and has little to do with the foundation of actual legislative authority in existing states. The necessity of the idea of a common act of will derives from the universal principle of right which in turn is grounded in practical reason itself. The ultimate legitimation of right is in the categorical imperative. Legislative authority therefore is only legitimate when derived from practical reason. If it is not derived from practical reason then it is not legitimate and there is no juridical condition to uphold right. But practical reason requires the upholding of right through legislative authority and thus justifies the *idea* that actual legislative authority derives from practical reason, whether it was founded by a common act of will or not. What must be the case dictates what is the case even when it seemed originally to contradict it.

A law that is so holy (inviolable) that it is already a crime even to call it in doubt *in a practical way*, and so to suspend its effect for a moment, is thought as if it must have arisen not from men but from some highest, flawless lawgiver; and that is what the saying 'All authority is from God' means. This saying is not an assertion about the *historical basis* of the civil constitution; it instead sets forth an idea as a practical principle of reason: the principle that the presently existing legislative authority ought to be obeyed, whatever its origin.

(VI: 319; 130)

Kant's insistence on the inviolability and irreproachability of the legislator is a consequence of his commitment to the deduction of right from practical reason. This is also what shapes Kant's sketch of what the rightful state must entail, given in the second part of his theory of right. Kant does not require that the sovereign body of the state take on any particular form in the sense of being democratic or autocratic, for instance. Instead, his only requirement is that the form of the state be in accord with the spirit of republicanism. For Kant, this means that the state must guarantee the separation of powers of the legislature, executive and judiciary.

These are like the three propositions in a practical syllogism: the major premise, which contains the *law* of that will; the minor premise, which contains the *command* to behave in accordance with the law, i.e. the principle of subsumption under the law; and the conclusion, which contains the *verdict* (sentence), what is laid down as right in the case at hand.

(VI: 313; 125)

For Kant, the separation of powers preserves the formal irreproacha- bility of sovereignty, which is always both inviolable and absolute (VI: 318; 129). In addition, it makes possible the ideal validation of each of the civic powers, by retaining their autonomy in relation to each other and legitimating them solely in relation to practical reason itself. The position of citizens in Kant's republican idea of a state is peculiar. Whether citizens are active participants in legisla- tion or not, all citizens ideally ground the law and are absolutely bound by it; they exist both noumenally and phenomenally within the state. This is demonstrated in Kant's discussion of both punish- ment and revolution. In the case of punishment, the criminal is responsible for the law in his noumenal self, whereas he breaks the law and is punished in his phenomenal self. This distinction enables Kant to avoid the Hobbesian predicament of explaining the possibility of people willing their own harm in the social contract. The self ideally involved in the common act of will which grounds legislative authority is an ideal self not a real one (VI: 235; 144). This is not to say that Kant forbids the involvement of real citizens in the legislative process. He does, however, restrict 'active' citizenship to persons who are independent of another's control, and thus properly free in the sense required by right. Thus self-employed men may be entitled to vote, but wage labourers and women may not (VI: 314–315; 125–126). This distinction between active and passive citizenship in no way undermines the freedom under the moral law of all human beings, or their ideal participation in the grounding of law. Virtues are not denied to wage labourers and women, only their rights are curtailed. In Kant's ideal state, each citizen is free as a human being, equal under the law as a subject and his own master. However, this ideal is, as he sees it, compatible with many different kinds of state being rightful. This is evident in his discussion of revolution, resistance and reform in relation to the examples he uses.

For Kant, revolution cannot be right, legally or morally, because there can be no legitimate contesting of the source of legitimacy and all legislative authority must be perceived as derived from that source, i.e. practical reason via the idea of a common act of will. Revolting citizens are in self-contradiction (VI: 320; 131). Kant's insistence on the absolutism of sovereign power appears, to say the least, inconsistent with the idea of a common act of will founding public law. However, it is perfectly in accord with the status of the original juridical act as a necessary purely formal supposition, legitimating the move to a juridical condition which guarantees intelligible possession. The sovereign is the law; to challenge the sovereign is to subvert the postulate of practical reason that demands the enforcing of right. With rigorous consistency, Kant acknowledges that this must mean that if a revolution is successful and a revolutionary government established, then it too may not be challenged by citizens. Change can only rightfully stem from the sovereign body itself (VI: 322–333; 133). The only example that Kant gives of when citizens may rightfully protest against the sovereign is when their agreement with a law would involve self-contradiction as much as the breaking of it. An actual example that Kant uses to illustrate this is if a hereditary privileged nobility is created, which conflicts with the idea of the equality of citizens under the law (VI: 329; 138–139).

However, even in this case, citizens would not be justified in rebelling against the law. It would be up to the sovereign body to obey the juridical commands of practical reason and bring itself, by reform, into accordance with the demands of right (VI: 329; 129). Thus there emerge two reasons for according empirical sovereigns absolute respect: first, because recognition of their legitimacy involves the acknowledgement of the ideal ground of their authority in practical reason; second, because through the reform from above of existing law, empirical states may rightfully approach the juridical ideal more closely.

In Kant's discussion of revolution and reform the tensions and peculiarities of his account of right come to the surface. Kant's account slips from the realm of ideas to the empirical realm and back again with bewildering consequences. The idea of a common act of will may be practically manifested in the power of an absolute monarch, the agent of ideal will. The ideal of freedom, equality and independence is actualized in a distinction between active and passive citizens. The concept of self-legislation becomes a complete submission to the powers that be, in the sense that the rights of the sovereign derive from pure reason and are unaccompanied by duties which he can be coerced to fulfil (VI: 319; 130). Structuring the whole discussion is the originating power of pure practical reason, which is beyond comprehension and a juridical ideal which is beyond attainment.

> Every actual deed (fact) is an object in *appearance* (to the senses). On the other hand, what can be represented only by pure reason and must be accounted among *Ideas*, to which no object given in experience can be adequate – and a perfectly *rightful constitution* among men is of this sort – is the thing in itself.
>
> (VI: 371; 176)

The doctrine of right begins with the clear distinction between right and virtue and the necessity of a separate metaphysics of right. Throughout the metaphysics of right, however, a dual message is presented. On the one hand, it seems that the realization of pure principles of right in experience is an unattainable goal, since legitimacy resides only in idea. On the other hand, it seems that right is realized in any actual legislative authority that guarantees ownership. This double consequence of the attempt to specify the nature of legitimate public authority reflects the dichotomous logic which can be traced in all of Kant's critical writings, but never so starkly as in his political work. Kant's own dissatisfaction with his attempts to ground right securely is evident in his unwillingness to end the argument of the first part of *The Metaphysics of Morals* with the account of legislative authority in the domestic state. In the final part of his discussion of right he moves on to the realm of the international, war and history in an effort to deduce a more substantive link between the real and ideal in politics.

HISTORY

The greater part of the argument of the theory of right is devoted to the question of legitimating public law within a domestic state. It is argued that any legislative authority which upholds intelligible possession must be treated as if it were legitimate. Thus right is seen to depend on the existence of absolute sovereign authority in relation to a group of citizens. By virtue of Kant's argument, any law must be preferable to no law, since the demands of practical reason compel an end to the state of nature. However, there is a sense in which all domestic states, regardless of how closely they correspond to the juridical republican ideal, are in a lawless condition, that is, in relation to one another. The demand of right that intelligible possession be guaranteed is continually under threat as long as states pose a threat to one another. Therefore, the demand of right goes beyond the necessity of the move to public law to the necessity of some kind of overarching authority that can ensure the possibility of stable inter-state relations or perpetual peace (VI: 343–351; 150–157). Such an authority cannot be the same as the legislative authority which grounds the domestic state, since this is itself an absolute authority. The ideal of perpetual peace is not an ideal of world government, but of a mutual, reciprocal agreement over international laws that in no way undermines the sovereignty of any of the parties to the agreement. It is this ideal that Kant puts forward in the concluding part of the metaphysics of right and expounds in detail in his essay on perpetual peace as the ultimate guarantor of right. In the case of the domestic state, the demands of right are fulfilled in idea by the common act of will and in reality by the existence of legislative authority backed up by coercive power. The problem for Kant, given that the demands of right extend to the inter-state realm, is how those demands are to be fulfilled without reference to original legislation. It is at this point that Kant's philosophy of right calls upon support from a philosophy of history.

Kant's writings on history are brief and fragmentary, but they are comprehensive enough to provide an argument for the nature of human development that can be used to substantiate practical reason's demand for progress toward perpetual peace. Texts such as *Anthropology from a Pragmatic Point of View*, 'Idea for a Universal History with a Cosmopolitan Purpose' and 'Perpetual Peace: A Philosophical Sketch' present a consistent account of world history. This account begins with the 'unsocial sociability' of individuals (that is, their incapacity and yet need for coexistence with others) (VIII: 20; 44), and through war, trade and culture potentially ends in international law.

Kant's reading of history derives from an account of human nature, which in turn is derived from the presuppositions of his critical philosophy. The dichotomous account of will given at the beginning of *The Metaphysics of Morals* is reflected in Kant's anthropological account of the human being. This is a being driven in part by the demands of practical reason, but largely incapable of fulfilling those demands due to the influence of the non-moral motivation of natural needs and desires. This fundamental limitation of the human being would appear to make the ends of practical reason eternally unattainable. However, Kant argues that this is not the case, because although practical reason may be powerless in practice, a substitute for it can be found in the work of nature itself. Natural self-interest propels human beings to coexist and ensure their mutual protection. In the same way, it pushes people in a state of nature into a juridical condition as a protection from the external threat of other groups.

> Thus that mechanism of nature by which selfish inclinations are naturally opposed to one another in their external relations can be used by reason to facilitate the attainment of its own end, the reign of established right.
>
> (VIII: 366–367; 113)

Similarly, the fact of war, which is an outcome of human greed and aggression, though evil in itself, can nevertheless be seen to serve the ends of reason. Kant argues that, given unregulated human desires for power, wealth and security, the interests of established states will necessarily clash and there will be war. As wars go on, more and more sophisticated weapons are developed, until mutual fear between states is so great that they are afraid to go to war. At the same time, human greed requires wider and wider markets and as war is bad for trade, this provides another motive not to go to war (VIII: 368; 113–114). In these circumstances, nature pushes humanity towards perpetual peace even as practical reason demands it.

> Though war is an unintentional human endeavour (incited by our unbridled passions), yet it is also a deeply hidden and perhaps intentional endeavour of the supreme wisdom, if not to establish, then at least to prepare the way for lawfulness along with the freedom of states, and thereby for a unified system of them with a moral basis.
>
> (V: 433; 320)

In the *Anthropology* and in the *Critique of Teleological Judgment* a further accomplishment of nature is suggested. This is the achievement of human culture, not simply as skill in the development of the arts and sciences, but as discipline in the capacity to overcome natural inclination itself. Kant argues that the inequalities and miseries of the human condition that result from the free play of human inclination will themselves lead humanity to master those inclinations (V: 433–434; 321). Once this is the case, practical reason will be freed from its practical impotence and the gap between the real and the ideal will have been genuinely overcome.

Thus Kant provides an account of history as progress to reinforce the possibility of right in the human condition. This reading of history, however, is throughout an ambiguous one. On the one hand, it appears as the triumphal account of the ironic success of a hidden hand in the realm of legality. There is an inevitability to the story given and the end of history seems to be within reach. On the other hand, Kant emphasizes the fragility of progress in the legal sphere and its constant liability to collapse back into war and conflict. This ambiguity is demonstrated in Kant's account of perpetual peace. Sometimes the goal of perpetual peace is presented as something close to a state of complete global harmony, substantively regulated by international law. Sometimes perpetual peace appears as little more than the uneasy coexistence of mutual deterrence, which is always liable to break down if technological or commercial advantage is held by one power. Once more we find a curious slippage between Kant's account of what is real and what is ideal, and yet on reflection it is unclear how this slippage is grounded. How can a self-interested reaction to the results of natural motivation be sufficient to ground the sphere of right? But then this is very much the same question as that of how the absolute power of an empirical sovereign can be grounded in right. Kant finds himself saying both that this is and that this is not possible. It is possible because in both cases coercion enables law; it is impossible because in neither case is it possible to deduce that coercion from the universal principle of right itself, the deduction can only be hypothesized. It is at this point in Kant's political thought that the discussion has to move beyond the realm of right and history to the realm of hypothesis which has always underlain them. Kant's arguments as to the legitimacy of states and the development of history both rely on Kant's own sleight of hand in mapping the relation of the real and the ideal. This is something Kant deals with self-consciously in his argument for the role of the philosopher's judgement in the realm of legality and its development.

JUDGEMENT

In one of his earlier political writings, the article 'An Answer to the Question: What Is Enlightenment', Kant sets out the political role of the scholar. In this essay, Kant defines enlightenment itself as the courage to use your own reason (*sapere aude*) and argues for the desirability of freedom of thought as the essential prerequisite of a fully enlightened age (VIII: 35–37; 54–55). Kant is aware, however, that there are dangers in a blanket encouragement of independence of thought in a people used to close guardianship. He argues that a sudden access to freedom may result only in the embracing of a new range of prejudices.

> Thus a public can only achieve enlightenment slowly. A revolution may well put an end to autocratic despotism and to rapacious or power-seeking oppression, but it will never produce a true reform in ways of thinking. Instead, new prejudices, like the ones they replaced, will serve as a leash to control the great unthinking mass.
>
> (VIII: 36; 55)

In considering the best way, therefore, to achieve enlightenment, Kant goes on to suggest that it is best served by encouraging a particular kind of freedom: the freedom to make public use of one's reason in all matters. Kant makes a sharp distinction between private and public uses of reason (VIII: 37; 55). The former is the use of reason by a government employee or citizen in contradiction to the law or to his orders from above. According to Kant, this use of reason both is and ought to be restricted, since a servant or citizen of the state is bound by absolute obligations to it, even when he or she considers that the state is wrong. It is a different matter with the public use of reason, which is the use of reason any scholar makes when he or she addresses the literate world about religious or political issues. While Kant accepts that the army officer who disobeys an order is definitely wrong, he argues that it should be perfectly acceptable for that same officer to write and publish an article explaining why a different order should have been given. The possibility of scholarly, public debate is essential to the possibility of enlightenment in a way that civil disobedience is not. Kant's argument in the essay on enlightenment remains one of the threads present in all of his political philosophy. Given the status accorded to legislative authority in all actual states, then it is clear that Kant cannot endorse the direct contradiction of this authority. All change must come from above. Scholarly debate, however, provides a way in which the powers that be may be influenced to bring existing legislation more into accord with the principles of right; the philosopher's judgement substitutes for political action.

> A high degree of civil freedom seems advantageous to a people's *intellectual* freedom, yet it also sets up insuperable barriers to it. Conversely, a lesser degree of civil freedom gives intellectual freedom room to expand to its fullest extent. Thus once the germ on which nature has lavished most care – man's inclination and vocation to *think freely* – has developed within this hard shell, it gradually reacts upon the mentality of the people, who thus become increasingly able to *act freely*. Eventually, it even influences the principles of governments, which find that they can themselves profit by treating man, who is *more than a machine*, in a manner appropriate to his dignity.
>
> (VIII: 41–42; 59–60)

Kant's essays on enlightenment, perpetual peace, the contest of the faculties, and theory and practice make clear that the value of public scholarly debate is lost if the realm of judgement passes over into the realm of action. In this sense the political judgement of the philosopher is parallel to aesthetic judgement, which can demonstrate the good without being able to put it into practice and which is fundamentally disinterested. Kant argues that philosophers should not become kings because 'power corrupts the free judgement of reason' (VIII: 368–369; 115). What he seems to be implying by this is that political judgement is a species of reflective judgement and can only be genuinely exercised when uncontaminated by empirical interest. A consequence of the assumption that true judges cannot act is, therefore, that the influence of the public use of reason is always uncertain and dependent on the attitude of the sovereign. Only one actual sovereign is quoted as having the appropriate attitude, and that is the Emperor Frederick with his maxim that freedom of argument is permissible on condition of obedience (VIII: 37; 59). That this is the best that can be asked of actual sovereign powers seems to leave little hope for the progress that Kant is arguing for. There is, however, another more indirect way in which he sees the philosopher's judgement as exerting its influence, one that takes us back into the realms of right and history.

In his essay on perpetual peace, Kant distinguishes between the concept of fate and the concept of providence within history (VIII: 361–362; 108). Both concepts involve the assertion that there is a necessity involved in the workings of nature in history. Fate implies a causal necessity, pushing us in a direction unknown. Providence is a teleological concept, involving the idea that there is purpose in history, 'the underlying wisdom of a higher cause', so that history is explicable in terms of its end. As Kant's readings of historical development demonstrate, it is the concept of providence that most obviously structures his account. However, it (providence) does so, as Kant quite clearly states, only by virtue of the philosopher's judgement, choosing to interpret history as if it were progress. This attribution of an end and direction to history is analogous to the role of teleological principles of reflective judgement in the understanding of nature as outlined in the *Critique of Teleological Judgment*. Kant explicitly describes the nature of this kind of judgement in the Ninth Thesis of his essay 'Idea for a Universal History with a Cosmopolitan Purpose'.

> It is admittedly a strange and at first sight absurd proposition to write a *history* according to an idea of how world events must develop if they are to conform to certain rational ends; it would seem that only a *novel* could result from such premises. Yet if it may be assumed that nature does not work without a plan and purposeful end, even amidst the arbitrary play of human freedom, this idea might nevertheless prove useful. And although we are too short-sighted to perceive the hidden mechanism of nature's scheme, this idea may yet serve as a guide to us in representing an otherwise planless *aggregate* of human

actions as conforming, at least when considered as a whole, to a *system*.

(VIII: 29; 51–52)

The argument of the Ninth Thesis is that there is value in prescribing a rational end to history, as giving hope for the future of mankind in accordance with the goals of practical reason. However, Kant is in no doubt that this is the contribution of the philosopher to history as opposed to the work of the empirical historian. What the empirical historian sees is the 'disjointed product of unregulated freedom' (VIII: 30; 52). Kant makes a similar argument in the text *The Conflict of the Faculties.* Here he reiterates the point that experience does not in itself provide hope for the future, since there is as much regress as progress in human affairs. However, as a philosopher, Kant argues that he can, indeed ought to, read particular historical events as symptomatic of the moral disposition of mankind and therefore of the possibility of progress. The event he singles out as indicative of the moral disposition of humanity is the French Revolution. The reason he singles it out is not because of the actions of the participants in the revolution, but because of the attitude of on-lookers to it, which he argues was publicly and consistently sympathetic. Whether the revolution succeeds or fails, the welcome given to it by those outside the fray and therefore capable of considered judgement signals the capacity of humanity to improve.

> It is simply the mode of thinking of the spectators which reveals itself publicly in this game of great revolutions, and manifests such a universal yet disinterested sympathy for the players on one side against those on the other, even at the risk that this partiality could become very disadvantageous for them if discovered. Owing to its universality, this mode of thinking demonstrates a character of the human race at large and all at once; owing to its disinterestedness, a moral character of humanity, at least in its predisposition, a character which not only permits people to hope for progress toward the better, but is already itself progress in so far as its capacity is sufficient for the present.
>
> (VII: 85; 153)

In addition, therefore, to the direct influence that scholarly discussion may have on the existing political and legal context, Kant suggests there is another political role for the philosopher's judge-

54

ment, the role of keeping the ends of reason before the eyes of the public and thereby inspiring the people to the possibility of their fulfilment. Thus the bringing together of the real and the ideal in the state and in history finally appears to come to rest in the reflection of the philosopher which, like aesthetic judgement, is a testimony to hope and faith. This is the hope that there is providence at work in self-interested inclination and nature will cultivate the moral character of humanity; and the faith in the influence that philosophers may exercise over kings.

CONCLUSION

Looking back over the different aspects of Kant's political thought, it is clear that Kant is caught in a continual struggle with the relation between the ends of practical reason, as they are defined in the universal principle of right, and empirical history and politics. The attempt to relate ideal to real is fraught with paradox, as Kant himself recognizes, and none of the ways in which Kant grounds a connection between right and reality is genuinely secure. The grounding of actual states in the principles of right becomes a defence of the status quo; the workings of history need not be read as progress, and the philosopher's judgement has no guarantee of effectiveness. In the previous chapter, it was concluded that the dual determination of critique by the assertion of both reason's limitation and its legislative power resulted in a series of struggles to fulfil tasks which the presuppositions of critique itself has made impossible. The political promise of critique explored in Chapter 1 is confirmed in Kant's explicitly political work. The ambition of reason in the practice of critique is repeatedly frustrated in a series of unsatisfactory resolutions to the dichotomies which grounded reason's ambition in the first place, i.e. to secure the legitimate territory of knowledge, morality, aesthetic judgement and right given reason's inherent limitation. Kant's theories of law, the state and history struggle to overcome the gulf between transcendent reason and the realm of empirical experience. Without recourse to judgement, however, these struggles are capable of resolution only through retreat to one or other side of the gulf, giving the possibility of either the utter condemnation or unquestioning endorsement of existing legal and political relations. Thus the philosopher may take refuge either in the moral law, from the standpoint of which all existing legal and political relations are inadequate; or he may construe actual states and inter-state relations *as-if* they instantiated the moral law. Judgement emerges as the place between the ideal and the real, but rather than resolving the tensions implicit in Kant's reading of right and history it occupies an inexplicable no man's land, in which the verdicts of practical reason and of empirical history are overturned by the philosopher. In the absence of determinate rules, the critic's political judgement becomes a peculiar invention, the legitimation of which, like that of aesthetic judgement, is mysterious.

The apparent divergence of the three aspects of Kant's political philosophy that have been identified as right, history and judgement, explains why interpretations of Kant's political thought can be so different (the Kant of the doctrine of right seems a much more authoritarian Kant than the Kant of the essays on history and culture). It also confirms that thinkers attempting to draw on the Kantian inheritance for an account of critical social and political theory are drawing on a volatile legacy. The different aspects of Kant's political thought are not neatly separable and the logic of their relation reflects the problematic logic of critique itself. The problem of the legitimation, application and enforcement of law is as much the problem of the political philosopher as of political philosophy, as the practice of critique demonstrates. In Kant's work the attempt to lay the foundations for a new metaphysics continually returns him to the question of the legitimacy of his own enterprise and leads to some peculiar consequences when it comes to the claims staked for the territory of the critical philosopher's authority.

In the following central section of this book, I will be examining the work of four different contemporary thinkers, Habermas, Arendt, Foucault and Lyotard, all of whom draw on Kant's work in accounting for the practice of their own critical social and political thought. In each case the Kant being addressed and used is a different Kant, although in each case it is a Kant recognizable in the critical philosopher's work as it has been outlined above and in the foregoing chapters. It will be argued that although Habermas, Arendt, Foucault and Lyotard all understand and use the critical philosophy differently, nevertheless they all become entangled in tensions analogous to those in which Kantian critique is caught and that this has profound consequences for the nature of their social and political theorizing. I will begin by looking at the work of Habermas. Habermas's work forms an appropriate starting point for the examination of the Kantian legacy in contemporary critical social and political thought because he embraces the Kantian project more wholeheartedly and holistically than the other three thinkers. Habermas claims that Kantian critique can be reconstructed in such a way as to avoid the problems that haunted Kant's own attempt to legitimate his (Kant's) arguments. In the following chapter the degree to which Habermas's critical theory succeeds in redeeming this claim will be assessed.

3

HABERMAS AND THE POSSIBILITY OF CRITICAL THEORY

INTRODUCTION

Habermas is well known both for the breadth of his scholarship and for his willingness to utilize ideas and insights from radically different fields and traditions to build his critical social theory. Mapping the range of thinkers that have exerted some influence on Habermas's mature thought would require a book in itself, and a further book could be devoted to arguments as to the centrality of particular influences on Habermas's project. However, it is not the purpose of this chapter to attempt to adjudicate between different sources of the theory of communicative action. The purpose of this chapter is to demonstrate the central importance of Kant's critical philosophy in Habermas's own conception of critical theory. The classification of Habermas as a Kantian thinker is a commonplace on the part of both Habermas and his critics. Since the publication of *Knowledge and Human Interests*, Habermas has found himself constantly defending and reformulating his critical theory in the light of accusations of Kantian foundationalism, formalism and utopianism.[1] Habermas has claimed, in his mature theory, to have captured what is useful in the project of Kantian critique without falling into any of the above errors, or at least without doing so in an indefensible way. It will be argued in this chapter that Habermas has not succeeded in taming or neutralizing the implications of the Kantian inheritance on which his work draws selectively. On the contrary, it will be argued that Habermas's mature work remains locked into the logic of Kantian critical thought and therefore shares its peculiar and paradoxical politics.

The chapter falls into four parts. The first will look at Habermas's account of a radicalized critique in *Knowledge and Human Interests* and at the nature of the moderated critique developed in response to the weaknesses of this early text. This will involve examining the nature of universal pragmatics, Habermas's concept of the evolution of society and the development of his thought into a theory of communicative action. The second section will examine the relation between Habermas's critical theory and Kant's critical philosophy, focusing in particular on the distinction between domains of reason or spheres of validity, the distinction between system and lifeworld, and the distinction between the logic and dynamics of historical development. The third section will explore Habermas's conceptions of morality and legality and the extent to which they follow the pattern of Kant's moral and political philosophy. The fourth section will demonstrate a parallel between Habermas's account of the philosophical discourse of modernity and Kant's argument for the discipline of pure reason. In conclusion, it will be argued that the politics of Habermas's critical theory repeats that of Kant's critical philosophy as described in the previous chapters.

RADICALIZING AND MODERATING CRITIQUE

In *Knowledge and Human Interests* Habermas argues for a revival of Kant's epistemological project, premised on a concept of knowledge which is neither equated with pure scientism nor with Hegel's absolute knowledge. In Habermas's view, Kant's recognition of the need to reflect on the limits of the validity of human knowing remains the crucial philosophical insight of modern philosophy (Habermas, 1971: 5). This insight was radicalized in the work of Hegel and Marx, but also significantly undermined first by Hegel's retreat into absolute knowledge and then by Marx's inadequate conceptions of reflection and action. According to Habermas, the unhappy result of the reworking of Kant's project in Hegel and Marx has been to defeat the possibility of radical epistemology and to open up the way for the irrelevance of philosophy to science and the essentially pre-Kantian dominance of positivism in the natural and social sciences. What is rejected in Hegel is not his phenomenology, which Habermas reads as an immanent critique of Kant, but his positing of the goal of absolute knowledge, which Habermas understands as a lapse back into the Kantian dilemma of knowing before knowledge and as the mark of an overweening ambition in philosophy which reaches beyond critique to metaphysics

(Habermas, 1971: 24). What is rejected in Marx is not his material-ism but his reduction of action to production. This results, according to Habermas, in the elimination of reflection as a motivating force in history and encourages the substitution of scientism for critique in social theory (Habermas, 1971: 44). Regardless of the merits of Habermas's reading of either Hegel or Marx, it is clear that his chief complaint against them has to do with the ways in which they sabotage rather than realize the potential of Kant's critical turn. It is this turn that Habermas wants to preserve, purged of any speculative taint. He accomplishes this in *Knowledge and Human Interests* by identifying transcendental conditions for different kinds of knowing in the concept of knowledge-constitutive interests and by following Fichte in subsuming theoretical under practical reason.

> Orientation toward technical control, toward mutual under-standing in the conduct of life, and toward emancipation from seemingly 'natural' constraint establish the specific view points from which we can apprehend reality as such in any way whatsoever.
>
> (Habermas, 1971: 311)

The natural sciences, therefore, are 'subject to the transcendental conditions of instrumental action', whereas the social/hermeneutic sciences are governed by the requirements of communicative action (Habermas, 1971: 191). However, the metacritical sciences, which are processes of self-reflection, are governed by the demands of emancipatory action in which knowing and acting are identical, and it is those sciences, for which Habermas takes psychoanalysis as a model, which reveal most clearly the essentially interested nature of reason (Habermas, 1971: 212).

At the end of *Knowledge and Human Interests* Habermas had hoped to have paved the way for a critical political and social theory necessarily linked to political and social practice. The concept of knowledge-constitutive interests, supposedly grounded in objective facts about the human condition and human evolution, made transcendental critique possible without being haunted by either transcendental ideals or the 'thing-in-itself'. It did not take long, however, for the critical reception of the notion of knowledge-constitutive interests to force Habermas to re-think the extent to which he had evaded the pitfalls of Kantian transcendental argument.[2] In particular, the notion of a constitutive relation between emancipation and critical theory was difficult to ground plausibly in facts about the human condition and appeared to be uncritically presumed rather than self-reflectively established. Without the guarantee of an emancipatory interest, the relevance of critical theory to the other aspects of knowledge becomes posited rather than necessary, putting the critic in danger of becoming the metaphysician and leaving science once more to scientism. In the light of these problems, among others, Habermas abandoned his first attempt to ground the possibility of critique in the concept of transcendental interest. He did not, however, abandon his commitment to the revival of the Kantian project of establishing the limits of the validity of claims to knowledge. Whereas Kant's search for the conditions of human cognitive and practical judgement led him into positing unknowable ideas in a transcendental beyond, for Habermas the search takes him to the analysis of the structure of language and an immanent, self-evident set of requirements for meaningful discourse. Metacritique has been reformulated as reconstructive science, the paradigm for which is provided by universal pragmatics (Habermas, 1979: 1). Universal pragmatics is Habermas's term for the analysis of the formal conditions on speech acts necessary for the arrival at understanding between speakers and hearers. Although Habermas has somewhat modified the boldness of his claims since the publication of *Communication and the Evolution of Society* (see Habermas, 1984: 137), his faith in the capacity of the analysis of the presuppositions of speech to deliver an adequate basis for critical theory has remained steadfast. As Habermas sees it, the understanding of any utterance, whether it be a claim to truth, a moral judgement or an aesthetic expression, depends on the possibility of the redemption of the validity claims implicit in the utterance. What is crucial to the truth or legitimacy of the utterance is its being recognized as being true or legitimate in the light of intersubjectively valid criteria, the validity of which in turn can be guaranteed only by their intersubjective agreement. Initially this appears to be a fairly uncritical description of how discourse works. It acquires a critical twist in that Habermas claims that the formal conditions of the intelligibility of utterance imply more than a *de facto* or transitory consensus. Instead, the formal conditions of all speech are logically implicated in an ideal of discursive validation in which all presuppositions are themselves discursively validated in free argument between equals. The grounds of truth, rightness and truthfulness can only be fully realized in the ideal speech situation. Universal pragmatics provides Habermas with a tool for the analysis of the logic of both individual cognitive development and the evolution of society. The idea of communicative rationality, which is intersubjectively based and oriented towards understanding, is both presupposed in all discourse and provides a standard against which both individual rational capacities and the organization of societies can be judged (Habermas, 1979: 205).

Since Habermas's turn to language in *Communication and the Evolution of Society* his theory has developed in line with the logical and historical claims made there for the critical potential of formal-pragmatic analysis. In *The Theory of Communicative Action* Habermas states that communicative rationality is already a given in modern social life (albeit in a fragmentary and distorted form) and that its universal potential for the grounding of critique can be expounded without recourse to foundationalism in three different ways.[3] First, in the reconstructive science of formal pragmatics; second, in the empirical usefulness of formal-pragmatic insights; and third, in an account of social theory since Weber worked up into a theory of societal rationalization.

> The programme of formal pragmatics aims at hypothetical reconstructions of that pre-theoretical knowledge that competent speakers bring to bear when they employ sentences in actions oriented to reaching understanding.
>
> (Habermas, 1984: 138)

In *The Theory of Communicative Action* emphasis is placed on the hypothetical standing of the universal rules transcendentally deduced through formal-pragmatic analysis. These hypothetical reconstructions can at best be supported by being checked against the intuitions of empirical speakers in different contexts, but they cannot be decisively legitimated. Habermas characterizes the rational internal structure of communicative action in terms of

> a) the three world-relations of actors and the corresponding concepts of the objective, social and subjective worlds; b) the validity claims of propositional truth, normative rightness, and sincerity or authenticity; c) the concept of a rationally motivated agreement, that is, one based on the intersubjective recognition of criticizable validity claims; and d) the concept of reaching understanding as the cooperative negotiation of common definitions of the situation.
>
> (Habermas, 1984: 137)

The argument of Habermas's formal pragmatics is that this internal structure is universally implicit in any discursive attempt to reach an understanding. The argument is based on an analysis of speech drawing heavily on the speech act theory of Austin and Searle but which transforms the vocabulary of locutionary, illocutionary and perlocutionary force into one of the positing and redemption of different validity claims. Claims *a* and *b* are derived from an examination of the ways in which it is possible to relate to the world in speech and are mutually supportive. According to Habermas, speakers/actors take up relations to three different worlds: an objective world of entities about which true statements can be made; a social world, which is composed of all legitimate interpersonal relations, which ground normative claims; and a subjective world, which is the world of private experience which the speaker/actor can truthfully express. This threefold classification is confirmed by the different kinds of validity claims made in all speech which is oriented towards understanding: that the statement made is true, that the speech act is right with respect to an existing normative context, and that the speaker means what is said. Claim *c* follows from the characterization of speech oriented to reaching understanding as the staking of claims to validity. Once speech is understood in this way it can obviously only be effective if there is intersubjective recognition of the kinds of claim being made. Once there is a conception of the nature of the claims there must also be a conception of what it means for the claim to fail, and therefore such claims are necessarily open to criticism. Habermas's fourth claim is not necessarily implicated in the characterization of communicative discourse in *a*, *b* and *c*. It is a claim that, over and above the grounding of validity claims in common conceptions of truth, right and authenticity, there is a sense in which the process of reaching understanding opens up the possibility of putting those grounds themselves into question and provides a procedure for discursively validating new grounds.

In *The Theory of Communicative Action* formal pragmatics plays a peculiar role. On the one hand, it is crucial to Habermas's second and third ways of expounding the universality of the concept of communicative rationality; on the other hand, the potential of formal-pragmatic analysis is seen to be much more modest than in Habermas's earlier work. Formal pragmatics provides the starting point and conceptual armoury for empirical analysis and a theory of societal rationalization and at the same time its findings are both hypothetical and incapable of conclusive validation. The path that

Habermas does not take in *The Theory of Communicative Action* is that of examining the empirical usefulness of formal pragmatic insights. He sketches out three ways in which this might be done, in

> the explanation of pathological patterns of communication, the evolution of the foundations of sociocultural forms of life, and the ontogenesis of capabilities for action.
>
> (Habermas, 1984: 139)

The first of these relies on the other two, since it presumes the adequacy of formal pragmatic standards of normality which may or may not be given support by empirical investigation of human evolution and psychological development. Although Habermas does not pursue these programmes here, it is clear from his writings on the evolution of the human species and the individual that he does think the insights of formal pragmatics can be supported empirically in a way that can buttress transcendental argument. In this context, however, he chooses the third and 'less demanding' way of developing a theory of societal rationalization. This is accomplished through a reconstruction of the history of social theory since Weber.

At first sight, Habermas's turn to a history of social theory as the means of grounding and developing his own critical theory is difficult to understand. In what sense can such a history help to establish the universality of the logic of communicative rationality? The answer, for Habermas, seems to lie in the way in which social theory in itself illustrates the self-understanding of the times in which it is produced and combines conceptual and empirical insights into the nature of rationality and action. By expounding, criticizing and reflecting on social theory, Habermas aims to arrive at his own interpretation of modernity and the possibility of critical theory within it. A full account of the details of Habermas's reconstruction of social theory is impossible here and I will confine myself to highlighting certain aspects of the argument only. However, it should be noted that Habermas employs the same tactic in his analysis of all the theorists with whom he engages. The arguments of the theorists in question are 'reconstructed' in the sense of being expounded and interrogated in terms of the concept of communicative rationality outlined in the first chapter of *The Theory of Communicative Action*. Thus Habermas contrives to appear to learn from Weber, Durkheim, Mead and Parsons, whilst at the same time teaching them a lesson.

Habermas's discussion of Weber's work is dominated by the claim that Weber's theory of the rationalization processes characteristic of modern societies has two aspects (Habermas, 1984: 140–141). One aspect concerns the mode of rationality opened up by the process of disenchantment, in which religious worldviews no longer provide a key to meaning. The other aspect concerns the mode of rationality characteristic of capitalism. The former mode of rationality is oriented towards understanding; the latter is oriented towards success.

> Unfettering normative contexts and releasing communicative action from traditionally based institutions – that is from obligations of consensus – loads (and overloads) the mechanism of reaching understanding with a growing need for coordination. On the other hand, in two central domains of action, institutions are replaced by compulsory associations – and organizations of a new type; they are formed on the basis of media that uncouple action from processes of reaching understanding and coordinate it via generalized instrumental values such as money and power.
>
> (Habermas, 1984: 341–342)

Habermas formulates his own distinction between lifeworld (action oriented towards understanding) and system (action oriented towards success) in the light of his reading of Weber, and criticizes Weber's emphasis on the logic of the latter over that of the former. In Habermas's case, it is the logic of communicative rationality in the lifeworld that motors systemic development. However, change is so complex and rapid that the mechanisms of co-ordination characteristic of the lifeworld (action oriented to understanding) are unable to cope. They become substituted by steering media which co-ordinate via strategic action and eventually recoil on the lifeworld which gave rise to them in the first place. It is this dualist conception of modern capitalist society that Habermas then fleshes out through an analysis of the work of Mead, Durkheim and Parsons.

The story told by Mead and Durkheim, according to Habermas, is the story of the rise of language as the medium for the formation of both individual and lifeworld (the 'linguistification of the sacred') (Habermas, 1984: 141). Mead's symbolic interactionist account of the development of subjective identity and the relation of ego to alter provides a reconstruction of individual development in terms of shifts in the nature of communication and 'the norming of behavioural expectations' (Habermas, 1987a: 43). The rise of language is reflected at the level of the species in Durkheim's sociology of religion and his account of the move from mechanical to organic solidarity in social systems. This shift, according to Habermas, operates at three levels in Durkheim's account: the rationalization of worldviews; the generalization of moral and legal norms; and the increasing individuation of individuals (Habermas, 1987a: 83). Habermas suggests that Durkheim came to understand this development as a process of rationalization towards a universalistic morality (Habermas, 1987a: 85). On Habermas's own reading of the logic of historical development, however, what Durkheim (like Mead) is drawing attention to is the release of the potential of communicative rationality that follows from the disenchantment of the world (Habermas, 1987a: 87–91). Habermas does not accept either Mead's or Durkheim's theories in total, and his most significant reservation about Mead is his tendency towards a 'disregard for dynamics in favour of the logic of societal development' (Habermas, 1987a: 110). By focusing on the logic of interaction and the symbolic reproduction of the lifeworld, Mead is led into an idealistic reading of history which ignores the way in which systemic reproduction distorts the logic of communicative rationality. It is at this point that Habermas turns to Parsons to supplement the theory of the lifeworld generated by the excavation of Mead and Durkheim. Although Habermas pays tribute to the usefulness and sophistication of Parsons's theory, he (Habermas) judges it to be too optimistic in one way and too pessimistic in another (Habermas, 1987a: 203). Pessimistic in that Parsons's conception of action is too narrow, leading him to accord conceptual primacy to his systems theory, too optimistic in that the inadequacy of Parsons's concept of action leads him to an over-sanguine account of social integration. Without a full concept of communicative rationality/action, Parsons has no critical tools to identify pathological patterns of development in modernity (Habermas, 1987a: 291–294).

At the end of his tour through the history of social theory, Habermas has identified the key elements of his own critical social theory. Three elements are crucial to this theory: first, there is the concept of communicative rationality/action and its utopian potential as opposed to rationality/action oriented to success. Second, there is the identification of lifeworld as the realm of communicative rationality and system as the realm of instrumental rationality. Third, there is an evolutionary theory about the relations between these two concepts of rationality/action in the histories of lifeworld and system.

According to Habermas, in this mature articulation of his theory, the strong transcendentalism of earlier formulations of his thought has been overcome. Although still acknowledging the significance of the Kantian philosophy in his work, Habermas sees himself as having evaded its dangers. In the next section this will be put to the test.

REASON AND HISTORY

For Habermas, as for Kant, the critique of reason involves addressing the problem of determining the conditions of judgement and delimiting the domains of reason, which are identified in both cases as theoretical, practical and aesthetic. In the previous chapters we saw how in Kant's case the critical project ran into a variety of problems. The assumption of the limitation of reason along with its legislative power led to the postulation of the thing-in-itself on the one hand, and transcendental ideas and ideals of reason on the other. The constitution and regulation of reason was itself placed beyond reason in the unknowable fiat of pure practical reason. The split between understanding and reason, or between theoretical and practical reason, reduced knowledge to knowledge only of appearance and elevated morality to a world apart from nature. In Kant's work the domain of the aesthetic becomes one in which the dualisms of the critiques of theoretical and practical reason are both confirmed and problematized. The possibility of aesthetic judgements of taste remains mysterious even as it is recouped through its subsumption in a transcendental and unknowable 'substrate'. The outcome of Kant's version of critique shifts constantly between authoritarian claims and the dissolution of all authority. Clearly Habermas is aware of the possible pitfalls into which a Kantian-inspired critique may fall. In particular, he is anxious to avoid 'metaphysical' connotations in the postulation of transcendental grounds. Abandoning his early attempt to establish these grounds in the concept of constitutive interests, Habermas turns to universal pragmatics and the way in which different claims are grounded in the logic of the use of language. The transcendental unity of apperception and the regulative ideas of reason are replaced by intersubjectivity and the idea of communication oriented towards understanding. However, a careful tracing of Habermas's grounding of the possibility of legitimate judgement, and of the relations between the domains of reason, suggests that his view that he has escaped Kantian pitfalls is over-optimistic.

Habermas bases the validity of claims to knowledge, right or truthfulness in the presuppositions of discourse, which can be identified through formal pragmatic analysis. The claim of formal pragmatics is that fundamental to all discourse is an orientation towards understanding which involves necessarily a threefold relation to the world, the mutual recognition of three kinds of validity claims and a concept of co-operative negotiation as to how those claims are to be understood (Habermas, 1984: 137). There are two important ways in which these transcendental conditions legislate for reason. First, they establish the priority of communicative over other kinds of rationality; second, they affirm the diremption of reason into separate realms. When examining the source of the authority of this legislation, however, there is recourse to a familiar Kantian move. The universal validity of the findings of formal pragmatics cannot be known but only hypothesized. It is a hypothesis, however, which like Kant's transcendental hypotheses is incapable of empirical proof or disproof, though it may be rendered more or less 'plausible' by reference to speakers' own intuitions (Habermas, 1984: 138). The hypothetical nature of the conditions enabling distinctions between valid and invalid judgement is claimed by Habermas to be a guarantee of his operating without metaphysical support and therefore *not* falling into Kantian traps. But this is to understand the critical philosophy as the static imposition of standards of reason rather than as the self-undermining of reason's authority which necessarily follows from the characterization of reason as both limited and legislating. In acknowleging the hypothetical status of his own transcendental presuppositions, whilst nevertheless assuming their legislative power, Habermas simultaneously grounds his critique and puts it into question. It is a testimony to his awareness of this that he looks beyond formal pragmatics to attempt to shore up the foundations of his critical theory in empirical research programmes and a theory of rationalization.

Perhaps the most glaring way in which Habermas reproduces Kantian logic in his mature theory is in his articulation of the domains of reason. As with Kant, the threefold modes of judgement in Habermas's work have a peculiar relation to one another and continually challenge their own demarcation. The relation of cognitive and moral judgement at a transcendental level in Kant's work, in which the conditions of the latter also guarantee the possibility of the former, is echoed by Habermas's grounding of judgements of truth about objects in the normative procedures of communicative rationality. At the level of empirical judgement, validity claims relating to all three realms of judgement are present, and yet judgement always relates primarily to one of those realms, which exist independently from one another. The role of aesthetic judgement in Habermas's work, again echoing Kant, is particularly odd. The aesthetic validity claim is essential to all discourse, since it involves the claim of truthfulness or sincerity. It therefore underwrites all cognitive and moral claims and yet its own domain of validity, the subjective world, is shadowy and inaccessible. The procedural legitimation of claims to truth and right is threatened by a form of judgement which, though essential to public discourse, is not essentially open to debate. Habermas's distinction of the realms of reason is one of the transcendental hypotheses of reason following from formal pragmatic analysis of discourse. The consequence of this demarcation is a constant tension between rigid analytic distinctions between different modes of judgement and aspects of the world and an undermining of these distinctions in the effort to secure the grounds of judgement (see Ingram, 1987: 183). In this, Habermas continues to follow the problematic logic of Kant's three critiques.

The concept of communicative rationality and its correlative distinction between the domains of reason is crucial to Habermas's idea of the 'lifeworld'. According to Habermas, the lifeworld comprises those aspects of social life that properly are co-ordinated through action oriented towards understanding, i.e. through the mechanisms of communicative rationality which enable understanding. This concept of lifeworld is contrasted analytically with systemic aspects of social life, which under capitalism are instrumentally oriented through strategic rationality. The lifeworld/system duality reflects the duality between communicative and strategic rationality and provides the context for the complementarity of different methodological approaches to the sociological explanation of the social world. Critics of Habermas have tended to focus on the extent to which he has gone too far towards systems theory in his acceptance of the autonomous logic of systemic steering media.[4] What is most striking about the lifeworld/system distinction in the context of argument, however, is the extent to which it maps on to the Kantian distinctions between reason and nature, noumena and phenomena. This is not to claim, of course, that Habermas understands his distinction as operating in this way. Habermas is quite clear that lifeworld and system reflect different aspects of empirical reality and that the distinction between them is much clearer analytically than in practice (Habermas, 1987a: 150–151). However, the way in which the distinction is used by Habermas and, in particular, his concept of the colonization of the lifeworld, echoes very closely Kant's assertion of both the authority and powerlessness of reason over nature. The concept of the lifeworld is not used by Habermas as a purely descriptive term to describe aspects of social life co-ordinated through symbolic interaction; instead it is used as, as it were, the proxy for what are identified as its transcendental presuppositions in communicative rationality. Lifeworld carries with it the utopian potential of the hypotheses of reason established through formal pragmatics and supported by a theory of rational evolution. Lifeworld embodies the real heart of rationality and therefore the possibility of critique. The rationality inherent in lifeworld is set against the rationality inherent in system, much as rational motivation is set against natural impulse in Kant's moral thought. The relation between the two rationalities results, as in Kant, in an assertion of the supremacy of the former over the latter, but the actual inability of the former to govern the latter. The parallel is continued in the claim of communicative rationality's inability to bring about its own ends in the world and the substitution of systemic steering media for action oriented towards understanding in the co-ordination of social life. The distinguishing of communicative rationality's theoretical from its practical power enables Habermas to condemn the colonization of the lifeworld from the standpoint of formal pragmatics, but paradoxically leads him to confirm the division between transcendental hypothesis and the empirical social order.

In his conception of the communicative rationality embedded in the concept of the lifeworld, Habermas does not simply rely on the findings of formal pragmatic analysis. Throughout his account of modernity the insights gained from linguistic analysis are bolstered by a complementary theory of individual development (which owes much to Mead, Piaget and Kohlberg) and of societal evolution.

> In this way I have attempted to free historical materialism from its philosophical ballast. Two abstractions are required for this: (i) abstracting the development of cognitive structures from the historical dynamic of events, and (ii) abstracting the evolution of society from the historical concretion of forms of life. Both help in getting beyond the confusion of basic categories to which the philosophy of history owes its existence.
>
> (Habermas, 1987a: 383)

Some critics have argued that Habermas's turn to an account of the evolution of individual and species represents the Hegelian/Marxist element in his work, to be contrasted with the formal Kantian elements which are to be found in his philosophy of language (Roderick, 1986: 100; Rasmussen, 1990: 56–58; White, 1988: 128). I would argue, on the contrary, that Habermas's reworking of historical materialism through his reading of the history of social theory follows the logic not of Hegel or Marx but of Kant.

Habermas frequently denies that he is engaging in philosophy of history (Habermas, 1984: 145–156). He supports this claim by arguing that in his account of human evolution he does not assert a linear progress towards the fulfilment of a kingdom of ends; nor does he conflate theoretical and practical reason; nor does he fall into Eurocentric universalism. Moreover, Habermas makes a firm distinction between the logic and the dynamics of development at both individual and social levels. This latter enables him both to differentiate the evolutionary levels of individuals from those of the social structure of which they are a part, and to separate the logic of evolution from the empirical directions of history. On examination, however, the distinction between the logic and dynamics of development that Habermas relies on to prevent a lapse into the old-fashioned philosophy of history raises some problems of its own. The possibility of making the distinction depends on the validity of formal pragmatic claims about the fundamental conditions that structure communication. These claims in turn, however, have a hypothetical character and are not open to proof. Nevertheless they provide standards for the assessment of both individual and social maturity. Given that there is no guarantee as to the direction of history, what status can be given to the logic as opposed to the dynamics of development? The answer seems to take us back to Kant's story of human and social maturation as one in which the dynamics of desire willy-nilly conform to a logic of development, which itself conforms not to history but to the philosopher's judgement. Of course, Habermas wants to defend his account of the logic of development as given in the analysis of the presuppositions of language, but even if this is the case, it is not clear why this should determine the reading of history. The lack of empirical support for the significance of this logic is demonstrated in the need to distinguish between logic and dynamics in the first place. Even if the distinction between logic and dynamics is accepted, it is also unclear whether it enables Habermas to evade the pitfalls of the traditional philosophy of history he rejects.

The logic of individual and social development he asserts is a linear one, with each stage being incorporated within its successor through individual and global learning processes. Communicative rationality *does* retain a utopian potential and the implication of a unified conception of reason. And the privileging of communicative rationality, in so far as it is specifically linked with the emergence of western secularized societies, *does* retain a strong flavour of Eurocentrism. Habermas abandons the Kantian ambition for philosophy to be the usher of the sciences for the more modest role for philosophy of stand-in and interpreter (Habermas, 1990a: 1–20). On close inspection, however, the distinction is not particularly clear. A philosophy that keeps the seat of empirical theories with strong universalistic claims, but is itself the keeper of the terms on which the seat should be abandoned (Habermas, 1990a: 15); and a philosophy that interprets the implicit totality of the lifeworld, but in terms that it has already articulated, continues to arrogate an authority to itself of Kantian dimensions, even as it struggles to support the pretensions of that authority (Habermas, 1990a: 18–19). Looking back at the three main elements of Habermas's mature critical theory, it is clear that his work still manifests a close relation to Kantian critique. This continues to be demonstrated in Habermas's attempts to develop a formalist ethics and his conception of, and treatment of the links between, the realms of morality and legality.

MORALITY AND LEGALITY

In *Moral Consciousness and Communicative Action* Habermas utilizes his theory of communicative action to specify the nature of moral consciousness and its relation to concrete social forms. In doing this Habermas draws on transcendental pragmatics, the psychological theory of Piaget and Kohlberg and his (Habermas's) evolutionary theory of society. The crucial element in Habermas's moral theory is derived from the analysis of the formal conditions for the redemption of normative validity claims. Implicit in the making and recognizing of such claims, according to Habermas, is a discursive procedure for the validation of norms which is universally binding. The principle of discourse ethics is summed up as:

> Only those norms can claim to be valid that meet (or could meet) with the approval of all affected in their capacity *as participants in a practical discourse.*
>
> (Habermas, 1990a: 66)

The rules governing pure practical discourse themselves derive from the transcendental conditions of successful communication oriented towards understanding. Breaching these rules involves the speaker in performative contradiction. In other words, the speaker 'makes performative use of something he expressly denies' (Habermas, 1990a: 129). The mark of moral consciousness on this account is a combination of universalism, formalism and openness/indeterminacy, it is oriented to normative validity rather than to value preferences. Habermas finds support for his moral theory in the accounts of moral development offered in particular by Kohlberg. The value for Habermas in Kohlberg's work arises from the way Kohlberg construes the stages of moral growth as hierarchically ordered in a logic of development which does not always correspond to the empirical dynamics of change in the child. This logic, in which each stage includes and sublates the previous stage, culminates in Kohlberg's hierarchy in the capacity for universal and formalistic moral thinking, which is not tied down to the concrete situation of the child. Thus Kohlberg's reconstructive science confirms Habermas's transcendental pragmatic analysis of the nature of moral consciousness.[5] Habermas's moral theory receives further support from his reading of the logic of species development, which complements that of the individual. The linguistification of the sacred, crucial to Habermas's account of rationalization, is the process in which questions of normative validity become open to discursive settlement. The mode of integration through action oriented towards understanding characteristic of the lifeworld, following the disenchantment of that world, is what makes discourse ethics possible. There has been a great deal of criticism of Habermas's concept of discourse ethics, mostly centred around the problems posed by the emptiness of an ethical principle which appears to have no substantive content and therefore no possibility of concrete application (see Benhabib and Dallmayr, 1990: 4). To these criticisms Habermas has two answers: the first relies on the distinction between norms and values mentioned above; and the second lies in the link between Habermas's conception of morality and the development of a specific kind of social order.

Habermas accepts that he has provided no guidance on the application of universal moral norms in context-specific situations. He argues that the question of the justification of normative principles is entirely separate from the question of the ways in which they can be applied. The latter question involves a knowledge of the ethical life of the lifeworlds in which individuals are situated and the concept of the good life towards which they are oriented. This is the realm of value-preference, which is not open to the kind of discursive validation that underpins universal principles, though it may be that universal principles rule out certain kinds of ethical practice.

> The question of the context-specific application of universal norms should not be confused with the question of their justification. Since moral norms do not contain their own rules of application, acting on the basis of moral insight requires the additional competence of hermeneutic prudence, or in Kantian terminology, reflective judgement.
>
> (Habermas, 1990a: 179–180)

Thus Habermas suggests the necessity of supplementing the formal procedures of discourse with the art of reflective judgement in the Kantian sense, as a way of bridging the gap between universal and particular, ideal and real.

Habermas's second response to the charge of empty formalism in his ethics is rather different from the first. It suggests the possibility of the direct concretion of the procedural requirements of universalist ethics in forms of life themselves. Habermas states that any universalistic ethics is dependent on a form of life that meets it halfway, both in terms of the education/socialization of individuals and in terms of social and political institutions.

> Moral universalism is a *historical result*. It arose, with Rousseau and Kant, in the midst of a specific society that possessed corresponding features.
>
> (Habermas, 1990a: 208)

Here Habermas returns to his theory of societal rationalization and the claim that, even if only partially, modernity has in its symbolic reproduction of the lifeworld embodied universal moral principles. If moral universalism is a historical result, then the possibility is opened up of the coming together of the justification and application of moral principles in a world in which the tension between actual discourse and its transcendental presuppositions has been resolved. This is the utopian moment implicit in Habermas's account of modernity (Habermas, 1984: 398).

In his essay 'Morality and Ethical Life: Does Hegel's Critique of Kant Apply to Discourse Ethics?' (Habermas, 1990a: 195–211),

Habermas accepts the affinities of discourse ethics with Kant's moral theory, but also identifies three differences between them. First, Habermas claims, the Kantian distinction between intelligible and empirical realms disappears in discourse ethics, which operates instead with the notion of the tension between actual discourse and its *counterfactual presuppositions*. Second, Kant assumes the individual tests his or her own maxims for action, whereas discourse ethics replaces this monological approach with an *intersubjective procedure*. Third, Kant is unable to ground the force of his 'ought', whereas discourse ethics derives its categorical imperative from the *universal presuppositions of argumentation*. On examination, the three ways in which Habermas differentiates himself from Kant all rest on the same point, i.e. the greater plausibility of the transcendental conditions of judgement identified by formal pragmatics. As has been argued above, however, it is not clear that Habermas's claims for the universal presuppositions of argumentation are any more plausibly grounded than Kant's hypotheses of reason. In both cases, universal claims have a hypothetical status and are incapable of being grounded by reference to purely empirical evidence. The parallels between the moral theories of Habermas and Kant are not significantly undermined by the difference in their transcendental reference points. In both cases, the limits of morality are traced using a universalization test and a principle of contradiction. In both cases, the formulation of the principle of morality poses problems for its actualization outside of a kingdom of ends or a fully rationalized lifeworld. In both cases, the difficulties of applying moral principles to the realm of legality (i.e. of natural motivation and tradition) leads on to the exploration of ways in which the promise of morality might be made good through the mediation of reflective judgement or through juridical development and political organization. In his most recent work, Habermas seems to be following both paths, but with the emphasis on the ways in which the capacity for reflective judgement is best nurtured through a particular kind of juridical system, which externally promotes what cannot be inwardly guaranteed. In *The Theory of Communicative Action*, the law plays a highly ambivalent role, both anchored in the communicative rationality of the lifeworld in modern societies and operating as a steering medium and colonizer of the lifeworld (Habermas, 1987a: 356–373). However, in *Faktizität und Geltung: Beiträge zur Diskurstheorie des Rechts und des demokratischen Rechtsstaats*, Habermas embraces more positively the idea of legal and political organization externally institutionalizing the procedures which are a transcendental requirement of moral judgement.

Habermas argues, it is clear that a post-conventional morality requires the complementary form of law. Law enables a society to regulate interactions without having to rely directly on the motivations of its members; indeed it vastly increases the scope for strategic action, yet in a manner still ultimately anchored in the principle of communicative consensus.

(Dews, 1993: 26)

The idea of the impartiality and autonomy of law in the liberal constitutional state provides a bridge between lifeworld and system, between validity and facticity, and between freedom and obligation (Habermas, 1990b: 98–99; 1992a: 599). Although Kant and Habermas clearly differ about the kind of state which provides the external complement to internal moral motivation, the logic of their arguments is startlingly similar and poses the same kinds of problems. In the first place it is the abstract nature of morality that necessitates a turn to politics. This is followed by an attempt to specify the principles of right which will fulfil the ends of practical reason. This attempt, however, remains dogged by the gulf that has been presupposed between morality and legality or between lifeworld and system. Two difficulties follow from this: the problem of how you ensure the shaping of law in the direction of right and therefore morality; and, perhaps more importantly, the problem of the relation between the realms of right and morality, even if the former is perfectly constituted. The formal procedural nature of Habermas's discourse ethics exhibits the same slipperiness as Kant's categorical imperative in its combination of rigour and permissiveness. On the one hand, discourse ethics is rigorous because it requires each individual to be motivated by the transcendental requirements of normative judgement; on the other hand, discourse ethics is permissive because it does not legislate substantively. This means that there are problems about recognizing when the perfect juridical constitution has been attained and about whether the gap between the juridical and the moral is bridged even if it is attained. The external enabling of communicative rationality may not be the exercising of that rationality, just as the externally motivated obedience to the moral law in Kant is not itself morality. This is something that Habermas himself recognizes in his use of the idea of the importance of autonomous public spheres acting in a sense as powerhouses of communicative rationality outside of the legal and political system yet in dialogue with it (Habermas, 1990b: 107; 1992b: 421–462).

> A public sphere that functions politically requires more than the institutional guarantees of the constitutional state; it also needs the supportive spirit of cultural traditions and patterns of socialization, of the political culture of a populace accustomed to freedom.
>
> (Habermas, 1992b: 453)

The role of the idea of the autonomous public sphere in Habermas's work is analogous to the mediations of reflective judgement which juridical and political development may support but cannot guarantee.[6] In the autonomous public sphere the distinction between norms and values collapses in a form of life which is internally motivated as well as externally governed by communicative rationality.

THE DISCIPLINE OF REASON

In the 'Transcendental Method' Kant demonstrates the discipline of pure reason whipping the warring philosophical perspectives into line. In the same way, in *The Philosophical Discourse of Modernity*, Habermas employs his paradigm of reason as communicative rationality to discipline the pretensions of other philosophical perspectives, all of which remain within the supposedly exhausted paradigm of the philosophy of consciousness.[7] The sword of the critique of reason cuts Hegel, Marx, Heidegger, Derrida and Foucault (among others) down to size. This text presents Habermas's mature reading of the history of reason as *Knowledge and Human Interests* presented his earlier ideas. The two texts share the same pattern; they both start with the Kantian distillation of modern thought and move on to consider the positive and negative aspects of the working through of the Kantian inheritance in later thinkers. Habermas's reading of Hegel and Marx is still essentially the same. Hegel's critique of Kant and Marx's of Hegel are seen to offer constructive ways beyond the Kantian paradigm, but are also seen as failing to fulfil their promise. In the later text, however, Habermas has a more systematic and unified conception of the way in which the two philosophers fail – they both remain within the paradigm of the philosophy of the subject or the philosophy of consciousness. Moreover, the Hegelian-Marxist tradition is characterized as only one trajectory of post-Kantian philosophy still caught in the philosophy of consciousness. What Habermas identifies as neo-conservative and young conservative traditions traced from Right Hegelian or Nietzschean sources are all caught up in the same paradigm. According to Habermas, this is the paradigm of knowledge as the knowledge of objects on the part of a subject-knower (Habermas, 1987b: 295–296). The implications of this model, which can be dated from Descartes, are that epistemology becomes fixated on the task of bridging the gap between knower and known. Kant's attempt to do this with its notion of the transcendental subject and its ultimate sway over the differentiated realms of reason is criticized by succeeding generations, but without the background presumption of the model of knowledge being fully challenged or replaced. As Habermas sees it, critics of Kant persistently either fall into the trap of positing a superior subject or transcendental condition of experience (e.g. Hegel, Heidegger, Derrida); or, like Marx, prioritize one particular aspect of the subject–object relation as of transcendental significance; or simply assert the opposite of the paradigm of subjective consciousness and assign an inexplicable transcendental force to some *other* of reason (e.g. Nietzsche, Foucault). Habermas constantly sees repeated the rigid dualism between transcendental and empirical and the more or less disguised spectre of foundationalism. These are, he claims, testimony to the exhaustion of this particular philosophical paradigm:

> the paradigm of the knowledge of objects has to be replaced
> by the paradigm of mutual understanding between subjects
> capable of speech and action.
>
> (Habermas, 1987b: 295–296)

Habermas's readings of the modern philosophical tradition are obviously highly contestable (see Rajchman, 1988; Wolin and Rajchman, 1990). Setting aside the defensibility of his characterization of other thinkers, however, what is most interesting about Habermas's argument is the extent to which it succeeds in establishing a paradigm of reason that does not fall into the offences of which he accuses the paradigm of the philosophy of consciousness. Kant's discipline of pure reason changes the terms of metaphysical dispute and thereby overrides the claims of scepticism and speculation. In a similar way, Habermas's new paradigm sets the disputes between Nietzschean scepticism and Hegelian speculation outside the boundaries of philosophical discourse. In Kant's case, however, the battles between scepticism and speculation continued to haunt his philosophy in the form of the thing-in-itself and the ideas and ideals of reason. The ghost that Habermas needs to lay is that of the transcendental/empirical distinction and its implications. The laying of this ghost takes us back to the three ways of validating the universality of the elements of communicative rationality: the findings of formal pragmatics; empirical science; and a theory of societal rationalization. As we have seen above, it is extremely questionable that any of these offer a way out of the dualisms and paradoxes of Kantian critical thought. The transcendental/empirical gulf is confirmed in the gap between actual speech and its counterfactual presuppositions, in the pre-judging of the results of scientific investigation, and in the recourse to a reading of history to close the gap between the destructive and constructive aspects of enlightenment reason. In setting out his alternative paradigm in *The Philosophical Discourse of Modernity*, Habermas invokes all of the above elements and tries to show how they do not repeat the logic of the philosophy of consciousness. As in his earlier work, however, the argument shifts uneasily between transcendental validation and the evidence of history, with a reading of the latter giving support to the former and the former dictating how the latter is to be read. The positive normative content of modernity is claimed to reside in the lifeworld, which takes the place of transcendental consciousness (Habermas, 1987b: 326). However, given the vulnerability of the lifeworld to systemic reproductive constraints, Habermas suggests that communicative rationality is enshrined most clearly in the autonomous public spheres which he invokes as both complementing and challenging the legal and political institutions that mediate between system and lifeworld.

> Centers of concentrated communication that arise spontaneously out of microdomains of everyday practice can develop into autonomous public spheres and consolidate as self-supporting higher-level intersubjectivities only to the degree that the lifeworld potential for self-organization and for the self-organized use of the means of communication are utilized.
>
> (Habermas, 1987b: 364)

At the end of *The Philosophical Discourse of Modernity* Habermas discusses autonomous public spheres as both dependent on the potential for communicative rationality and action embodied in the lifeworld and as helping to realize that potential. However, the implication of the closing passages of Habermas's argument is that the capacity of the lifeworld and autonomous public spheres to realize communicative rationality is constantly threatened, both by imperatives of systemic co-ordination and by the problem of mediating the gap between specific contextual needs and interests and universal normative requirements (Habermas, 1987b: 365–367). According to Habermas, philosophy, like the autonomous public sphere, draws its critical capacity from the rationalization of the lifeworld (Habermas, 1987b: 365). This implies a twofold account of the potential of modernity: on the one hand, modernity is a state of constant tension between lifeworld and system; on the other, in so far as the philosopher reads history as the development of communicative rationality, modernity is progress to a moral end. Philosophy is both locked into the perpetual struggle between communicative and strategic rationality and holds the key to the transcendence of that struggle.

CONCLUSION

At the end of the previous chapter I stated that, for Kant, the problem of the legitimation, application and enforcement of law is as much the problem of the political philosopher as of political philosophy as such. This is true for any critical theorist whose critique is premised on the limitations of reason. The theorist becomes caught in the double difficulty of accounting for his or her own critical practice even as he or she engages in that practice. Habermas's self-conscious utilization of Kant's critical philosophy to deal with this double difficulty has direct consequences for both the politics of his theory and his theorization of politics. In both cases Habermas shifts between claims to authoritative judgement and the impossibility of legitimating that authority. In an effort to ground critique Habermas employs the idea of knowledge-constitutive interests, then moves on to universal pragmatics, a theory of rationalization and the art of reflective judgement. However, none of these ways of overcoming the divisions of reason is sustainable except as hypothesis or as hope. Similarly, the development of the lifeworld and of autonomous public spheres, which promises progress in history, remains permanently fragile outside of the philosopher's judgement. Rather than exemplifying the success of critique, Habermas's theory, like Kant's critical philosophy, is a testimony to critique's impossibility and its persistent tendency to lapse back into the speculative and sceptical alternatives it is designed to overcome.

4

ARENDT AND THE POLITICAL PHILOSOPHY OF JUDGEMENT

INTRODUCTION

Arendt's work is difficult to classify under traditional political or philosophical labels. Her politics appear to veer between conservatism and anarchism, elitism and radical democracy; and the nature of her philosophical practice cannot be straightforwardly categorized as 'rationalist' or 'deconstructionist', 'modernist' or 'postmodernist' (Hansen, 1993: 4; 76–88; Ingram, 1988). Arendt herself has bequeathed the story of her formation as a political activist and thinker. Once upon a time there was a gifted student of philosophy being tutored by masters in the life of the mind, without a great deal of interest in politics. Suddenly, however, history happens and the philosopher is claimed by politics, snatched from the life of the mind into the horrors of exile, statelessness, war and the eventual task of comprehending the final solution (Young-Bruehl, 1982: 42–76). When Arendt's story is told in this way it is easy to neglect the fact that the ways in which Arendt responded to the cataclysmic happenings of history are always mediated by her relation to philosophy and to the work of certain philosophers. Kateb notes how Arendt's last work *The Life of the Mind* both accuses and excuses philosophy (Kateb, 1984: 189). Throughout her work Arendt displays a paradoxical willingness to blame philosophy for the fate of modernity and yet at the same time find in it the possibility of modernity's salvation. In order to understand the nature of Arendt's political thought and the reasons for her eventual turn to Kant for the beginnings of a new political philosophy, it is necessary to understand Arendt's indictment of the political philosophy of the past and the role she sees it as having played in the modern world.

For Arendt, Heidegger and Plato represent the two aspects of the threat that philosophy poses to politics. Heidegger is the philosopher who turns away from the world and in gazing at the stars risks Thales' fate of falling down the well at his feet (Arendt, 1978a: 82–83). Plato is the philosopher who turns towards the world and in an effort to make it safe for philosophy conceptualizes the world as both inferior and manageable (Arendt, 1958: 14). Significantly, Heidegger can be forgiven: his error can be laughed at as the product of absorption in the life of the mind; and as long as a divorce between thinking and acting is respected, such errors can be avoided. It is Plato, with his insistence on the submission of the world of appearance to a higher truth and his subordination of politics to philosophy who cannot be forgiven. It is Plato who initiates the great mistake of western political thought, that of seeing the task of politics as essentially the task of legislation and government; and the task of political philosophy, therefore, as the discovery of the fundamental principles underlying legislation and rule (Arendt, 1958: 12). According to Arendt, this mistake has huge consequences for thinking and acting, both of which cease to be valued in themselves and acquire value only in so far as they serve other higher ends. The emphasis on ruling as the key concern of politics encourages, in Arendt's view, the presumption of the determinability of human action. Infinite legislative power and complete manipulability of people provide the twin ingredients that Arendt identifies as the hallmark of totalitarian thinking, in which everything is determined and yet anything is possible (Arendt, 1986: 437–459). Although Arendt does not take a crudely Popperian view of the role of Plato in the origins of totalitarianism, she does see the tradition of political philosophy founded by Plato as part of the conditions of possibility of totalitarian development. At the very least Arendt claims that the understanding of politics on which traditional political philosophy is premised could do nothing to hinder the rise of Nazism and Stalinism. It is therefore not surprising that in her own political writings she attempts to offer a completely different account of the nature of politics and the role of the philosopher in politics from the one she reads in Plato's *Republic*. The aim of this chapter is to examine the way that Arendt makes use of Kant's critical thought in her effort to write a new kind of political philosophy. Unlike Habermas and Kant himself, Arendt overtly rejects the role of the prescriptive political theorist. Her work is therefore much more selective in its use of Kant than is the case with Habermas. Nevertheless, it will be argued that in spite of her attempts to avoid the legislative aspect of critical political theory, Arendt's use of Kant's work has consequences that problematize her own aims for a rebirth of politics and a new kind of political philosophy.

THE *VITA ACTIVA*

Arendt was one of the first to attempt to explain and define totalitarianism as a unique phenomenon, and there has been extensive debate as to the merits of the historical and conceptual argument that she formulates in *The Origins of Totalitarianism* (see Bittman, 'Totalitarianism: The Career of a Concept', in Kaplan and Kessler, 1989: 56–68). What is clear is that Arendt herself came to see totalitarianism, as defined in the chapter added to the second edition of *The Origins of Totalitarianism* (Arendt, 1986: 460–479), as the complete opposite of genuine politics. The most distinctive characteristic of totalitarian rule for Arendt is the way in which it abolishes the space between people. Under totalitarianism people are welded together as a single whole rather than having a distinct identity. This whole then exists at the whim of the higher forces of nature or history (Arendt, 1986: 466). All distinctions are overridden in the interests of the logic of an idea. Totalitarian regimes are distinguished by a fictitious but complete rationality in which all aspects of life are explicable and controllable; yet at the same time there is a complete abandonment of traditional standards of rational self-interest. In this realm of rigorous absurdity both the vocabulary and the inner resources for dissent are lost.

> Present totalitarian governments have developed from one-party systems; whenever these became truly totalitarian, they started to operate according to a system of values so radically different from all others, that none of our traditional legal, moral, or common sense utilitarian categories could any longer help us to come to terms with, or judge, or predict their course of action.
>
> (Arendt, 1986: 460)

The account of politics that Arendt formulates as an alternative to this nightmare vision of totalitarianism takes its starting point from the idea of the necessity of space in political life, and from the conviction of the uselessness of truth, morality or law as adequate protection against totalitarian development. It is important to note that the kind of shrinking of public space that is carried to its extreme in totalitarian regimes is characteristic, according to Arendt, of the development of the modern capitalist state in general and that therefore her view of politics is not only set against Nazism and Stalinism but the trend of liberal democratic rule as well. Arendt's most systematic statement of her own political thought is to be found in *The Human Condition*. Originally Arendt had wanted to entitle the book *Vita Activa*, a phrase which sums up the other of the philosophical *vita contemplativa* (Arendt, 1958: 12–17). The *vita activa* covers all modes of human activity in the world including political activity. Arendt argues that the tradition of western philosophy has been to ignore or denigrate the *vita activa*, with the result that its true scope and meaning has not been understood. In offering a thorough comprehension of the *vita activa*, Arendt sees herself as rescuing the possibility of a conception of genuine politics.

The three different modes of the *vita activa* identified in *The Human Condition* are labour, work and action. Labouring is the activity humans need to engage in in order to sustain and reproduce themselves. Arendt sees as significant the fact that the word 'labour' is also used in many languages to mean the process of giving birth (Arendt, 1958: 115). Labour is a never-ending process with no enduring result, the products of labour are essentially consumable and are swallowed up in the service of self and species preservation. Labour is necessary for life, but as a labourer the human being is the equivalent of a slave. In *The Human Condition* Arendt relies heavily on models of human organization drawn from the ancient world to provide the ideal types for her categorizations. According to Arendt's model of Ancient Greece the sphere of labour maps onto the sphere of the household, the private economic realm where the primary movers are slaves and women. The lack of political freedom of these groups helps to underline Arendt's point that labour is a necessary precondition of any other activity, but in itself it is not far removed from an animal existence. Indeed she refers to the labourer as *animal laborans* and is deeply critical of what she sees as the mistaken idealization of labouring activity in Marx's work (Arendt, 1958: 101–109; Hansen, 1993: 35). Arendt argues that the incredible increase in human productivity in the nineteenth and twentieth centuries has led to the identification of labour and production as the highest ends of human existence. In both communist and capitalist contexts the concerns of the household have come to dominate the public sphere so that governments are preoccupied with 'social' issues (Arendt, 1958: 313–325). For Arendt this is a highly dangerous development because she sees economic and social questions as essentially resolvable, a matter of understanding, organization and management. On one frequently quoted occasion, at a conference in which Arendt was being asked to define the terms of the political, she was adamant in refusing to accept the issue of housing as a genuinely political issue precisely because she argued that in principle all rational persons should be able to agree on housing policy. Like other economic questions, housing is part of the sphere of necessity which is a precondition of politics but is not itself the stuff of which politics is made (Bernstein, 1986: 249–254).

Although housing is an economic or social issue and therefore, ideally, an aspect of the private sphere of human activity, there is a sense in which Arendt does see it as also part of the public sphere; more specifically that part of the public sphere in which the boundary between the private and the public is drawn. In so far as houses are artificial, humanly constructed objects, which exist independently through time, houses are a product not of labour but of the second mode of the *vita activa*, work. In Arendt's view labour is very much a natural activity, one that humans share with other species in the naturally given world. Through work, however, humans create an artificial world of their own, a lasting and objective context for uniquely human activity (Arendt, 1958: 137). It is work that literally creates the space that Arendt sees as necessary for political life. The worker (*homo faber*) is above all a builder of walls; the city walls that divide the human realm from the natural and the household walls that divide the private from the public sphere. Work covers a range of creative activities for Arendt: builders, architects, craftsmen, artists and legislators are all examples of *homo faber*, because all are involved in making a context for human life that will transcend both labour and work. What all the activities included in work have in common is that they are governed by a specific end or intention and are under human, sovereign control. Work is inherently both violent and constructive, it violates the given world of nature and reshapes it and, unlike labour, it is a process with a definite beginning and end (Arendt, 1958: 139). The ideal type of the worker creates the public world physically and institutionally through constructing buildings and making laws. However, he does not himself act in the space he has made. As bad as the idealization of labour and the domination of the public realm by private interest, according to Arendt, is the conceptualization of political man in the form of the sovereign maker of the world. This is the fundamental mistake of Plato repeated throughout the history of western political thought until Marx compounded the error by substituting labour for work as the end point of the *vita activa*. While Arendt is prepared to accept that, unlike labour, work is at least a distinctively human activity, she argues that to understand the public realm in terms of work would be to destroy the world that work has created. What work makes possible is a chance for human beings to begin afresh, to be reborn into an artificial as opposed to a natural world. The end of work itself, however, is its own finite product; there is no more to do once it is completed except to destroy it.

> Alone with his image of the future product, *homo faber* is free to produce, and again facing alone the work of his hands, he is free to destroy.
>
> (Arendt, 1958: 144)

The worker works alone in a battle to erect bulwarks against the natural world and to build a new theatre for human activity. However, the stage he creates is in itself meaningless. It is only in acting and speaking on that stage to an audience that the achievement of *homo faber* finds its full realization, and Arendt implies that any one acting in the role of *homo faber* will only ruin the play. This brings us to the third mode of life in the *vita activa*, action. In action humanity escapes both the slavery of necessity involved in labour and the violent sovereignty of *homo faber*. Action represents for Arendt the highest moment of the *vita activa*. In essence, the human capacity for action is the capacity for spontaneous new beginning undetermined by either prior causes or articulated ends (Arendt, 1958: 176). In *The Human Condition* Arendt draws most obviously from the example of the Athenian polis to demonstrate her understanding of action. In this context, action covers both acting and speaking as a kind of heroic self-disclosure in which individual actors begin themselves again in the artificial public world in the eyes of their fellow citizens. In labour, humanity is united as a species; in work, human agents are in an isolated relation to nature; but in action, Arendt claims, we have 'men in the plural', people act for and with each other. It is action which is the political form of human activity, taking place within the free, open space of a shared, constructed public realm. Politics is not a matter of achieving ends; it is an ongoing activity of beginnings and new beginnings over which no actor can exert absolute control. In acting, the actor reveals him- or herself to others, discloses who he or she is, but never with full knowledge of what the consequences of this might be. An actor initiates and suffers but is not the author or producer of his or her act; he or she is not in sovereign control. Labour has neither beginning nor end, work has both beginning and end, action is beginning but the end cannot be known to the actor (Arendt, 1958: 144, 190). Arendt is aware that the boundlessness of her characterization of action appears to make the realm of politics completely anarchic and unpredictable. In an effort to introduce some stability into the political arena without sacrificing the necessary indeterminacy of action, she introduces the concepts of promising, forgiveness and power. Promising gives binding direction to the future of action; forgiveness redeems the unintended consequences of action (Arendt, 1958: 237); and power is generated through working with others in political action in contradistinction to the violent imposition of a unilateral will that characterizes work (Arendt, 1958: 199–207). However, it is difficult to see how promising, forgiveness and power stabilize the political realm, since they all rely on the spontaneous self-disclosure characteristic of action in the public realm but can in no way be guaranteed by it. In the context of *The Human Condition* Arendt is not centrally concerned with the issue of political stability. However, in her later text, *On Revolution*, Arendt focuses much more closely on the significance of both the foundation and preservation of the political sphere and returns to the importance of promising and of power.

> The grammar of action: that action is the only human faculty that demands a plurality of men; and the syntax of power: that power is the only attribute which applies solely to the in-between space by which men are mutually related, combine in the act of foundation by virtue of the making and the keeping of promises, which, in the realm of politics, may well be the highest human faculty.
>
> (Arendt, 1973: 175)

According to Arendt, it is the mutual contract between the founding fathers of the United States that creates the public space in which violence is transformed into power. It is this act of beginning, saved from arbitrariness by the principle of mutual promise and common deliberation which it carries within it, that grounds the authority of the United States' constitution (Arendt, 1973: 213–214). This is not, however, an authority that predates the act of foundation, but an authority created within the act itself. According to Arendt, this presents the founding fathers with a difficulty, because authority traditionally must be seen to derive from something over and above the contingency of action (Arendt, 1973: 206). Paradoxically, the genuine authority (in Arendt's terms) of mutual promise and mutual deliberation has to be subsumed under some pre-existing absolute in the language of the founding fathers, whether this is the absolute of truth (self-evidence), precedent or of divine or natural law. Arendt is surprisingly indulgent towards this tactical invocation of a higher ground for action because it functions to keep open the public space opened up by the constitution.

The predominant metaphor in Arendt's account of the political in general is a theatrical one. Actors need labour to sustain them and a stage to act upon, and acting itself is essentially public and revelatory. It is at this point that the metaphor breaks down, since there is no sense in which Arendt's actors have a script written down in advance. Rather, the actors are improvising the play as they go along and they cannot know the direction it is going to take. There is, however, a character in *The Human Condition* whose role in some sense complements and completes that of the actors and this is the storyteller or historian.

> Action reveals itself fully only to the story teller, that is, to the backward glance of the historian, who indeed always knows better what it was about than the participants.
>
> (Arendt, 1958: 192)

At first sight the introduction of the storyteller into Arendt's political realm seems out of keeping with the centrality of action to the public sphere. An open-ended orientation towards the future is definitive of action, yet the storyteller looks backwards and endows events in the public world with a finite meaning. Arendt makes a clear distinction between the stories woven by actors themselves and the finished account produced by the historian (Arendt, 1958: 181–188). In fact, the position of the storyteller in relation to the political realm is ambiguous. It is not clear whether the reading of history is itself political or whether it is simply the means for the preservation of the idea of the political through the immortalizing of great words and deeds. Arendt introduces the storyteller as the counterpart of the legislator; the latter creates the framework for action, the former supplies action with meaning and purpose (Arendt, 1958: 196–197). Unlike the legislator, however, the storyteller does not exercise sovereignty but interprets without recourse to any rule or law, so that storytelling is like action in being neither legislative nor legislated. Moreover, the storyteller deals in meaning and has, as it were, one foot in the *vita contemplativa*, the life of the mind. It is this that provides the clue to the likely significance of the figure of the storyteller in Arendt's account of politics. It is the only role possible for the philosopher in politics once the nature of politics is properly understood, and it provides Arendt with a way out of the paradox of stressing the centrality of action in politics at a theoretical level. The traditional subordination of politics to philosophy and action to contemplation is only properly reversed in a philosophical text if a place for philosophy can be found in politics. Contrary to Arendt's own protestations, there are already signs in *The Human Condition* of a project to return philosophy to politics rather than to insist on a rigid division between the life of the world and the life of the mind.

In *The Origins of Totalitarianism* and *The Human Condition* Arendt does not draw explicitly on Kant's work; indeed, in the latter text, Kant's political philosophy is summarily dismissed as the culmination of a modern trend in political thought which sees political activity as primarily legislative (Arendt, 1958: 63). Nevertheless Arendt's conceptions of truth and morality as law-governed, the rigid distinctions she draws between theory and practice, and between the animal and the distinctively human, all reflect the influence of Kant on her thought (see Beiner, 'Hannah Arendt on Judging', in Arendt, 1982: 141). The distinction between the three modes of the *vita activa* mirrors Kant's distinction between the three human dispositions in *Religion Within the Limits of Reason Alone*: 'animality', 'humanity' and 'personality' (Kant, 1960: 21).[1] In distinguishing between these different dispositions, Kant contrasts the drive for physical satisfaction; the capacity to fulfil the ends dictated by desire; and the predisposition to unconditional self-legislation (Kant, 1960: 23). However, the most significant Kantian element in Arendt's exposition of the human condition is Arendt's characterization of the political as a realm of pure spontaneity which can acquire meaning through the judgement of the storyteller. This concept of political life is very close to Kant's notion of history and the distinction he draws between the recording of empirical events and the role of the transcendental historian, who gives what is inherently arbitrary meaning and purpose. The role of the storyteller in *The Human Condition* is the beginning of a shift in the focus of Arendt's political thought facilitated by her coverage of the Eichmann trial (Arendt, 1965; 1971). This is a shift towards the role of thought in the political world of action and is accompanied by an increasing tendency to return to Kantian categories and insights for the way forward to a more adequate political philosophy. Central to this development in Arendt's thought is the concept of judgement as in some way mediating between the *vita activa* and the *vita contemplativa* or, in Kantian terms, between empirical and transcendental realms.[2]

THE *VITA CONTEMPLATIVA*

In her coverage of the Eichmann trial, Arendt coined the phrase 'the banality of evil' to describe the phenomenon of the human being who does not think. This was not a claim that Eichmann did not know what he was doing or did not understand the consequences of his actions. Rather it was a claim that Eichmann did not, and in the end *could* not, internally reflect on what he was doing. He had lost the capacity to converse with himself, so that he could neither enjoy the harmony of a good conscience nor the torments of a bad one. Instead, Eichmann, chameleon-like, absorbed the standards of others and perceived no contradiction in being supported by one law and condemned by another. According to Arendt, her assessment of Eichmann formed the starting point of a series of reflections on the relation between thinking, conscience and judgement; reflections which culminated in her work on the life of the mind. On the surface this appears to be a significant departure from the focus on the *vita activa* in *The Human Condition*. However, it is clear (from Arendt's contextualization of this shift in relation to the Eichmann case) that Arendt is primarily interested in making a connection between a certain kind of mental life and the possibility of politics as she formulated it in the earlier text. Between the Eichmann trial and her death, Arendt continues both to articulate her concept of political action *and* returns repeatedly to the problem of the connection between thought and action – the relation of philosophy to politics.

The Life of the Mind was intended to be a three-volume examination of the three key mental faculties: thinking, willing and judging.[3] For each of the faculties explored in *The Life of the Mind* one particular philosopher is crucial: in the case of thinking, it is Socrates; in the case of willing, it is St Augustine and in the case of judging, it is Kant. It is clear from Arendt's discussion of these three faculties that although both thinking and willing may be destructive of life in the world, judging is always productive of and central to politics. Thinking, which Arendt distinguishes sharply from cognition, involves a turning away from the world into an endless internal dialogue about the meaning of invisibles, i.e. concepts and ideas. Thinking does, however, have important side effects in terms of both moral conscience and the capacity to judge. The connection between these is not fully explained by Arendt but she does insist that the connection is there.

> If thinking, the two-in-one of the soundless dialogue, actualizes the difference within our identity as given in consciousness and thereby results in conscience as its by-product, then judging, the by-product of the liberating effect of thinking, realizes thinking, makes it manifest in the world of appearances, where I am never alone and always much too busy to be able to think.
>
> (Arendt, 1978a: 193)

Arendt wants to argue that thinking creates a kind of internal space which liberates both conscience and judgement from determination by either the laws of the land or the rules of cognition. It is in this sense that the individual's capacity for thought may enable him or her to resist the external pressures of a totalitarian regime. Having said this, however, Arendt is insistent that thinking is essentially an activity that requires withdrawal from the political world of appearance, in essence it is an anti-political faculty because it is inherently solitary (Arendt, 1978a: 52–53).

In the lectures on willing, Arendt looks to the philosophical tradition for an exposition of willing, but argues that philosophy has tended to distrust and deny the existence of a separate faculty of will (Arendt, 1978b: 34); although exceptions are to be found in the tradition founded by St Paul and furthered most notably in the work of St Augustine and Duns Scotus. For Arendt, will is a pure capacity for spontaneous new beginning, which cannot be said to fall under any determination other than itself. For this reason, Arendt argues that Kant has no proper conception of the will, since for him either reason or nature determines the will to action (Arendt, 1978b: 63). As Arendt explains it, the nature of the will must always be both elusive and offensive to philosophy, because as soon as it is theorized its absolute contingency becomes anchored in some other determination and the meaning of will is lost. Even in the realm of political action Arendt identifies the same tendency to disguise the 'abyss of pure spontaneity' in other terms, such as those of return or renewal (Arendt, 1978b: 214–217). What emerges from Arendt's examination of will are two main points: first, that the will individualizes human beings, it is what makes one human different from another (Arendt, 1978b: 195); second, that the will is an ungoverned capacity for beginning, a capacity inherent in all human beings which Arendt terms 'natality' (Arendt, 1978b: 217). Will is a necessary condition of human plurality and spontaneity but it is in itself a principle of pure arbitrariness and contingency. Attempts to tame will in thought by reducing it to some other principle are argued by Arendt to lead to a behaviourist understanding of the human condition which is the death of the political. Arendt suggests that the proper way to manage the unmanageability of will is through the faculty of judgement. Judgment, unlike thought, may be able to do justice to will without doing violence to the nature of action (Arendt, 1978b: 217).

The significance of judgement for Arendt's political thought is already signalled in *The Human Condition* in the role of the historian and storyteller, but this significance is not fully apparent until it becomes clear in the lectures on thinking and willing how judgement is the mental faculty that properly relates the life of the mind to the life of the world. Arendt's account of judgement draws heavily on Kant's account of reflective judgement in the third critique. She sees it as the capacity to discriminate and decide without recourse to any specific rule or law. This capacity is essential to action as it is outlined in *The Human Condition*, but is even more essential to the writing of the story in which the meaning of action is revealed. In her lectures on Kant, Arendt produces a political reading of the *Critique of Aesthetic Judgment*, which, in establishing the primacy of judgement for politics, shifts the emphasis from the political actor of *The Human Condition* towards the storyteller or historian. This figure becomes increasingly identified with the Kantian account of the spectator of the French Revolution, whose judgement provides evidence for progress in history (see the discussion in Chapter 2, pp. 54–55).

Arendt is dismissive of Kant's doctrine of right as being part of the Platonic tradition of western political philosophy which she rejected in *The Human Condition* (Arendt, 1982: 8). Instead, Arendt constructs an alternative Kantian political philosophy on the basis of a selective reading of Kant's essays on history and politics and on the *Critique of Aesthetic Judgment*. For Arendt, politics is about human beings in the plural acting with others in a defined public space; it is not about legislation and government. Thus neither the critique of theoretical nor of practical reason can be relevant to politics since they concern the subsumption of particular claims or maxims under universally determining rules. In the *Critique of Aesthetic Judgment*, however, Arendt claims that the consideration of the faculty of judgement is fundamentally political. In this context, judgement is based on a plurality of individuals whose particular judgements acquire general significance without this being a relation of subsumption under law. Arendt argues that Kant's theorization of judgement radically redefines the relationship between philosophy and politics (Arendt, 1982: 27–29). Instead of philosophers turning to politics in order to close off a space for thought and premising their political philosophy on the inferiority of the political realm, the life of the mind itself acquires political significance.

Arendt bases her claim as to the essentially political nature of judgement on her reading of the role of the *sensus communis* in the *Critique of Aesthetic Judgment*, and on her reading of the figure of the spectator or philosophical judge which emerges from Kant's essays on enlightenment, peace, history and the contest of the faculties. The *sensus communis* is that faculty which enables us to abstract from our own subjectivity in judgements of taste and compare them with the possible judgements of others, thus guaranteeing the general communicability of those judgements (Kant, V: 293–294: 160). The use of the *sensus communis* in Kant's grounding of the judgement of taste, according to Arendt, testifies to the necessity of a shared public world and to the possibility, by virtue of that shared public world, of the capacity to transcend one's own particularity and put oneself in the place of another. This in turn implies, though it does not ensure, the possibility of agreement between the inhabitants of the public realm (Arendt, 1982: 27; 68–74). Arendt bases her account of Kant's philosophical judge on his defence of the public use of reason as it is articulated in the essay 'What is Enlightenment?'; and on his endorsement of the judgement of the spectator as opposed to the actor in 'The Conflict of the Faculties'. Arendt draws a parallel between the relation of actor and spectator in politics and that of genius and taste in aesthetics. In both cases it is the latter capacity to judge and discriminate between the fruits of the former that takes precedence because it is this capacity which presupposes the shared public space that makes creativity possible (Arendt, 1982: 63). Judgement, it appears, rescues action from pure arbitrariness and philosophy from its irrelevance to action. Whereas in *The Human Condition* the philosopher seemed to be in danger of vanishing from the polis altogether, in the political philosophy of judgement the role of the spectator is celebrated and made crucial to action. As Arendt sees it, judgement is a mental process including the ability to think from the standpoint of others. Judgement therefore implies an ideal of an 'enlarged mentality' that can be extended to cover all humanity. It is this ideal, according to Arendt, which is implicit in Kant's reference to an original contract dictated by our very humanity in the *Critique of Aesthetic Judgment* (Kant, V: 297; 164), a reference made in the context of a discussion of the empirical human interest in the communicability of beauty. This ideal takes on the status of a Kantian regulative idea for Arendt, by and towards which both judgement and action should be oriented.

> It is by virtue of this idea of mankind, present in every single man, that men are human, and they can be called civilized or humane to the extent that this becomes the principle not only of their judgments but of their actions. It is at this point that actor and spectator become united; the maxim of the actor and the maxim, the 'standard', according to which the spectator judges the spectacle of the world become one.
>
> (Arendt, 1982: 75)

Arendt's aim in her work on judgement is to create a political philosophy that does not violate her concept of politics. Crucial to Arendt's concept of politics is a notion of human activity which is not structured by the violence of truth, morality or law. The last three involve the coercion of particulars by universal determinations, whether these are the rules of the understanding or the commands of practical reason. In Kant's concept of reflective judgement, the human faculty which is lawful without law, Arendt argues that she has found what she is looking for, a political philosophy which is not a philosophy of right. There are two closely related questions that arise for the assessment of Arendt's annexation of Kant's critique of judgement: first, a question about the sustainability of her reading of Kant's concept of reflective judgement; second, a question about the implications of the use of Kant for the kind of political philosophy Arendt is attempting to create.[4]

Arendt's reading of Kant's political philosophy is distinguished in particular by her unwillingness to recognize any relation between the project of the first two critiques, of limiting and legislating for the realm of theoretical and practical reason respectively, and the project of either the critique of the aesthetic judgement of taste or of the writings on enlightenment, history and providence. It is also the case that Arendt runs together the notions of judgement at work in both

Kant's aesthetic and political texts, presuming rather than substantiating the claim that the relation of genius and taste in aesthetics is equivalent to that between the actor and spectator in politics. Let us go on to examine Arendt's reading more carefully.

> Taste, like the power of judgment in general, consists in disciplining (or training) genius. It severely clips its wings, and makes it civilized or polished; but at the same time it gives it guidance as to how far and over what it may spread while still remaining purposive.
>
> (Kant, V: 319; 188)

In Kant's *Critique of Aesthetic Judgment*, the aesthetic judgement of taste commands universal assent whilst being subjectively located in the sense of pleasure or displeasure. Crucial to Kant's account of this kind of judgement is the explanation of how it carries legitimate authority a priori. Only if in possession of such authority is taste in a position to clip the wings of genius. For Kant, the authority of the judgement of taste is tied to the concept of the *sensus communis*. However, the nature of the *sensus communis* is difficult to pin down from Kant's exposition of it. It is clear both that the *sensus communis* implies or is implied by human community and sociability; and that the *sensus communis* is intrinsically and mysteriously bound up with the conditions of both cognition and morality (Kant, V: 293–296; 159–162). Arendt's account of Kant's concept of the *sensus communis* draws on two different aspects of Kant's exposition. Arendt does not distinguish between Kant's examination of the aesthetic judgement of taste as empirically linked to the evolution of human community (Kant, V: 296–298; 163–165); and his account of that judgement as rooted in the transcendental conditions of judgement in general and linked to the supersensible grounds of theoretical and practical reason (Kant, V: 345–347; 219–220). It is only the latter account that, for Kant, endows the aesthetic judgement of taste with a priori authority. In the passage Arendt quotes to support her use of the idea of an 'enlarged mentality' as the standard of judgement, Kant in fact goes on to dismiss the empirical interest in the beautiful as a possible ground for the a priori power of judgement 'on which all legislation must depend' (Kant, V: 297–298; 164).

The tension in Kant's exposition between the *sensus communis* as a product of human community and the *sensus communis* as a transcendental condition of judgement is not explicitly addressed by Arendt and reappears in her own account of political judgement. Her notion that such judgement should be regulated by the idea of the original contract of mankind implicit in the enlarged mentality of the *sensus communis* brings together the empirical and transcendental moments in Kant's account (Arendt, 1982: 75). On the one hand, the idea of an original contract is clearly linked to the notion of authority grounded in mutual promising, which is exemplified by the American founding fathers. On the other hand, the fact that it is an idea elevated to a regulative principle abstracts the authority of judgement from history and prompts the question of the ground of judgement. Arendt's reading of Kant reproduces the problem of the link between the empirical and transcendental ground and goal of aesthetic judgement. At the same time as judgement is given a historical location, it is also de-historicized as an eternally indeterminate condition (Kant, V: 340; 213). Arendt treats the concept of the *sensus communis* as if it has resolved the problem of the authority of judgement rather than as part of the radical problematizing of that authority. This enables Arendt to introduce the concept of the *sensus communis* as being relatively straightforward; and encourages her to identify the complex and always contestable authority of the *sensus communis* in the aesthetic judgement of taste in relation to genius with the authority of the judgement of the political spectator in relation to the political actor. Let us now return to Arendt's reading of Kant's account of the latter.

The starting point of Kant's political philosophy is the division between morality and legality and the demand of the pure principle of right to secure externally the obedience to the categorical imperative that is internally secured by virtue. Because Arendt dismisses Kant's philosophy of right, she adopts the actor/spectator split suggested to her by Kant's account of both taste and enlightenment without locating the origins of that distinction in Kant's broader political thought. For Arendt, the priority of the spectator over the actor is a necessary consequence of the spectator's access to the 'enlarged mentality' which is the mark of judgement. For Kant, however, the actor/spectator distinction is a consequence of the idea of law, according to which political actors cannot challenge law without attacking the source of legitimacy itself. The position of the spectator is the only political resource that the citizen has and even this is governed by the prescriptions of right, in that judgement must be with reference to the idea of progress towards the indeterminate ideal of the perfect juridical community. As a philosopher and judge, Kant appreciates the French Revolution as progress and at the same time condemns all of its participants. Arendt explains this split by reference to a transcendental principle of publicness which Kant formulates in the essay on perpetual peace (Arendt, 1982: 48). Arendt argues that, 'For Kant, the moment to rebel is the moment when freedom of opinion is abolished' (Arendt, 1982: 50). However, it is apparent that in Kant's own account the parameters of the judgement of the spectator restrict the philosopher to the *vita contemplativa* and there is no space for the philosopher to rebel without contravening both right and morality. The relation between the actor and spectator in politics in Kant's work remains constrained by the transcendental principle of right. The authority of the political judge is ultimately the authority of practical reason, which demands the *as-if* identification of history with progress. This kind of judgement is the privilege of the archetypally enlightened individual, the philosopher – as opposed to the political actor, the king. In the case of both the aesthetic judgement of taste and political judgement, Kant's exposition returns us to the problems posed by the split between the realms of theoretical and practical reason. Although there are clear links between the two kinds of judgement, both being species of reflective judgement and both holding out hope for a bridging of the gap between reason and nature, they cannot be completely identifed with one another. Political judgement retains a clear link to the idea of the legislation of reason. The aesthetic judgement of taste, on the other hand, in demonstrating the principle peculiar to judgement, brings home the difficulty of understanding the conditions of reason's authority. In Arendt's use of the Kantian conceptions of judgement, both the ambiguities of aesthetic judgement and the role of the categorical imperative in political judgement tend to become lost. The result of this is that the coming together of the *vita activa* and the *vita contemplativa* in judgement is expounded as simple and straightforward, whereas in fact the authority of judgement is ambivalently located in empirical community and transcendental legislation, an ambivalence which represents the separation of the realm of action from the realm of thought.

It is possible to argue that the adequacy of Arendt's reading of Kant makes no difference to the strength of her political thought. However, I would claim that, on the contrary, Arendt's use of Kant leads to the compounding of problems inherent in Arendt's concept of politics and the relation of the philosopher to politics (or of the *vita activa* to the *vita contemplativa*). These problems centre on Arendt's ambivalence about the place of legislation in politics in relation to both the political actor and the political spectator. In *The Human Condition* Arendt refers approvingly to the Greeks:

> The Greeks, in distinction from all later development, did not count legislating among the political activities. In their opinion, the lawmaker was like the builder of the city wall, someone who had to do and finish his work before political activity could begin.
>
> (Arendt, 1958: 194)

In her early work Arendt is anxious to distinguish political action from legislation because legislation involves a determinate end, whereas action cannot be governed by design. She returns to the political significance of legislating in her later work on revolution and on the founding of new constitutions following both the American and French Revolutions. Having marginalized lawmaking as a form of action in *The Human Condition*, in *On Revolution* Arendt comes to see the primary authoritative legislation of a constitution by the American founding fathers as exemplary politics. Nevertheless, in Arendt's discussion of the making of the American constitution it is clear that lawmaking still remains a problem for politics. Lawmaking may, in certain cases, be simply an opening out of the possibilities of political action, and therefore itself capable of being understood as action, but it always poses the problem of its own legitimacy. If the grounding principles of law cannot be justified in terms of a determinate end, then they require justification in terms of their beginning. In order to resolve this problem, the founding fathers resort to a 'noble lie', by claiming divine inspiration or by denying the newness of their state and claiming it as the rebirth of an old authority, a new Rome. The problem of the grounding of law is not only a problem for the founding fathers, it is also a problem for Arendt. Once lawmaking is no longer consigned to the sphere of work and the spontaneous will of *homo faber*, how is it to be legitimated? The answer is the same as the answer to how action is to be rescued from pure contingency; it is judgement that is invoked as the ground of law; in this case, the judgement of the founding fathers in their mutual promising and mutual deliberation. Arendt's discussion of legislation in *The Human Condition* and *On Revolution* is, in both cases, inspired by her desire to keep political action from being law-governed. In the earlier text, this results in political action being characterized as a kind of pure spontaneity; an arbitrary and purposeless process which is matched by the arbitrary violence of the legislator, and only recouped by the judgement of the storyteller. In the later text this results in a recourse to judgement, as opposed to law, as the standard for legislation and political action more generally. Thus the question of legislation in the *vita activa* returns us to the question of the legitimacy of judgement, the *vita contemplativa* and the noble lies of the philosopher.

In Arendt's account of the political spectator, she is as anxious to avoid the idea of judgement as being law-governed as she is in the case of political action. This means that neither rules of the understanding nor moral principles may legislate for judgement; it is neither a matter of truth nor of right.

> Judgment is not practical reason; practical reason 'reasons' and tells me what to do and what not to do; it lays down the law and is identical with the will, and the will utters commands; it speaks in imperatives. Judgment on the contrary arises from a 'merely contemplative pleasure or inactive delight'.
>
> (Arendt, 1982: 15)

Arendt identifies genuine political philosophy with the Kantian disinterested judgement of taste, which, on the basis of the *sensus communis*, enables discrimination in the assessment of political life and progress in history. This identification endows the Arendtian judge with authority. However, in explaining the basis of the capacity for such judgement, Arendt glosses over the distinction between the *sensus communis* as an empirical capacity and as located in the transcendental ground of judgement. This leads to a fundamental ambiguity in Arendt's account of the authority of her own philosophical practice. On the one hand, political philosophy is a contribution to political dialogue which is located in the realm of action and which has no power to legislate for action in advance. On the other hand, political philosophy is detached from the realm of action and has the power to legislate for what does or does not count as action in the political realm.

> When one judges and when one acts in political matters one is supposed to take one's bearings from the idea, not the actuality, of being a world citizen and, therefore, also a *Weltbetrachter*, a world spectator.
>
> (Arendt, 1982: 75–76)

Arendt's aim is to free both the practice and comprehension of politics from the constraints of law, truth and morality. As she sees it, preoccupations with law and questions of rule and government have diverted attention away from the distinctively human capacity for action and new beginning, allowing the encroachment of private concerns into the public realm and reducing political power to violence. Preoccupation with truth and morality, on the other hand, has encouraged the subordination of politics to supposedly higher ends, leading to the dismissal of the intrinsic value of political action. Judgement represents a way forward for politics and for political philosophy which is in principle antithetical both to the conditions that make totalitarianism possible and to the standpoint of the philosopher-king. Paradoxically, however, in her use of Kant's concept of reflective judgement, Arendt in practice reinforces the authority of the *vita contemplativa*. The idea of being a world citizen or the idea of an original contract of humanity is an abstract regulative principle with no meaning outside of the spectator's judgement as to whether or not it can be said to orient political practice. In the end, the status of these ideas seems little different from that of the noble lies of Plato or of the founding fathers.

CONCLUSION

Arendt's political thought might be said to begin where Habermas's leaves off, with the problems of mediating between the realms of the ideal and the real or of the *vita contemplativa* and the *vita activa*. Arendt is anxious to avoid the consequences of philosophical authoritarianism in both theory and practice and therefore cannot draw holistically on Kant's critical philosophy as Habermas does. The double implication of Arendt's rejection of traditional political theory, including Kant's philosophy of right, is the exclusion of legislation from politics and the divorce between contemplation and action. However, the conception of political life and of political philosophy that follows from Arendt's account of the human condition, precisely because of the exclusions and separations on which it is premised, in fact repeats, even as it challenges, the elements of the tradition which are being rejected. Arendt's use of Kant helps to explain the tensions within her thought noted at the beginning of this chapter. The ways in which her work combines elements of radical democracy with elitism reflect Arendt's attempt to underwrite the removal of legislation from politics without rendering political action arbitrary through a political philosophy of judgement. When the concept of judgement used in this attempt is itself formulated in terms of the tensions it is intended to overcome, then it is unsurprising that Arendt's own philosophical practice remains poised between legislative authority and arbitrariness.

The relation of Habermas and Arendt to the Kantian legacy is very different. Nevertheless, Habermas's critical theory and Arendt's political philosophy of judgement both repeat the complexities, ambiguities and tensions of the politics of Kantian critique. In order to fulfil the requirements of the universal laws of reason, Habermas makes use of the concept of reflective judgement to enable his reading of history in theory, and the role of autonomous public spheres in practice. In order to mobilize a conception of politics and political philosophy without law, Arendt makes use of the identification of empirical conditions with transcendental ideals of reason in theory; and then interprets the legislation of the founding fathers in terms of this identification in practice. In both cases, Kant's concept of reflective, aesthetic and political judgement is used to retrieve both the practice of philosophy and the practice of politics from the fate of either abstract universal legislation or incomprehensible particularism. In both cases, however, the use of Kant's work results in a repetition rather than a resolution of the philosophers' problems.

5

FOUCAULT'S CRITICAL ATTITUDE

INTRODUCTION

Foucault is closer to Arendt than to Habermas as a thinker, in that he has no desire to found a new critical theory as such. Instead, the majority of Foucault's published work consists of histories of madness, medicine, knowledge, prisons and finally sexuality. These are, however, always histories with a difference; they are critical histories, archaeologies or genealogies. What characterizes all of these critical histories is that they challenge the received wisdoms of the historians of psychiatry, medicine and penal reform. Implicit in this challenge, moreover, is a critique of standard assumptions in philosophy, social theory and politics. It is the latter critical aspect of Foucault's work that leads Habermas to accuse him of 'cryptonormativism' (Habermas, 1987b: 294); because Foucault himself is very careful to avoid endorsing specific alternative values or principles on the basis of which contemporary theory and practice can be condemned. For some commentators it is Foucault's strength, for others his weakness, that he seems to be a critical theorist without a theory.[1] Foucault's own view, explicit in his late work but implicit throughout, is that critique relies not on substantive theory, but on working with a critical *attitude*.

Foucault explicitly rejects the Kantian project of the critique of reason. As several comentators have pointed out, however, Foucault's attitude to Kant in relation to modern thought and to his own *transgressive*, as opposed to *transcendental*, critique is an ambivalent one (Rajchman, 1985; Hacking in Couzens-Hoy, 1986: 239; Norris, 1993: 29–99). This ambivalence is expressed by Foucault himself in his later work as a difference in his relation to two aspects of Kant's critical philosophy. The first aspect is labelled an 'analytics of truth' and the second is labelled an 'ontology of ourselves' (Foucault, 1988: 95). Foucault identifies the former aspect of Kantianism with the search for transcendental presuppositions of truth. In both his archaeology of knowledge and his genealogies of power relations, Foucault is engaged in contesting the possibility of an analytics of truth and the idea that critique is governed by transcendental legislation. Foucault identifies the second aspect of Kantianism with a specific kind of relation between the philosopher and his present. In his late work on ethics, subjectivity and freedom, Foucault draws on this aspect of the Kantian inheritance to help to explain the nature of his own critical practice. In this chapter a reading of Foucault's work as the struggle to retain the possibility of critique without reference to any transcendental regulation or orientation will be offered. In the final section, it will be argued that Foucault's formulation of this struggle as being both with and against Kant brings the agonistic politics of Foucault's critique closer to the politics of Kantian critique than Foucault's bifurcation of the critical philosophy acknowledges.

In reflecting on Kant's essay on enlightenment, Foucault outlines the nature of his own project as involving three areas of analysis: relations of control over things; relations of action upon others; and relations with oneself. Foucault then poses three crucial questions for the critical thinker:

> How are we constituted as subjects of our knowledge? How are we constituted as subjects who exercise or submit to power relations? How are we constituted as moral subjects of our own actions?
>
> (Foucault, 1984b: 49)

The focuses of these three questions can be mapped onto the chronological development of Foucault's work, and I have used the distinction between the early work on knowledge, the genealogical work on power relations and the late work on ethics to structure the argument of this chapter.[2] This analytic distinction helps to foreground the ways in which at each of these stages Foucault is thinking with and against Kant's critical questions: What can I know? What ought I to do? What may I hope for? (see Bernauer, 1990: 18). I will begin my exploration of Foucault's critical attitude with his work on the conditions of theoretical reason in *The Order of Things*.

103

THE CRITIQUE OF THOUGHT

Like the works on madness and medicine that preceded it, *The Order of Things* is a critical history or archaeology. However, whereas the earlier works had focused on radical shifts in the perception and treatment of madness and illness, the later text is concerned with the question of the possibility of thought in different historical eras. In a sense, however, although the subject matter is different, the purpose of all of these earlier works appears the same; that is, to demonstrate that what seems to be self-evidently rooted in a continuous development is actually the result of a recent radical disjuncture in theory and practice. Foucault's lesson is that we cannot think otherwise than we do, within the context of a specific era, but he hints at the promise that in realizing this limitation we may be able to challenge it. A concern with limits and the transcendence of limits is characteristic of all of Foucault's work and it is the central preoccupation of *The Order of Things*. In the Preface, a short story by Borges is cited, in which the classification of animals in a Chinese encyclopaedia is so bizarre that it brings the reader up short against the limits of his thought, making the reader (Foucault) laugh (Foucault, 1970: xv). This laughter signals the reader's inability to comprehend another way of thinking as being thinking at all, and Foucault uses this demonstration of a radical gap in comprehension to illustrate his understanding of the history of thought in contradistinction to the usual assumptions of the history of ideas. Where the history of ideas emphasizes development and continuity and a temporal ordering of its elements, Foucault's archaeology of thought emphasizes radical change and discontinuity and a spatial ordering of elements in an epistemological field or *episteme*. The emphasis shifts from the tracing of ideas to the excavation of their conditions of possibility: this is what Foucault labels, with a self-consciously ironic echo of Kant, the historical a priori.[3]

> This *a priori* is what, in a given period, delimits in the totality of experience a field of knowledge, defines the mode of being of the objects that appear in that field, provides man's everyday perception with theoretical powers and defines the conditions in which he can sustain a discourse about things that is recognised to be true.
>
> (Foucault, 1970: 158)

Although in *The Archaeology of Knowledge* Foucault modifies the generality of his claims about the historical a priori, in *The Order of*

Things the concept of the episteme encompasses the conditions of possibility of thought in any given era, legislating for and establishing the limits of understanding (Foucault, 1970: 168). Foucault's own apprehension of different epistemes in western thought is possible only when those epistemes no longer regulate thought, and through a patient historical reconstruction that attempts to explore them from within, using contemporary evidence. Foucault states that it cannot be possible to acquire the same comprehension of one's own episteme as of those that have been superseded; neither is it possible to explain why there are historical shifts from one episteme to another (Foucault, 1970: 217–218). In *The Order of Things* three epistemes are identified within European thought since the sixteenth century: Renaissance thought with its episteme of resemblance; classical thought, with its episteme of representation; and modern thought since the end of the eighteenth century, with its foundationalist/ anthropological episteme.

What Foucault's treatment of the limits of both classical and modern thought reveals is that the nature of those limits is inevitably twofold. First, the limit is the episteme, the conditions of possibility which constitute the nature of science in a given era. Second, the limit is what is excluded by the episteme, the ways of thinking which are not possible. In the normal course of events the limit is not itself in any way experienced or thought, but the archaeology of knowledge, according to Foucault, opens up the unthought to be thought and therefore focuses attention not only on what it is possible to think but on what it is impossible to think. Foucault's thinking of the classical episteme, which is excluded by the episteme of his own time, orients his examination of the modern episteme around what it is not or what it fails to be.

Foucault's most famous claim in *The Order of Things* is that man is a recent invention in the history of thought. In the Renaissance and classical epistemes, man was not a structuring principle for knowledge in the sense of being a condition of its possibility. At the end of the eighteenth century, however, Kant's critical philosophy heralds a radical shift away from previous modes of thinking by locating the conditions of knowledge and thought outside of the space of representation, and inside of the transcendental subject. Foucault's treatment of the Kantian Copernican revolution is interesting in that he focuses very little on Kant's critical turn in itself, beyond suggesting that it can be seen as in some ways occupying a position on the cusp between classical and modern epistemes. It is not Kant's critique in itself which decisively shifts the conditions of possibility of knowledge, but the way in which it makes possible the idea of man as both origin and object of knowledge, a 'transcendental-empirical doublet'. Foucault suggests that from the early nineteenth century onwards Kant's distinction between transcendental and empirical is confused by being subsumed under the question 'What is man?' (Foucault, 1970: 241–243; 321–323). Thought falls into an anthropological sleep caught up in a hopeless and endless search for the grounds of man's finitude in man himself. The effect of this is to condemn the human sciences to an unhappy fate in which positivism and eschatology form the alternative conceptions of true discourse.

> Comte and Marx both bear out the fact that eschatology (as the objective truth proceeding from man's discourse) and positivism (as the truth of discourse defined on the basis of the truth of the object) are archaeologically indissociable: a discourse attempting to be both empirical and critical cannot but be both positivist and eschatological; man appears within it as a truth both reduced and promised.
>
> (Foucault, 1970: 320)

According to Foucault, modern thought is inevitably entangled in the effort to find a way between the truth of man as reduction or as promise. In this sense, modern thought, it is implied, is constantly brought up against its limits in a way that has not been true of previous epistemes. Foucault makes this explicit first by rejecting the idea that phenomenology constitutes a way out of the tension between empirical and transcendental (Foucault, 1970: 320–323) and then by suggesting that the proper contestation of positivism and eschatology would have to be by questioning the foundations of modern thought itself. This can be done by raising the 'aberrant' question 'Does man really exist?' (Foucault, 1970: 322). Only by uprooting anthropology can a new space for thought be constituted which will take us beyond the new dogmatism of the modern episteme. As Foucault sees it, it is the human sciences that will open up the way to a new constitution of thought.

> The human sciences, when dealing with what is representation (in either conscious or unconscious form), find themselves treating as their object what is in fact their condition of possibility. They are always animated, therefore, by a sort of transcendental mobility. They never cease to exercise a critical

examination of themselves. They proceed from that which is given to representation to that which renders representation possible, but which is still representation.

(Foucault, 1970: 364)

It is, in particular, the human sciences of psychoanalysis and ethnology that, for Foucault, constitute a challenge to the modern episteme. This is because it is these sciences that, rather than becoming hooked up on the project of grounding the analytic of finitude in man, recognize and trace the boundaries of that finitude in what cannot be thought in the sense of being subsumed under an anthropological model (Foucault, 1970: 373–380). Instead, it is the model of language that Foucault argues will replace that of man in the human sciences; structuralism will replace historicism and anthropocentrism (Foucault, 1970: 385). Foucault's welcoming attitude to the rise of the 'question of language' derives from his recognition that it is within language that man experiences his limit not within himself but as something ineradicably other.

From within language experienced and traversed as language, in the play of its possibilities extended to their furthest point, what emerges is that man has 'come to an end', and that, by reaching the summit of all possible speech, he arrives not at the very heart of himself but at the brink of that which limits him; in that region where death prowls, where thought is extinguished, where the promise of the origin interminably recedes.

(Foucault, 1970: 383)

In this account, the experience of language is like the experience of the sublime, a painful and dramatic encounter with our limits.[4] It is this experience, which is also that of the laughter provoked by the classification in the Chinese encyclopaedia, that for Foucault restores the possibility of a critique of reason. However, this seems by now to have become something more radical and universal in its implications than the critical history of an archaeology of knowledge. The limit is not now simply what is constituted by specific historical epistemes as being either within or without the conditions of possibility of knowledge. Instead, the limit appears as presenting, without being able to represent, an eternal other to thought.

It might appear that Foucault has decisively surpassed the resources of Kantian transcendental critique in *The Order of Things*. There are two principal reasons for this: first, the concept of the historical a priori appears antithetical to Kant's transcendentalism; second, Foucault cites Kant as the first thinker to subsume thought under the question 'What is man?' On reflection, however, although it is clearly the case that Kant would not have agreed with Foucault's historicization of the a priori, it can be argued that Foucault's approach to thought remains fundamentally Kantian. The interrogation of the conditions of possibility of thought follows the logic of Kantian critique in that it is premised on the same presumption of the necessary limitation of reason as a prerequisite of its power to regulate what can be known. And Foucault, like Kant, finds his tracing of the limits of the knowable in an uneasy relation to that which cannot be known, which includes both what cannot be thought within a particular episteme and the reasons why that episteme has, as it were, taken power. Moreover, it is not the case that Foucault rejects the Kantian critical philosophy in his condemnation of the turn to anthropology in nineteenth-century thought. In fact Foucault is very careful to make clear that it is not Kant's philosophy itself, with its careful distinction between empirical and transcendental and its raising of the question of the limits of representation, that is at fault. On several occasions in the text, Foucault refers to the possibility of a new critique of reason analogous to that of the Kantian critique, which, on the threshold of modernity, opened up a new space for thought. At the end of *The Order of Things*, Foucault argues that the new possibilities for thought heralded by structuralism are already implicit in the modern episteme that was inaugurated by Kant. In many ways, Foucault's own archaeological project is an attempt to return to the moment of rupture in which, on his own account, the episteme of representation is confronted with the question of its limits in *The Critique of Pure Reason*. Foucault is anxious to restore to contemporary thought the awareness of radical limitation which has been lost in positivism and eschatology.

Given the parallels between the archaeology of knowledge and the critique of reason, it is not surprising to find problems reminiscent of those encountered in Kant's work in Foucault's text. At the heart of Foucault's endeavour is the critical discourse of the archaeologist. But what are the conditions of the possibility of that discourse? Like Kant, Foucault offers alternative answers to this question, all of which return us to the difficulty of attempting to speak from a place that is inaccessible to reason. The first answer is that critical discourse is made possible by difference. Because of the radical difference between epistemes, it is possible to grasp their limitations from the position of hindsight. But how is difference identified? And how does the archaeologist understand the conditions of possibility of a thought that is no longer his? Foucault is quite clear that what he is investigating is not the surface patterns but the fundamental presuppositions of thought. Since the limits of an episteme are never explicit to the thought thinking in terms of it, the critical reconstruction of the archaeologist is necessarily located in an outside judgement, the authority of which is mysterious. Foucault's second answer, in which he shifts towards a less historicized basis for critical discourse in the experience of limitation enabled through language, transports us to an even more mysterious place. The sublime moment recognizes our limits and what lies beyond them in a way that is radically inarticulable. In some sense Foucault clearly sees the apprehension of this limit as legislating for the future of thought in which the figure of man is to be replaced by that of language. But the nature of this legislation is outside comprehension, signalled only by laughter or silence, and its authority can be understood only via the authoritative account of the archaeologist himself.

It is clear that Foucault himself perceived the dangers of a new transcendentalism in the conception of archaeology in *The Order of Things*. In particular he became anxious to disassociate himself from the structuralist label and from the pitfalls of a critical discourse that simply substituted the mysterious being of language in place of the anthropological ground of knowledge. In *The Archaeology of Knowledge* and 'The Order of Discourse' (Foucault, 1972; 1980a: 51–77) Foucault moves away from the static notion of the episteme towards a much more complex and fluid idea of the conditions of the possibility of knowledge as embedded in historical practice.

> In the enigma of scientific discourse, what the analysis of the episteme questions is not its right to be a science, but the fact that it exists. And the point at which it separates itself off from all the philosophies of knowledge (*connaissance*) is that it relates this fact not to the authority of an original act of giving, which establishes in a transcendental subject the fact and the right, but to the processes of a historical practice.
>
> (Foucault, 1972: 192)

The Archaeology of Knowledge and 'The Order of Discourse' are both texts in which Foucault attempts to formulate the nature of his approach to history. In these texts the grander scale of the project of *The Order of Things* gives way to a more specific and technical theoretical discourse. The same philosophies that in *The Order of Things* were identified as the hallmark of the modern episteme, historicism and anthropologism, are still the target of critique. What changes in these texts is Foucault's own conception of what he is both investigating and criticizing; instead of the episteme or, more generally, 'thought' or knowledge, there are the concepts of 'discursive formation' and 'will to truth'. This is not the abandonment of Foucault's established terrain, but its reconceptualization in more dynamic, practical and positive terms. Knowledge is both a practice in itself and the product of practices: it is accomplished by events and itself accomplishes them; not in the sense of a continuous development or an intended outcome but as part of the complex, fragmentary, discontinuous, chance workings of the material of history (Foucault, 1980a: 69).

> We must call into question our will to truth, restore to discourse its character as an event, and finally throw off the sovereignty of the signifier.
>
> (Foucault, 1980a: 66)

In setting out these requirements, Foucault is not only challenging other historians and philosophers, he is guarding his own critical discourse against transcendental pretensions. The critic cannot occupy a space apart from the object of criticism since his discourse is also implicated in the material of history. Instead, critique becomes the practice of the principle of reversal (Foucault, 1980a: 70). Whereas the genealogical aspect of the task involves the investigation of the practical conditions of possibility of specific discourses, the critical aspect involves identifying what is excluded, limited and controlled by those discourses. However, critical discourse about the way the limits of discourse are policed is itself policing its own limits and is equally open to the principle of critical reversal.

The outline of the principles of genealogy and critique in 'The Order of Discourse' marks a decisive shift in Foucault's work from the analytic demarcation of the limits on thought to the analysis of how those limits are dynamically constituted.[5] There is also a significant change in the vocabulary of Foucault's discourse, which moves from a modified Kantianism to a strongly Nietzschean tone. The genealogy of power relations which becomes the focus of Foucault's work confirms the implication both of Foucault's new characterization of his critique and of his new style. This is the implication that genuine critical discourse is grounded in the failure of the project of transcendental critique and the complete rejection of a legislative role for the critic. In the next section the nature of critique as genealogy will be examined.

STRATEGIC CRITIQUE

In *Discipline and Punish* Foucault's critical examination of the constitution of knowledge and subjectivity is carried out as a genealogy of power relations in the context of a history of prisons. The ubiquity of the concept of power relations as a reference point in this genealogical work and in the first volume of *The History of Sexuality* is such that it is difficult to grasp the nature of Foucault's critical discourse without understanding how Foucault uses the terms 'power' and 'power relations'. *Discipline and Punish* is the text in which Foucault's concept of power is most obviously developed and put to work.[6] It is in this text that Foucault formulates the contrast between juridical and disciplinary power and takes issue with traditional political theory. It is also in this text that the connection between disciplinary power, the subject, the modern human sciences and humanism is demonstrated. The book is subtitled 'The Birth of the Prison' and is dominated by two images, the horror of the execution of Damiens at the beginning and the model of Bentham's panopticon (Foucault, 1977a: 3–6; 200–202). The first represents juridical power, the second its supersession by disciplinary power. *Discipline and Punish*, like Foucault's earlier histories, offers a challenge to histories of modernity that work in terms of a model of continuity and progress. There is a radical discontinuity between the repressive juridical power characteristic of the system of crime and punishment in the classical age and the productive disciplinary power of modern penal systems. Moreover, the latter does not constitute an improvement or reform of the former in any meaningful sense. In spite of the chronological framing of Foucault's argument, he is also not suggesting that juridical power is wholly replaced by disciplinary power; the two modalities of power may coexist. As with the earlier histories also, Foucault does not restrict the significance of his analysis to the area explicitly under investigation. Just as the episteme underlying the specific subjects of linguistics, biology and economics is seen to characterize the episteme of an age, so the regime in nineteenth-century prisons characterizes what Foucault identifies as the general normalizing power produced by and producing the 'carceral system' (Foucault, 1977a: 293–308). What does distinguish Foucault's history of prisons from his other histories is its reluctance even to gesture towards the other of what is being analysed. The silence of madness and the philosopher's laughter seem to have disappeared as critical reference points.

Crucial to Foucault's account of disciplinary power is the figure of the subject. Power produces and works through sovereign individuals, the panopticon is organized around them. In *The Order of Things* Foucault has already announced both the birth and death of man in the history of modern thought. In *Discipline and Punish* the same story is dealt with rather differently. The construction of the subject is detailed in such a way as to demonstrate that liberal ideas of subjectivity and autonomous individuality as ahistorical givens are an illusion. Instead, Foucault stresses the materiality of the soul and the docility of the body and the way in which individuals are channels and vehicles of power. In *The History of Sexuality Volume I* the claims of *Discipline and Punish* are confirmed in the demonstration that discourses such as psychiatry and psychology are not concerned with the liberation of a repressed and 'genuine' sexual self, but are themselves techniques and strategies of power which produce sexuality as an effect.

> Never have there existed more centers of power; never more attention manifested and verbalized; never more circular contacts and linkages; never more sites where the intensity of pleasures and the persistence of power catch hold, only to spread elsewhere.
>
> (Foucault, 1976: 49)

The overall impression given by the argument of *Discipline and Punish* is that power is everywhere and in everything (Foucault, 1977a: 304–305). Thus the founding reference points of enlightened modern thought, the rational subject, disinterested knowledge, the importance and possibility of human emancipation are transformed in Foucault's account to effects and channels of power. The rational subject is an unintentional product of complex techniques and strategies of power, imbued with power, policed and policing self and others. Knowledge is power/knowledge, again an unintentional product of complex techniques and strategies of power with unintended political consequences. The ideal of human emancipation is the illusion of humanitarian reformers, unwittingly feeding power with their model prisons, public health measures, schools and hospitals. The language and tone of the description of the emergence of the disciplinary society is highly critical and subversive of the dominant understanding of modern liberal democracy. To some extent it echoes the stories of madness and medicine Foucault has already told, with nineteenth-century thinkers and reformers cast as the unwitting villains of the piece. Nevertheless, there appears to be a difference between the way that power as a condition of possibility of modern discursive formations works in Foucault's text and the role of concepts such as madness and the episteme in earlier histories. In working at the limits of madness and knowledge, part of Foucault's critical task was to signify, however gesturally and incomprehensibly, to the other side of the limits which condition our grasp of madness or knowledge. But there seems to be no other side to power, even in imagination. Power appears to be an inescapable and inexplicable force in terms of which everything else can be interpreted, but which is not itself a subject of critique. However, whatever impression may have been given by the role of power in *Discipline and Punish*, Foucault himself in a host of other contexts explicitly denies that power is either an ultimate determining force or occupies a place outside of the scope of critical discourse.

> There have been gross misunderstandings, or I have explained myself badly: I have never presumed that 'power' was something that could explain everything.
>
> (Foucault, 1991a: 148)

In a number of articles and interviews during and after the work on prisons and the initial work on sexuality, Foucault introduces a variety of refinements to the concept of power and denies that his own discourse is rendered uncritical by the ever-presence of power.[7] He stresses that the term 'power' is always a shorthand for 'power relation'. Power does not signify an ahistorical transcendental force but a mode of relation which itself requires the capacity of resistance or freedom. One of the most useful sources for Foucault's later reflections on the nature of power is the article 'The Subject and Power' (Dreyfus and Rabinow, 1982: 208–226).

> Power is exercised only over free subjects, and only insofar as they are free. By this we mean individual or collective subjects who are faced with a field of possibilities in which several ways of behaving, several reactions and diverse comportments may be realized. Where the determining factors saturate the whole there is no relationship of power; slavery is not a power

relationship when man is in chains. (In this case it is a question of a physical relationship of constraint.) Consequently there is no face to face confrontation of power and freedom which is mutually exclusive (freedom disappears everywhere power is exercised), but a much more complicated interplay. In this game freedom may well appear as the condition for the exercise of power (at the same time its precondition, since freedom must exist for power to be exerted, and also its permanent support, since without the possibility of recalcitrance, power would be equivalent to physical determination).

(Dreyfus and Rabinow, 1982: 221)

In 'The Subject and Power' the nature of Foucault's critical discourse is reminiscent of the language of perpetual overturning of the principle of reversal in 'The Order of Discourse'. In the later text, however, critique and resistance are understood in strategic terms as the mobilization of forces in the struggle to overturn relationships of power. Relationships of power in turn are presented as inherently limited; they represent the management or government of adversaries and not a permanent victory over a vanquished enemy (this would constitute power as domination). The implication of this characterization of resistance and power is that strategic relations are always potentially power relations and vice versa.

For, if it is true that at the heart of power relations and as a permanent condition of their existence there is an insubordination and a certain essential obstinacy on the part of the principles of freedom, then there is no relationship of power without the means of escape or possible flight. Every power relationship implies, at least *in potentia*, a strategy of struggle, in which the two forces are not superimposed, do not lose their specific nature, or do not finally become confused. Each constitutes for the other a kind of permanent limit, a point of possible reversal. A relationship of confrontation reaches its term, its final moment (and the victory of one of the two adversaries) when stable mechanisms replace the free play of antagonistic reactions.

(Dreyfus and Rabinow, 1982: 225)

The perpetual tension between power and freedom and between relations of power and strategies of resistance raises the question of how the distinction can be drawn between the two sets of terms. Foucault clearly rejects the idea that there can be any universal criteria of judgement which would settle this question. Relations of power and strategies of resistance are always specifically located and the recognition of what counts as either power or freedom depends on the particular context. However, the question still remains for actors in specific contexts as to what would count for them as practices of liberation. In the discussion of some specific examples of resistant practice in 'The Subject and Power' (Dreyfus and Rabinow, 1982: 211–212), Foucault concludes that central to these struggles (examples include the women's movement, movements for children's rights, the anti-psychiatry movement) is the attack on the form of power which makes individuals subject. This form of power encompasses both external control of individuals and their internal self-governance (Dreyfus and Rabinow, 1982: 212). Participants in these resistances ask the question of who they are and refuse the definitions and relations through which the question has previously been answered. A little later in the same essay, Foucault draws a contrast between two kinds of philosophy: the universalist philosophy of Descartes, which asks about the nature of the 'I' as an unhistorical subject; and the specific analysis of ourselves and our present which he ascribes to Kant's reflections on enlightenment (Dreyfus and Rabinow, 1982: 216). In parallel with the political movements of resistance he has already discussed, Foucault maps out the practice of the critical philosopher as raising the question of who we are, refusing what we are and imagining what we could be beyond the form of power as subjection (Dreyfus and Rabinow, 1982: 216). The exposition of both resistance and of critical philosophy gestures towards different kinds of subjectivity and returns us to that 'certain essential obstinacy' within subjectivity which always remains a condition of power. The possibility of strategic critique, therefore, and of practices of liberation in the 'realm of thought' (Foucault, 1988: 155), seems to require an orientation of thinking in relation to freedom. Foucault is quite clear that the practice of critique is not a matter of legislating for judgement or positing a direction for history (Foucault, 1991a: 157). Nevertheless, the later discussions of power, freedom, resistance and criticism suggest that the specific intellectual, in operating with the critical principle of reversal first outlined in 'The Order of Discourse', is engaged in a practice which has general as well as specific implications. It has specific implications in terms of whatever is revealed about the particular network of power relations under investigation; and it has general implications as an example of the practice of freedom.

At the point of transition between his archaeological critique and his genealogical work Foucault turns from a Kantian to a Nietzschean critical vocabulary. The resources of Kant's critical philosophy are decisively rejected as being of no use to the contemporary critic. However, as Foucault works through the question of the nature of power relations and their connection to both situations of domination and strategies of resistance, Kant's work again becomes a reference point in Foucault's characterization of his own critical practice. As Foucault himself expresses it, this is no longer the Kant of the 'analytics of truth', but is instead the Kant of an 'ontology of ourselves', a relation to self which Foucault characterizes as ethical. At the beginning of the essay 'The Subject and Power', Foucault makes the following claim:

> I would like to say, first of all, what has been the goal of my work during the last twenty years. It has not been to analyse the phenomena of power, nor to elaborate the foundation of such an analysis. My objective, instead, has been to create a history of the different modes by which, in our culture, human beings are made subjects.
>
> (Dreyfus and Rabinow, 1982: 208)

Foucault goes on to elaborate three modes of objectification of subjects which he has examined: through scientific inquiry; through the dividing practices characteristic of clinics and prisons; and through the work of subjects on themselves. As Foucault presents it here and in other contexts in his later work, the three dimensions of his studies exist in parallel; one is not superseded by the other. However, this disguises the extent to which the shift from the archaeology of the episteme to the genealogy of discursive formations and relations of power marks a significant change in Foucault's critical discourse; from the invocation of the philosopher's laughter at the limit of understanding to the dynamic fluidity of the principle of reversal. The turn to the examination of the work of subjects on themselves represents a further development in Foucault's critical attitude. Foucault is still engaging in genealogy, but his genealogy of ethics (forms of relation to self) becomes entangled with the question of the form of ethics involved in his genealogy.

116

CRITIQUE AND ETHICS

The second and third volumes on the history of sexuality have a very different subject matter from the first. In them, the focus shifts from the idea of sexuality as an effect of power conceived in disciplinary terms, to sexuality as intrinsically linked to an aesthetics of existence. Central to this aesthetics of existence is the work done by individuals on themselves to make themselves subjects of sexuality. Foucault calls this work *ethical* work. The emphasis changes from the idea of power working through subjects, to the idea of subjects playing games of truth and power with themselves. In attempting to uncover the problematizations and practices underlying this relation, Foucault introduces an alternative to the vocabularies of force and warfare characteristic of *Discipline and Punish* and of strategic conflict/resistance common to the later glosses on power relations; this is a vocabulary of aesthetic creativity. Moreover, the object of his analysis is no longer the modern subject but the subjects of the ancient world from the fifth century BC in Greece to the first two centuries AD in Rome.[8] Throughout the second and third volumes on the history of sexuality, Foucault chronicles in detail the kinds of relation to self characteristic of Ancient Greece and Rome. He also notes the differences between Greece and Rome and explains how the ethics of late paganism introduce a concept of care for the self which has strong affinities with the Christian confessions of the flesh which are to supersede it. The discussion is densely detailed and seems to take one a long way from the question of the constitution of the modern subject of sexuality which was originally Foucault's theme. However, the significance of Foucault's work on the concept of care of the self in the ancient world lies not in what it tells us about Greek and Roman ethics, or about the development of the subject of sexuality through the centuries. Instead, it lies in the focus of the work, which is on modes of relation to self that do not operate in the form of the 'government of individualization' that Foucault discusses in 'The Subject and Power' (Dreyfus and Rabinow, 1982: 212). This is not to say that Foucault is suggesting that a revival of Ancient Greek ethical practices is the way to overthrow the modes of subjection of the modern subject. Nevertheless the ancient ethical practices that Foucault uncovers do exemplify a mode of relation to self outside of both juridical determination and determination by universal moral principles within a conscience. Moreover, these practices depend on the presumption of a capacity for self-creativity.

117

> The idea of the *bios* as a material for an aesthetic piece of art
> is something which fascinates me. The idea also that ethics can
> be a very strong structure of existence, without any relation to
> the juridical per se, with an authoritarian system, with a
> disciplinary structure.
>
> (Foucault, 1984b: 348)

The characteristics of self-creativity and self-rule in the Greek
practices of care of the self are specific to that particular context.
However, the possibility of self-creativity and self-rule is not confined
to a particular historical era, even if the ways in which it is
manifested will differ. Both the examples of resistance and the
account of critical philosophy given in 'The Subject and Power'
depend on a relation to self which is ethical. Without ethical relations
to self, all power relations would be a matter of domination, because
all choices would already be decided according to external or
internalized effects of power. Foucault is adamant that he is not
positing an existentialist 'authentic' self; what is significant is not the
self as an authentic or inauthentic product, but the capacity of
creativity itself.

> From the idea that the self is not given to us, I think that there
> is only one practical consequence: we have to create ourselves
> as a work of art.
>
> (Foucault, 1984b: 351)

Foucault's concept of ethics as an aesthetics of existence is developed
through the examination of practices of relation to self in late pagan
and early Christian contexts. However, when it comes to reflecting
on the nature of a modern aesthetics of existence, Foucault's most
sustained examinations of what this might mean focus on the kind of
philosophical practice implicit in Kant's essays on enlightenment and
the conflict of the faculties. The significance of these minor Kantian
texts for Foucault has already been signalled in the references to
Kant in 'The Subject and Power' discussed above. At the beginning
of the second volume of his history of sexuality, *The Use of Pleasure*,
Foucault again contrasts universalist critical philosophy with a different
kind of critique. The latter is identified as the critical work of thought
on itself in which the possibility of thinking differently is essayed
(Foucault, 1985: 8–9). This implies that non-universalist critical
philosophy is an example of ethical work as Foucault defines it: a
practice of relation to self or an aesthetics of existence. This

implication is confirmed in the two articles in which Foucault explicitly compares his philosophical practice to that of Kant: 'What is Enlightenment?' (Foucault, 1984b: 32–50) and 'The Art of Telling the Truth' (Foucault, 1988: 86–95). In these essays, Foucault argues that Kant's reflections on enlightenment and, in the case of the latter essay, on revolution are an example of philosophy as the critical ontology of ourselves.

> The critical ontology of ourselves has to be considered not, certainly, as a theory, a doctrine, nor even as a permanent body of knowledge that is accumulating; it has to be conceived as an attitude, an ethos, a philosophical life in which the critique of what we are is at one and the same time the historical analysis of the limits that are imposed on us with the possibility of going beyond them.

> (Foucault, 1984b: 50)

In place of the search for transcendental foundations for theory and practice which characterizes critique as an 'analytics of truth', the 'critical ontology of ourselves' is a constant calling into question of the present. It consists in reflection upon the limits of what and who we are and the consequent potential for identifying and pursuing what lies beyond those limits. In 'What is Enlightenment?', Foucault argues that Kant's reflections on his time signify a departure in philosophical critique from preoccupation with universals to preoccupation with the specificities of the present. Foucault goes on to link Kant's text to an attitude of modernity (Foucault, 1984b: 39). This 'attitude' is then explained as exemplified by Baudelaire in both his conception of his relation to the present, 'in which extreme attention to what is real is confronted with the practice of a liberty that simultaneously respects this reality and violates it' (Foucault, 1984b: 41); and a relation to self as one of self-production. It is not easy to recognize how Foucault is able to make the link between Baudelaire's modernism and Kant's reflections on enlightenment and revolution. Crucial to Foucault's reading is his understanding of Kant's commitment to the public use of reason in relation to the events of his time (Foucault, 1984b: 35–37). In the text on enlightenment this commitment is not contextualized in a philosophy of history, but in the idea of the development of humanity from childhood to maturity. As such, Foucault argues, it demonstrates the direct responsibility of each individual for the process of enlightenment, including the reponsibility of the philosophical critic for his intervention in the debate about what enlightenment is.

> But it seems to me that it is the first time that a philosopher has connected in this way, closely and from the inside, the significance of his work with respect to knowledge, a reflection on history and a particular analysis of the specific moment at which he is writing and because of which he is writing. It is in the reflection on 'today' as difference in history and as motive for a particular philosophical task that the novelty of this text appears to me to lie.
>
> (Foucault, 1984b: 38)

The value of Kant's philosophy here is not in its substantive claims but as an exemplar of what Foucault terms a *limit attitude* (Foucault, 1984b: 45). In a way elicited but not determined by the events of his time, Kant detaches himself from and reflects self-consciously on the limits of his present and how they may be transcended. Foucault goes on to explain what critique as a 'limit attitude' involves in contradistinction to transcendental critique. He argues that such critique is both archaeological and genealogical: archaeological in that it 'will seek to treat the instances of discourse that articulate what we think, say and do as so many historical events'; genealogical in that 'it will separate out, from the contingency that has made us what we are, the possibility of no longer being, doing, or thinking what we are, do, or think' (Foucault, 1984b: 46). What this means, it transpires, is that critical ontology is always both localized and experimental. It does not lay claim to radical and global alternatives to present conditions, but restricts analysis to specific practices and ways in which they might be transgressed. Critique aims to give new impetus to the work of freedom. It is a kind of perpetual agitation (Foucault, 1988: 155). As such the work of critique is never finished, 'we are always in the position of beginning again' (Foucault, 1984b: 47). In 'What is Enlightenment?', Foucault indicates the value of this critical work by spelling out what is at stake for the critical ontologist.

> What is at stake, then, is this: How can the growth of capabilities be disconnected from the intensity of power relations?
>
> (Foucault, 1984b: 48)

The practice of critical ontology has a double relationship to what Foucault has defined as what is at stake in that practice; this is implied by the invocation of both Kant and Baudelaire in Foucault's exposition. On the one hand, critical ontology in *reflecting* on limits flushes out the contingency of the modes of thought on which accepted practices rest (Foucault, 1988: 154–155). This aspect is represented by the way in which both Kant and Baudelaire theorize in relation to the present in all its specificity. On the other hand, as the *work of thought*, critical ontology exemplifies the exercise of a capability which operates in disconnection from power relations.

> Thought is not what inhabits a certain conduct and gives it its meaning; rather, it is what allows one to step back from this way of acting or reacting, to present it to oneself as an object of thought and question it as to its meaning, its conditions, and its goals. Thought is freedom in relation to what one does, the motion by which one detaches oneself from it, establishes itself as an object, and reflects on it as a problem.
>
> (Foucault, 1984b: 388)

The capacity to reflect on limits in all their contingency and historicity is intrinsically linked by Foucault to the capacity to make oneself a work of art (Foucault, 1984b: 42). As a process of constant creative engagement with the given limits of existence, the critical ontology of ourselves is intrinsically ethical. It represents in itself an aesthetics of existence in that the work of thought is not coerced by an external law, but is self-judging and self-legislating.

In critical ontology the specificity of time and place is brought together with the practice of freedom in a way that recalls not only the reflective judgement of history in Kant's writings, but also the realm of aesthetic judgement and genius. The notion of the disinterested reflective judgement of taste is recalled in the idea that critical ontology involves the exercise of thought that operates with no given principle of judgement. Kant's characterization of the work of genius is recalled in the way in which critical ontology exemplifies creative self-legislation without in any sense being able to lay down the law for others.

> Genius is the exemplary originality of a subject's natural endowment in the *free* use of his cognitive powers.
>
> (Kant, V: 318; 186)

Kant goes on in this passage:

> The other genius, who follows the example, is aroused by it to a feeling of his own originality, which allows him to exercise in

121

art his freedom from the constraint of rules, and to do so in such a way that art itself acquires a new rule by this, thus showing that the talent is exemplary.

(Kant, V: 318; 187)

For Kant, of course, the practice of self-legislation involved in both the judgement and creation of art is linked, however obscurely, to the 'supersensible substrate' of all judgement. In the same way, when Kant reflects on both enlightenment and revolution, his thinking is oriented by philosophies of right and history which depend on the idea of the transcendental legislation of practical reason. Foucault attempts to detach Kant's reflections from their broader context, since he is expounding a critical discourse which does not claim to hold the key to progress. However, there is a sense in which Foucault's critical ontology does not avoid the authoritative pretensions of Kantian critique. The perpetual criticism of genealogy depends on the capacity to think and re-think the given limits of existence. This capacity exemplifies an aesthetics of existence which is a practice of self-legislation. Freedom is both the beginning and the end of critique, which is always a matter of both specificity and transcendence. Kant's questions of what one ought to do and what one ought to hope for are unanswerable for Foucault in the sense that, like the work of genius, they cannot be legislated for in advance. However, in the examples of critical ontology as an aesthetics of existence as well as in the examples of political resistance that Foucault gives in 'The Subject and Power', the answer to Kant's questions is already given in terms of an ethic of self-legislation and self-government.

CONCLUSION

I carefully guard against making the law. Rather, I concern myself with determining problems, unleashing them, revealing them within the framework of such complexity as to shut the mouths of prophets and legislators: all of those who speak *for* others and *above* others.

(Foucault, 1991a: 159)

Foucault's refusal of the role of legislative critic mirrors Arendt's refusal of the idea of the philosopher legislating for politics. In some ways Foucault's relationship to Kant's work is similar to Arendt's in her political philosophy. Both thinkers reject the grounding of philosophical practice in transcendental legislation and therefore reject the Kant of the first two critiques; both thinkers use Kant's writings on judgement. However, in Arendt's case, the use of Kant's critique of judgement as resolving the question of the ground of judgement results in the repetition of Kantian paradoxes in her thought. The politics of Kantian critique are clearly reflected in the tension between the authority of the political judge and the undecidability of political action. In Foucault's case, there is no such crude repetition of the dynamics of Kantian critique. Foucault premises his use of Kant on the necessary impossibility of any general answer to the question of the ground of judgement; in Foucault's work, it is not Kant's *answers* to any of the questions of the transcendental critic that are of interest, instead it is the *questions* that Kant asks and the ways in which he asks them. In both Foucault's early and later work, Kant's posing of the question of reason's limitation remains a reference point for what Foucault is arguing against and for what he is arguing for. In so far as Kant's questions are posed in terms of finding the universal transcendental conditions of possibility for theory and practice, then Foucault argues against Kant. However, in so far as critique is construed as the calling into question of limits and conditions of possibility for theory and practice, then Foucault argues with Kant. The bifurcation of Kant's thought into an 'analytics of truth' and a 'critical ontology' enables Foucault to account for his use of Kant in the exposition of his (Foucault's) own critical practice, without succumbing to the perils of universalist philosophy. Nevertheless, in spite of the historicization and location of the work of the specific intellectual, the orientation of the work of critique towards the idea of an ethical relation to self keeps Foucault's thinking closer to the politics of Kant's critique than is acknowledged. The link between critical ontology and self-making problematizes the clarity of the distinction between an 'analytics of truth' and 'critical ontology'. Foucault may not legislate for either judgement or action, but he does make freedom a condition of possibility of both judgement and action and indicates that freedom (in the sense of self-legislation and self-government) is the orientation of both exemplary judgement (critical ontology/the constant calling into question of limits) and exemplary action (resistance). The authority of Foucault's critical discourse derives from the tensions within the work of the critic between specificity and generality. Like the Kantian critic, the Foucauldian critic works at the limit. Transgressive critique, like transcendental critique, displays a political logic which shifts between the conditioned and the conditioning. Because Foucault accepts that critique cannot be universally grounded, he cannot attempt to lay down the rules for either critique or transformation (Foucault, 1988: 155). However, in the same way as Kant's work operates in Foucault's late essays, the critical ontologist is able to rule by example.[9]

6

LYOTARD: PHRASING THE POLITICAL

INTRODUCTION

Lyotard, like Arendt and Foucault, rejects a legislative role for the critic and finds his chief debt to Kant in Kant's writings on aesthetic and political judgement. Throughout his work, Lyotard is preoccupied by the problem of how to resist and disrupt dominating orders, both discursive and economic. From his early political writings on Algeria to his most recent work on art, time and language, Lyotard remains philosophically engaged in challenging and undermining the theoretical and practical status quo of late-twentieth-century capitalism. However, this is not to say that Lyotard's work has not changed, both in the way it conceives of its target and in the ways in which it considers its dissident work to be possible. The most crucial shift in Lyotard's conception of his own critique and what it is criticizing came with his eventual abandonment of a Marxist framework for critique in the 1960s.[1] Following on from this, Lyotard can be seen first exploring the disruption of the *discursive* by the *figural*; then going on to examine the violence of *libidinal intensity* breaking through systemic order; then moving on again to the destruction of *grand narrative*; and most recently focusing on *judgement* and *witness* as displacing the ruling *genres of discourse*.[2] In all of these different incarnations, Lyotard is concerned with opposing what he frequently labels 'terror'. What is terroristic is what is totalitarian in the sense that it eliminates not just dissidence but plurality – whether in theory or in practice. Lyotard is, therefore, very much alive to the key problem inherent in any critical philosophy. That is the danger that critique may itself come to usurp the authority of that which it criticizes, replacing one totality with another. In this chapter I will be focusing on the way that Lyotard's more recent work relates to the Kantian inheritance. It will be argued that both the *pagan republican's* rejection of *grand narratives* (see pp. 131–135) and the *critical nightwatchman's* readings of the *signs of history* (see pp. 135–140) return us once again to the paradoxes of the politics of critique and the ambivalences inherent in the position of the critical political philosopher.

AGAINST CRITIQUE

Both capitalism and the Marxist theory of capital are the targets of Lyotard's critical attention in *Libidinal Economy*, but he is insistent that what he is engaged in is not critique.

> We laugh at critique, since it is to maintain oneself in the field of the criticized thing and in the dogmatic, indeed paranoiac, relation of knowledge.
>
> (Lyotard, 1993a: 95)

The 'we' of the above quotation stands for 'we libidinal economists', the laughter of whom, unlike Foucault's laughter at the classification of the Chinese encyclopaedia, indicates a complete rejection of the project of critique. This applies to any kind of critique, whether it be a Kantian critique of reason, or a Marxist critique of political economy, or a critique of those critiques. The problem with critique, from the viewpoint of the libidinal economist, is that in seeking to assess, understand, limit and improve its object, critique is simply reproducing the same kind of object. Both critique and what is criticized are, for the libidinal economist, just examples of the appropriative power of the ego. The libidinal economist is uninterested in judging between alternative orderings or economies of signs at the level of the theoretical explanation or practical organization of human existence. Instead, the libidinal economist is interested in tensors, which are signs operating at the level of the order of meaning but which also produce intensities through 'force and singularity'. These intensities open up a radically different time and space from that of the economies premised on what Lyotard sees as the constitutive western phantasy of the unified subject. In *Libidinal Economy* the conception of force pulsating the 'great ephemeral and labyrinthine skin' (Lyotard, 1993a: 210) is set against the conception of power as systemic regulation and control. The former abolishes distinctions and hierarchies; fragmenting, linking and revaluing what is unified, separated and valued at the level of the latter. However, it is misleading to represent the two kinds of economy as completely distinct. As portrayed by Lyotard, the libidinal economy continually forces its way through both the theoretical mastery of Marxist readings of capital and the development of capitalism itself, the 'white terror of truth' is fought by the 'red cruelty of singularities', or alternatively, a 'thousand cancerous tensors' are deployed in the bodies of signs by the libidinal economist acting as a good 'intensity-conductor' (Lyotard, 1993a: 241–262).

> What is this discourse? How is it legitimated? Where is it situated? Who authorizes you to speak in this way? Are you the manager . . . of the great skin? But how could you be, when it is ephemeral and offers nothing to hold onto or secure? Aren't you concerned with pure imagination and rhetoric? Are you looking for truth, do you claim to speak it, to have spoken it?
>
> (Lyotard, 1993a: 241)

The series of questions with which Lyotard broaches the final chapter of *Libidinal Economy* demonstrates his determination to break with the language of legitimation which is inherent in critique. In his account of the economy of his writing, Lyotard contrasts it with theoretical discourse which is caught in an endless cycle of reproduction and power. Instead, his writing aims at powerlessness, it is a bottle without a message, containing only a few energies of unpredictable effect. The libidinal economist is not a critical theorist, pronouncing on the evils of capitalism or reformulating the critique of political economy; he is a vehicle for the intensification of forces. He cannot, therefore, speak truth to power or occupy a position beyond reproach, he can only testify to violence and stay where he is. In setting out his view of what the libidinal economist does, Lyotard suggests it is in keeping with contemporary scientific research, which has become something very different from critique with its presumptions of the a priori authority of a knowing subject.

> The modern scientist no longer exists as a knower, that is to say as a subject, but as a small transitory region in a process of energetic metamorphosis, incredibly refined; he exists only as a 'researcher', which means on the one hand, of course, as part of a bureaucratic apparatus of scientific power, but on the other hand, indissociably, as an experimenter, indefatigable and not enslaved, with new junctures and combinations of energy; the statements he proposes count only in terms of their novelty.
>
> (Lyotard, 1993a: 253–254)

However, in spite of the explicit rejection of libidinal economy as critical theory, Lyotard acknowledges that, simply by virtue of being a theoretical text, *Libidinal Economy* must be read as a message and not only experienced as the transmission of unpredictable energies. Read as a text, the message of the book is, paradoxically, a highly critical one. The reader is clearly encouraged to support the 'red cruelty of singularities' against the 'white terror of truth' and to condemn the manifestations of the latter to be found in universal theories, unified conceptions of the subject and global capitalist systems of exchange and reproduction (Lyotard, 1993a: 241). The celebration of *jouissance* and intensity is counterposed to the rejection of regulation and control. The question is therefore inevitably raised as to the basis of the affirmation of violence against power on the part of the libidinal economist, and Lyotard recognizes its inevitability in his attempt to establish the libidinal significance of his own writing. The difficulty is that the only way the question can be answered is in terms which push against the dynamic of a libidinal economy as the play of intensities across the great ephemeral skin. Two kinds of answer are suggested in *Libidinal Economy*, both of which threaten the return of a language of critique. One is the suggestion that force and intensity operate as, as it were, the transcendental conditions of possibility of power and system, so that in favouring the libidinal economy one is returning to some kind of authentic origin of understanding and action. The other is the suggestion that late capitalism is developing historically towards the facilitation of the libidinal economy (becoming increasingly libidinized), so that in endorsing force, intensity and singularity one is already celebrating an approaching end of history. Lyotard is clearly not endorsing either of these possibilities in so far as he remains faithful to the project of the libidinal economist. Nevertheless, the questions that the critical theorist will necessarily ask (i.e. those cited above, Lyotard, 1993a: 241) and the ways those questions may be answered combine to unsettle the confidence of Lyotard's account of the economy of his writing.

Libidinal Economy aimed at providing a radical critique (non-critique) primarily of Marxist analyses of capitalism, though by implication also of any totalizing theory that attempts to subsume either knowledge or practice under a single principle. At the same time, libidinal economy continues to rely heavily on a Freudian vocabulary, a vocabulary from which Lyotard increasingly distances himself in his subsequent writings. In place of Hegel, Marx and Freud, the philosophical reference points of Lyotard's thought become the sophists (Protagoras, Gorgias), Aristotle, Kant, Wittgenstein and Levinas. However, the target of critique remains the 'white terror of truth' conceived more mildly as the pretensions of grand narratives.

> Humor does not invoke a truth more universal than that of the masters; it does not even struggle in the name of the majority by incriminating the masters for being a minority. Humor wants rather to have this recognized: *there are only minorities.*
>
> (Lyotard, 1993b: 83)

In *Libidinal Economy* the idea of the tensor as the moment of intensification, the disruptive force that inhabits another time and space, undermines the pretensions of power and subverts the economy of signs. However, in later texts, although the subversion of dominant orders continues to be referred to in the language of force, the overturning is no longer represented violently; it becomes a much more gentle, playful challenge. Instead of intensity, difference becomes Lyotard's weapon in what is grandiosely conceived as a war against totality. This is most clearly demonstrated in the text for which Lyotard is most famous, *The Postmodern Condition: A Report on Knowledge,* and in the interviews published in English as *Just Gaming.*

PARALOGICAL THINKING

The Postmodern Condition purports to present an overview of the state of knowledge in modern western societies. The argument of the book takes its starting point from the demise of the grand narrative, i.e. the incapacity of any universal theory to make sense of either the natural or social world. The challenge that the book poses is that of how to legitimate knowledge in a world in which there is no longer a belief in common foundations or a common direction to human development. Lyotard finds his answer to this question in a concept of language games.

> Most people have lost the nostalgia for the lost narrative. It in no way follows that they are reduced to barbarity. What saves them from it is their knowledge that legitimation can only spring from their own linguistic practice and communicational interaction.
>
> (Lyotard, 1984: 41)

Although this quotation is reminiscent of Habermas, Lyotard is insistent that linguistic practice and communicational interaction are fundamentally pluralist; there is, contrary to Habermas, no common underlying language game. Lyotard traces two trajectories within science of the turn away from grand narrative and suggests tentatively how these might be reflected in social relations more generally. The first development within science is a shift to performative criteria for the legitimation of knowledge. According to this 'little narrative', scientific research is essentially legitimated with reference to its success in solving problems and bringing about technological advances. This is a criterion of power and control. However, the introduction of pragmatic, performative grounds for the assessment of scientific development leads, on Lyotard's account, to a second development of a different kind. Lyotard argues that the pressure of performative criteria results in rapid progress in problem solving within the sciences. At a certain point the limits of the disciplinary boundaries will have been reached and scientists will be forced to challenge the rules of their own problem-solving discourse (language game). This means a shift towards what Lyotard calls 'paralogical thinking' in which the constitution of linguistic practices is recognized and re-invented.[3] In paralogical thinking, the parochialism of language games is transcended and incommensurables are thought together. This means that rather than all scientific thought being narrowed down to a project of control, it works instead to open up new horizons and possibilities. It is obviously in the idea of paralogical thinking that Lyotard finds the positive moment in the postmodern condition. Paralogy functions like intensity and force in the earlier work in that it disrupts the hegemony of power and control. However, even more than with the workings of the libidinal economy, there is no sense of a guarantee of hope. Instead, the postmodern condition remains fundamentally ambivalent between control and paralogy, and both moments are reflected in the changes in social relations brought about by scientific and technological revolutions. Lyotard ends the work with a reference to temporary contracts as exemplifying both the power of the system and the creative possibilities that are not subordinate to the system which it nevertheless permits. It is suggested that this ambiguity is the best that can be hoped for in a society that has given up the project of any wholesale revolution or reconstruction.

> This bears witness to the existence of another goal within the system: Knowledge of language games as such and the decision to assume responsibility for their rules and effects. Their most

significant effect is precisely what validates the adoption of rules – the quest for paralogy.

(Lyotard, 1984: 66)

In the essay added as a postscript to *The Postmodern Condition*, 'Answering the Question: What is Postmodernism?', Lyotard further clarifies his concept of the postmodern, and it is the idea of paralogy, of the transcendence and invention of rules, that assumes greatest importance in his account. He links this idea to the Kantian concept of the sublime as the feeling accompanying the presentation of that which is unpresentable, the pain of the failure of imagination to exemplify ideas (Lyotard, 1984: 78). On this account certain kinds of art and philosophy appear to be accorded a privilege in capturing the postmodern moment within modernity, but Lyotard is clear that this privilege does not encompass any reference to a kingdom of ends.

> Finally, it must be clear that it is our business not to supply reality but to invent allusions to the conceivable which cannot be presented. And it is not to be expected that this task will effect the last reconciliation beween language games (which, under the name of faculties, Kant knew to be separated by a chasm), and that only the transcendental illusion (that of Hegel) can hope to totalize them into a real unity. But Kant also knew that the price to pay for such an illusion is terror.

(Lyotard, 1984: 81)

Paralogical thinking is not only essentially linked to the recognition of difference and plurality but is also to do with the creative transcendence of rules and limits. In *Just Gaming* it becomes apparent that paralogy is part of a new conception of justice. It also becomes apparent that Kant is an increasingly important reference point for Lyotard in his effort to formulate an anti-terroristic account of what it means to be critical in the postmodern condition.

The argument in *Just Gaming* reinforces the parallel between postmodern language games and Kantian faculties made by Lyotard in the above quotation. The reference is not so much to the discrete concerns of different disciplines as recorded in Kant's *The Conflict of the Faculties*, but more fundamentally to the division between the faculty of the understanding and the faculty of reason established in Kant's first two critiques. In *Just Gaming* Lyotard claims that the language game of truth and the language game of justice (prescription) are absolutely different and that neither can be grounded in the

131

other. This means that the 'pagan' postmodernist's account of the language game of justice must be a republican one, in Kant's sense of a republican politics as the separation of powers. For Kant, a state is republican if in it the powers of the legislature, executive and judiciary are distinct. The reason for Kant's insistence is that he needs to preserve the formal irreproachability of the sovereign body since it is identified ideally with the common will, while at the same time recognizing the distinction between ideal and real which necessitates rulers to punish and courts to judge (Kant, VI: 313–318; 124–129; Kant, VIII: 349–353; 99–102). The relation of the three powers to each other is complex; each has its own ultimate authority and yet each works in subordination to the other, so that the sovereign may neither judge nor punish, the ruler may not legislate or judge and the judge may not legislate or rule. In so far as each carries authority, it is by virtue of its identification with pure practical reason in idea; in so far as each has its authority limited, it is by virtue of the others' identification with pure practical reason in idea. Kant's account of republicanism in the political realm carries clear echoes of the relation between the three faculties explored in each of his critiques: understanding, reason and judgement. The legislation of the understanding, the command of reason and the adjudication of reflective judgement are like the political powers in their domains of authority as well as in the complexity of their relation to one another.

Lyotard relates his study of language games to Kantian republicanism in that it too is premised on respecting the difference between the faculties; but more importantly than this, the language game of justice becomes identified with republicanism because it (the game of justice) is nothing other than respect for difference itself.

> The examination of language games, just like the critique of the faculties, identifies and separates language from itself. There is no unity to language; there are islands of language, each of them ruled by a different regime, untranslatable into the others. This dispersion is good in itself and ought to be respected. It is deadly when one phrase regime prevails over others.
>
> (Lyotard, 1993c: 20)

In *Just Gaming*, therefore, Lyotard is dealing with the equivalent of critique itself, the examination of the language game on which the examination of language games itself is premised, the question of what makes prescription possible. This is a question to which there can be only one answer for the postmodern republican, and that is that *nothing* makes it possible. The language game of justice has no origin and no author. However, this is only the starting point of Lyotard's analysis. The absence of authority in justice opens up the question of what, therefore, is signified in the pragmatics of obligation implicit in the word 'ought'? Lyotard's answer takes us back to the undeduceability of the moral law, the Kantian concept of 'idea' and the Kantian account of reflective judgement and the sublime.

According to Lyotard, the words 'you must' can be articulated in the language game of description as an account of the way in which someone is/has been obliged; *or* they can be articulated as an instruction in the language game of prescription. The latter is not in any sense reducible to the former. However, the latter does in some way mark the point of transcendence of the former from the game of description in which the aim is knowledge of the given to another descriptive game – of the exploration of the possible. In order to try to explain this, Lyotard invokes the relation between the undeduceability of the moral law in Kant's *Critique of Practical Reason* and the role of the ideas of reason in setting up an *as-if* ground for moral judgement (Lyotard and Thébaud, 1985: 58–59). Like the moral law, the language game of prescription cannot be deduced; it stands as absolute obligation to the unknown and unknowable. In its relation to nothingness, however, the language game of prescription follows the moral law in opening up the possibility of a realm beyond the given and thus also the possibility of judging *as if* one were in another world beyond the given. It is the mark of our capacity to move beyond the language game of truth and both explore and invent other games. To play the game of the just is to acknowledge the inescapability of incommensurable difference as an obligation, a debt that can never be paid (Lyotard and Thébaud, 1985: 64–65; 71). For Lyotard the way in which Kant uses the notion of 'ideas of reason' as unknowable but regulative pinpoints the postmodern moment in the modern in which the enlightenment project is disrupted from within by an ethical imperative which transcends the terror of the legislation of reason. This transcendence does not imply an answer to questions of truth, morality and right, instead it demands a respect for the unanswerability of those questions.

> Absolute injustice would occur if the pragmatics of obligation, that is, the possibility of continuing to play the game of the just were excluded. That is what is unjust.
>
> (Lyotard and Thébaud, 1985: 66)

By this point it is clear that Lyotard's analysis of the ungrounded nature of prescription goes beyond a comfortable endorsement of pluralism and relativism. The imperative for the respect for plurality is not simply the recognition of a gulf between 'is' and 'ought'. Rather, this imperative is based on the striving to transcend given reality, a striving which is itself a given in the fact of obligation towards nothing that describes the prescriptive language game. The relation to nothingness makes all moral and political judgement necessarily a matter of hypothesis and invention or, as Lyotard sees it, of reflective judgement in the Kantian sense. This is not the reflective judgement of beauty, in which the faculties are in harmony, but the judgement of the sublime – the pain of the inadequacy of any attempt to bridge the gap between the real and the possible, the present and the unpresentable. Lyotard supplements his reading of Kant with a reading of Levinas and draws on both to argue that the game of the just *is* equivalent to an absolute obligation to an unknowable and unpresentable other (Lyotard and Thébaud, 1985: 71).[4]

At one point in *Just Gaming*, Lyotard claims that he is hesitating between a 'pagan' and a Kantian position in his examination of language games (Lyotard and Thébaud, 1985: 73). In the exchange with his interviewer, it becomes clear that underlying this hesitation is the issue of moral and political judgement in the postmodern reality of incommensurable language games. The pagan approach appears to be more playful; a matter of policing the boundaries of language games and preventing any hegemonic moves on the part of one game to take control of another. On this approach, the game of justice is simply a response to the inability of any one narrative or language game to sustain a claim to all the territories of reason. The pagan has no response, other than laughter, to the relativist paradox that it is itself usurping the position of totalization; nor to the charge that he or she provides no grounds for the condemnation of what is absolutely unjust other than pure opinion, a blind preference for plurality over unity. The Kantian approach, on the other hand, appears to make room for a stronger accounting for of the game of justice and also of the possibility of judgement. According to this account, the sea that separates the islands of language, uniting and distinguishing them at the same time, is the idea of pure practical reason itself. Just as Kant's account of the separate powers in the republic depends on their ultimate grounding in the idea of a common will, so Lyotard's account of the separate language games of description and prescription relies on an inescapable fact of relation to otherness, which can only be understood in idea. In *Peregrinations*, Lyotard confirms the argument of *Just Gaming*: the fact of obligation cannot be directly legislative; but it can and should orient and regulate ethical judgement and ethical practice.

> I shall call the law the fact that there is a question or that we are questioned about what we ought to become and what we ought to do to become it. That fact Kant calls a 'factum rationis', the indisputable fact that practical reason is an a priori transcendental condition for any morality whatsoever. It is a pure obligation, a duty, not one, however, to do this or that, but rather the pure 'fact' of duty, of being obliged.
>
> (Lyotard, 1988b: 35)

In *The Postmodern Condition* and *Just Gaming* Lyotard departs radically from the celebration of the disruptive force of the libidinal economy. However, he is still fundamentally concerned with countering systemic power and control in modern society. In *The Postmodern Condition* the postmodern moment within modernity of paralogical thinking, invention and the challenge to the bounds of little narratives substitutes for intensity in the subversion of the hegemony of performative criteria in knowledge. In *Just Gaming* the language game of justice and its debt to nothing demands the transcendence of the limits of the descriptive language game and the invocation of other possible worlds. It seems as if in his exploration of the game of justice, Lyotard is, in effect, providing support for his endorsement of paralogy in his report on knowledge. Paralogy exemplifies obedience to the imperative that forces us to look beyond the boundaries of our particular island of truth. It is this that is essential to justice and, as the essay 'What is Postmodernism?' and Lyotard's reflections in *The Differend* and *Peregrinations* all suggest, it is this which is essential to art and to the practice of philosophical writing. The dismissal of the theoretical text as a reliable vehicle for libidinal energies is turned, in Lyotard's later work, into the elevation of philosophical writing into a practice of justice. The pagan republican becomes the critical nightwatchman and the reader of the signs of history.

PERPETUAL PEACE

A *différend* takes the form of a civil war, of what the Greeks called a stasis: the form of a spasm. The authority of the idiom in which cases are established and regulated is contested. A different idiom and a different tribunal are demanded, which the other party contests and rejects. Language is at war with itself, and the critical nightwatchman posts guard over the war.

(Lyotard, 1989: 357)

Since the publication of *The Differend*, Lyotard has been engaged in bringing together consideration of the question of the legitimation of knowledge in the postmodern condition, and the concern with justice expressed in *Just Gaming*. He has elaborated a more complex account of language games and of their incommensurability in the concepts of regimes of phrases and of the differend itself. And he has identified this elaboration with the practice of a deliberative politics, which shifts between the roles of the critical nightwatchman in guarding the wars between genres, and the more positive task of abetting the invention of new genres of discourse. Crucial to both Lyotard's epistemological and ethical concerns is the conceptualization of both theory and practice in terms of regimes/clouds of phrases and the peculiar position of proper names in relation to these regimes (Lyotard, 1988a: 50). Crucial to both also is the understanding of philosophical writing as operating in some sense between the lines of the families of phrases. Unlike other genres of discourse, philosophical phrasing does not have its 'rules of linkage' fixed in advance (Lyotard, 1988a: 29; 60–61).

In *The Differend* Lyotard moves from an account of theory and practice in terms of language games to one in which the basic element is the phrase. He argues that the phrase is inescapable in the sense that phrasing is involved even in the denial of phrases or in silence (Lyotard, 1988a: 13–14). All phrases are open to linkage with other phrases in the future and are the product of past linkages. Depending on the nature of the linkages made with any given phrase, the phrase regime will belong to a different genre of discourse (language game). It is the genre that establishes the means by which any given phrase or group of phrases may be legitimated. This means that the judgement of disputes can only be accomplished within a given genre. A differend occurs when a dispute arises, but the means of litigation are inappropriate to one side of the dispute; in other words, they belong to a different genre. Lyotard uses the example of a worker taking a case about her contract to a tribunal. In order to bring the case, the worker must adopt the idiom of labour-power as a commodity; becoming a plaintiff by bringing a case involves confirming the genre of social and economic law and leaves no space for a different phrasing of one's relationship to one's productive capacity. In the case of a differend, becoming a plaintiff is also at the same time becoming a victim.

> If the labourer evokes his or her essence (labour-power), he or she cannot be heard by this tribunal, which is not competent. The differend is signalled by this inability to prove. The one who lodges a complaint is heard, but the one who is a victim, and who is perhaps the same one, is reduced to silence.
>
> (Lyotard, 1988a: 10)

The differend is the experience of a wrong which cannot be recognized, perhaps not even articulated, within the dominant genre. Its importance for Lyotard lies in the way in which it directs the speaker beyond the limits of one genre towards the task of constructing new means of litigation within which their wrong can find expression. The differend marks both the heterogeneity of phrase regimes and genres and the tensions between them. It also, however, marks a possibility of relations between genres by suggesting that new litigations might be attempted that could adjudicate the dispute differently, perhaps more fairly. Implicit in the notion of the differend is a link with Kantian ideas of reason, which represent the capacity to think of new possible worlds. Without ideas there could be no grasp of the differend in the first place, no intimation of a genre in which the wrong could be recognized as wrong. However, the nature of the relations implied by the differend emphasize struggle rather than harmony, and Lyotard draws a parallel between those relations and the relations of war and commerce characteristic of Kant's account of perpetual peace. Always contrasted with the differend is the idea of the absolute hegemony of a single genre or regime of phrases. This is the situation where there is no conceivable way that a wrong could be addressed (Lyotard, 1988a: 106).

Lyotard likens his account of phrases governed by genres to an archipelago of territories. The differend, in which an idea of reason fuels a challenge to the authority of one particular sovereign, encourages a voyage across the passages which separate the islands. This voyage, however, by definition does not itself come under the governance of any particular regime; its relation is to the gap, the nothingness which is the space/pause between a phrase and its linkages. Philosophical phrasing, politics and art are all cited by Lyotard as examples of this voyaging and all of them are understood as involving the conception of reflective judgement that Lyotard derives from Kant.[5]

> This is the faculty which has enabled the territories and realms to be delimited, which has established the authority of each genre on its island. And this it was only able to do thanks to the commerce or to the war it fosters between genres.
>
> (Lyotard, 1988a: 131)

Philosophy, politics and art all involve judgement without the presence of determining rules. In a sense, they *are* the differend because they are grounded not in a specific genre of discourse but in nothing, i.e. in the relation to absolute otherness expressed in Lyotard's account of the undeduceability of Kant's categorical imperative. In other words, it is philosophy, politics and art that capture the possibility of going beyond a particular genre, because for them no rules are given, they can only be invented. The task of philosophy, politics and art, as Lyotard sees it, is to seek out the differend and exacerbate it. This feeds the relations between the genres and helps to confirm and delimit the boundaries of their sovereignty. It is this role that characterizes the critical nightwatchman, patrolling and policing the seas within which the archipelago is situated. However, the differend is not just a matter of the distinction between different genres of discourse. The differend poses a challenge to discourse, a challenge to create *'new rules for the formation and linkage of phrases'*. It is in this constructive task that judgement shifts from a delimiting role to one of guidance and regulation (Lyotard, 1986: 115).

> Is the only purpose of the reflective function which is ours to transform, as Kant thought, dispute (*différend*) into litigation, by substituting the law-court for the battle-field? Is not its aim also that of emphasizing disputes even at the risk of aggravating them, of giving a language to what cannot be expressed in the language of the judge, even if he is a critical judge?
>
> (Lyotard, 1989: 410)

The inspiration for Lyotard's positive account of judgement is once more to be found in Kant's work, in particular in a reading of Kant's account of the historical-political significance of the attitude of the spectators to the French Revolution given in *The Conflict of the Faculties* (Lyotard, 1986: 45–77). In this text, Kant argues that the enthusiasm expressed by spectators for the revolution can be taken as confirmation of a reading of history as progress. According to

Lyotard, enthusiasm is an example of a sublime reflective judgement. It is the outcome of a striving towards the ideal; towards the presentation of that which is unpresentable or, in Lyotard's own terms, it is a passage between cognitive and prescriptive genres, belonging to neither.

> However, the episodic unleashing of excessive enthusiasm retains an aesthetic validity, it is an energy giving sign, a tensor of *Wunsch*. The infinity of the Idea draws all other capacities to itself, that is to say all the other faculties, and produces an *Affekt* 'du genre vigoureux' [ibid.] characteristic of the sublime.
>
> (Lyotard, 1986: 64)[6]

The enthusiasm of the spectators of the French Revolution has an exemplary validity for Lyotard. This enthusiasm is a 'sign' of history and provides a kind of case study of what signs of history are and how they may be comprehended. According to Lyotard, signs of history are, like proper names, unsubsumable under the cognitive genre of discourse (Lyotard, 1988a: 32–58). In the case of a sign, it is not just that it is possible to link it to a heterogeneity of phrases, it is also that it challenges the genres which attempt to subsume it. Signs are linked to historical events, but it is not the events themselves but the judgement they evoke that constitutes the sign. This is a kind of judgement (sublime) which is liberated from the confines of determined genres and reaches towards a new litigation. Sublime feeling oscillates in the abyss between nature and reason, its indetermination enables the cultivation of new possibilities for judgement: 'There is no sublime, therefore, without the development of the speculative and ethical capacities of the mind' (Lyotard, 1988b: 41). This is why, on Lyotard's account, it is possible for Kant to argue that the judgement of the spectators of the French Revolution can be read as evidence of progress in history.

Signs of history are characterized by the way in which they liberate judgement, pushing it towards the invention of new rules for phrasing. But what exactly does this liberation mean? In Kant's case, the judgement of the French Revolution is oriented by a teleological account of history as progress towards the moral law. This regulative idea is presented as an attempt to close the gap between the realm of the understanding and that of reason, given the actual impotence of practical reason itself. The striving to close the gap, which is the reading given by the philosopher to the sign of the spectators' enthusiasm, is then interpreted as evidence of the cultivation of people's moral sensitivities. The philosopher, by reading the sign of history in the way that he does, substitutes for the direct rule of reason, much as the ruler and judge carry out their work, without in any sense challenging the law which legitimates their activity. For Kant, therefore, the sign of history liberates judgement in that it allows it to become detached from the determining rules of cognition, i.e. empirical history, but it certainly does not liberate judgement to think beyond the ideas of reason which themselves underlie the possibility of cognition in the first place. For Lyotard, however, the liberation of judgement appears more radical.

> But however negative the signs to which most of the proper names of our political history give rise, we should nevertheless have to judge them *as if* they proved that this history had moved on a step in its progress; i.e. in the culture of skill and of will. This step would consist in the fact that it is not only the Idea of a *single* purpose which would be pointed to in our feeling, but already the Idea that this purpose consists in the formation and free exploration of Ideas *in the plural*, the Idea that this end is the beginning of the *infinity of heterogeneous finalities*.
>
> (Lyotard, 1989: 409)

Whereas for Kant the cultivation of judgement involves its orientation towards the moral law, for Lyotard the cultivation of judgement involves its orientation towards the exploration of a plurality of Ideas. The signs of history to which Lyotard bears witness for contemporary judgement are evoked by the names: Auschwitz; Budapest 1956; May 1968. Unlike Kant, Lyotard's witness is not to the ultimate rule of the moral law but against terror; it is a witness negatively directed against the danger of totalitarianism, positively directed towards respect for heterogeneity.

PHILOSOPHERS AND KINGS

Judgement, in the sense of reflective judgement – the practice of philosophy, art and politics – is not a genre according to Lyotard. Judgement operates in the passage between disparate territories, encountering the differend and inventing new rules of phrasing for it. All of Lyotard's philosophical writing from *Libidinal Economy* onwards is an attempt to divorce his philosophy from power so that he can emulate the critical judge without uncritically presuming the legitimacy of his own discourse. In this, of course, Lyotard is following closely in the footsteps of Kant's critique of reason. Since his abandonment of libidinal economy, Lyotard has come to rely more and more heavily on a reading of Kant to sustain a practice of philosophy which is not totalizing and prescriptive. In doing this, Lyotard follows Arendt and Foucault in using one aspect of Kant's writings to undermine the legacy of another. Kant's critical thought is premised on the twin assumptions of reason's limitation and its legislative power. As discussed in Chapter 1, the presumptions of critique result in a series of dichotomies which reason must, yet cannot, overcome. Lyotard rejects the totalizing and unifying themes in Kant's critique and adopts a non-authoritarian, non-terroristic version of Kant's critique as the guardian of limits and boundaries. There are two ways in particular in which Lyotard identifies his mature thought and its epistemological, ethical and political implications as Kantian: first, he claims to be a republican thinker in the Kantian sense; second, he claims to be using the Kantian concept of ideas of reason. How successful is Lyotard (or can he be) in utilizing these aspects of the Kantian inheritance without lapsing back into the language of sovereign legislation which he seeks to avoid?

Republicanism in the Kantian sense means support for the separation of powers, and over and above that respect for the uniqueness of the authority of each of those powers within their own domains. Lyotard is a Kantian republican in that he supports, respects and sees it as his task to reinforce the separation of the territories that make up the archipelago of genres. No power is entitled to encroach onto the ground of another, just as the judge must not interfere with the ruler or the legislator, and so on. Kant argues that the republican constitution is the best defence against despotism. Lyotard argues that the recognition of the validity of a plurality of genres is the best defence against terror. On what are both of these arguments based? For Kant, the desirability of republicanism rests on the presumption that a rightful state is one grounded on the idea of the common will of the people. The principle of right can be protected in actual states by preventing the identification of rulers with legislators, thus preserving the formal irreproachability of law. Moreover, in that the idea of a common will continues to ground law, all members of the state can count themselves as self-legislating, and rulers will be deterred from acting in such a way as the people would not choose to act (e.g. in starting wars, etc.). Legislators should see themselves as representatives of the common will, and rulers should be obliged to respect this.

> The republican constitution is not only pure in its origin (since it springs from the pure concept of right); it also offers a prospect of attaining the desired result, i.e. a perpetual peace.
>
> (Kant, VIII: 351; 100)

Kant's support for republicanism is not based on a kind of liberal pluralism. It is essentially justified by a concept of right and a reading of history, both of which are themselves determined by the idea of pure practical reason. Neither is republicanism a separation of powers in the sense of the distinction of defined and incommensurable territories. The legislature, executive and judiciary are all measured in terms of and defined in relation to the demands of practical reason; they derive their powers from a higher power which explains them. The fact that this power is not itself comprehensible does not mean it is not both the ground and end of any rightful, republican politics. That republicanism is contrasted to despotism is a consequence of the moral limitation of human beings. A nation of angels could be a democracy, since actual will would always be the equivalent of ideal will. Because a human state is made up of beings divided between alternative motivations, there has to be a buffer between law and rule, so that there is no danger of the identification of a private *Willkür* with *Wille* itself (since this would be despotism). For Kant, it is the legislation and rule of pure practical reason that is ultimately desired and desirable.

Turning now to Lyotard's republicanism, there are interesting parallels with Kant's argument. At first sight, particularly when he is working with the concept of language games, it is possible to read Lyotard's republicanism as a loose adaptation of Kant to the language of an 'anything goes' postmodern pluralism. What texts such as *The Differend* and *L'Enthousiasme* make clear is that Lyotard is much closer to Kant than this. The focus shifts more and more from the language games or genres themselves to the context in which they are situated, from the archipelago to the sea. What separates the islands of language, uniting and distinguishing them at the same time, is variously presented as nothingness, as pure obligation to otherness, as the unpresentable, as the realm of judgement, art, politics and philosophy. However, it is clear that it is from the sea that the islands emerged, from the sea that they may be comprehended and from the sea that new lands will be discovered.

Moreover, like the Kantian critic of reason, it is the postmodern philosopher/judge voyaging across the sea who usurps the legislative authority of the sovereigns of the islands themselves, establishing limits and boundaries, punishing incursions or alternatively encouraging war and commerce (Lyotard, 1986: 29–30). There are parallels also between Lyotard's philosophical interventionist force and the Kantian critic in that, in both cases, the authority of the philosopher derives from the originary authority of an unknowable law and from the idea of respect for that law as an end of history. In Kant's case it is the moral law, in Lyotard's the principle of respect for otherness which exerts an absolute obligation over the practice of the political philosopher. The task of the philosopher is to present the unpresentable and read the unreadable – to judge and bear witness. Republicanism, therefore, does not mean for either Kant or Lyotard a philosophical practice which respects difference in the weak sense of merely acknowledging plurality. Both thinkers see difference as underwritten by and dependent on something else, pure practical reason or the game of the just, unsubsumable under any genre. Despotism or terror is defined as the illegitimate identification of an actual sovereign with what can only be understood in idea. But as the keeper of the idea, the philosopher holds out the ideal of knowing the unknowable, comprehending the law as a possible end of history which can be read in events themselves.

The ideas and ideals of reason play a crucial part in Kant's critical philosophy. They underpin the legislation of the understanding in theoretical reason and represent the possibility of morality and right in the realm of practical reason. Lyotard finds the concept of the idea of reason useful because it is a principle of judgement which is not a concept and which can subsume only *as if* it were a concept. In Kant's moral philosophy, ideas of reason provide *as-if* notions of an ideal order which can then be used in the judgement of actions/maxims within the actual world. There is no sense in which these hypothetical grounds for judgement can be known to be true. These judgements are inherently indeterminate and must be comprehended differently from cognitive judgements. The gulf between descriptive and prescriptive language games is understood by Lyotard as the same as the fundamental incommensurability of concepts and ideas. Lyotard thus faces the same problem for judgement as Kant as to the relation between empirical and ideal worlds. Ideas of reason represent the answer for Lyotard to this problem, in that he sees them as precisely the invention of ways of crossing the passage/gulf between the realm of the understanding and reason. At the same time, however, ideas of reason as attempts to represent the unrepresentable play another role – that of orienting judgement in a particular direction, towards the goal of an ideal end of history as plurality, invention and heterogeneity. In the discussion of signs of history, ideas of reason are more than what can be postulated by the inventive powers of judgement, they have become the guides of judgement. The consciousness of the space between real and ideal in the sublime judgement has been transmuted into the philosopher's judgement of history as if it were progress. In his Kantian republicanism and in his use of the Kantian idea of reason, Lyotard follows Kant towards the moment of the philosopher's judgement as bridging the gap between real and ideal history. In *L'Enthousiasme*, Lyotard refers to Kant's writings on history and, in particular, to Kant's reference to the way in which philosophical history might be compared to fiction, the production of a novel (Lyotard, 1986: 96).

> In writing the *Conjectures*, the critical judge delivers a favourable verdict on the pretensions of the novel to phrase the historical-political. The latest condition on this favour is that it will be a novel of cultivation, a *Bildungsroman*, in the critical sense of the cultivation of the will, that of its hero and that of its reader.
>
> (Lyotard, 1986: 103–104)[7]

There are differences between the *romanesque* phrasing of the political to be found in Kant's writings on history and politics and Lyotard's. Kant's story is written in terms of the unifying idea of a kingdom of ends demanded by pure practical reason. Kant's heroes and readers have their sensibilities and capacities cultivated through the judgement of beauty as much as through sublime feeling. For Lyotard, however, the story must be written in terms of an idea of heterogeneity and an ultimate respect for the incommensurability of phrase regimes. It is only the judgement of the sublime that genuinely captures and therefore cultivates our sensibilities and capacities in the appropriate way.

> The sublime feeling is neither moral universality nor aesthetic universalization, but is, rather, the destruction of one by the other in the violence of their differend.
>
> (Lyotard, 1994: 239)

The stories that Kant and Lyotard tell may not be the same stories but what does remain the same is the peculiar role of the storyteller.

In Kant's work, it is the spectator's judgement of the French Revolution that exemplifies progress, in the sense of invoking the ideal of politics as the self-legislation of reason in a kingdom of ends. The judgement of the spectator thereby becomes privileged over both the legislation of legitimate monarchs and the violent revolt of subjects in so far as these are not governed by respect for the moral law. In Lyotard's work, the critical nightwatchman's reading of the signs of history also exemplifies progress, in the sense of invoking an ideal of politics as the respect and cultivation of plurality and heterogeneity. The judgement of the Lyotardian political philosopher thereby becomes privileged over the practice of political actors in so far as they fail to be oriented by the ideal implicit in the game of the just.

CONCLUSION

On the surface, Lyotard's critical discourse might seem closer to Foucault's critical ontology than to Habermas's critical theory or Arendt's political philosophy of judgement. Lyotard, like Foucault, sets out to be a critical thinker who refuses to legislate universal grounds or ends for either theory or practice, and he consistently opposes totalizing conceptions of the true and the good. However, Lyotard's reliance on strongly Kantian presumptions about the abyss between the realms of 'is' and 'ought' in practice brings his theorizing closer to Habermas than to Foucault. The Lyotardian critic testifies to the simultaneous impossibility and possibility of progress by first asserting the unbridgeability of the gap between empirical and transcendental realms; and then going on to locate progress in a particular kind of philosophical practice that is identified with exemplary politics. The logic of this argument mirrors Kant's movement from the failings of the philosophy of right to the resources of reflective judgement. At any given stage in the critic's journey, the impossibility of synthesizing the diremptions on which critique is founded is made possible through the critic's mysterious capacity to voyage across unchartable seas. The result is a critical practice which veers between the acknowledgement of its own lack of authority and a claim to occupy the absence which is the ground of absolute obligation.

7

THE CRITIQUE OF INTERNATIONAL POLITICS

INTRODUCTION

The preceding chapters of this book have been concerned with examining the politics of Kantian critique in Kant's own work and as it re-surfaces in different ways in the ideas of contemporary thinkers drawing on Kant's work. In the first two chapters of this book it became clear that the politics of Kantian critique were both complex and contradictory. The presumptions of both reason's limitation and its legislative power created a problem of authority for the critic from the beginning. In conceiving his critical project initially as a matter of securing those territories to which reason has legitimate claim given reason's inherent limitation, Kant institutes a series of splits between transcendental and empirical realms, the faculties of reason, understanding and judgement. The difficulty for the critic is that his work depends on a capacity to transcend the divisions on which critique is premised. Critique becomes the exploration of its simultaneous possibility and impossibility, an exploration which is characterized politically in the variety of roles that the critic plays. The Kantian critic acts at different points as legislator, warrior, warmonger, peacemaker and judge in an effort to establish the authority of critique. At no point, however, are the diremptions of reason overcome and each effort of the critic is undermined and unsettled by the terms of its own institution. The complexities of the politics of critique are nowhere better illustrated than in Kant's conception of perpetual peace. The concept of perpetual peace has both a theoretical and political significance within Kant's work. In the first critique, perpetual peace is the aim of the critical philosopher in arbitrating between the warring parties of speculation and scepticism. The critic seeks to bring about the peace of a legal order, which will mediate between the despotism of dogmatic rationalism and the anarchy of sceptical empiricism. In Kant's political philosophy, the concept of perpetual peace is introduced to underwrite the power of right within the state by mediating between the despotism of world government and the violence of war. However, the meaning of the concept of perpetual peace in either of these contexts is a paradoxical one. It always involves the tension between sovereign authorities (theoretically those of the faculties of reason, politically those of autonomous states) and the difficulties of demarcating and policing the legitimate boundaries between them. It is always shadowed by the threat of war, chaos and anarchy (theoretically in the sense of critique's tendency to reopen the battles of reason that are supposed to have been transcended, politically in that Kantian perpetual peace depends on the threat of war). And it always involves a promise of transcendence (theoretically in the capacity of the critic to legislate for reason, politically in the orientation of history towards the moral law to which the judgement of the critic bears witness). The options of despotism and anarchy are repeated rather than resolved in the ways in which the critic attempts to make peace through law, war and judgement in both theory and practice.

Habermas, Arendt, Foucault and Lyotard all engage in different ways with the legacy of critical philosophy, both in their efforts to locate their own critical discourses and in their reflections on their own time and place. All of these thinkers are acutely aware of the difficulties inherent in Kant's attempts to establish the legitimate scope of theoretical, practical and aesthetic judgement. Therefore they do not offer a crude repetition of Kant's critique of reason. Instead, they seek to refine and to select from aspects of Kant's work in such a way as to create a new kind of critical theorizing. Only in Habermas's work is there an attempt to re-think critical philosophy wholesale. But what we find in Habermas is that (in spite of attempts to tie in transcendental conditions to the pragmatics of language or the orientation of history to communicative evolution) the dominance of the Kantian terms in which his critical theory is set up continually puts into doubt the ways in which he is trying to mediate the transcendental/empirical divide. We are returned to the tensions of the Kantian theoretical perpetual peace, in which the critic hovers between the possibility and impossibility of judgement and relies in turn on universal legislation, the conflictual dynamics of history and the capacity to read history to bring about the ends of reason.

Arendt, Foucault and Lyotard are much more careful than Habermas to avoid one of the roles of the Kantian critic, that of the legislator. All of these three thinkers select for their critical purposes the Kantian texts which are traditionally identified as problematic or marginal; those on beauty, culture, politics and history. For all three of them, the idea of judgement is crucial to what they can productively use in the Kantian legacy. In aesthetic judgement and in the judgement of history, Kant is seen as having displaced the terms of his own critique and made possible both a different conception of the critical philosopher's role and a different ethical and political theory. However, the examination of the use of Kant in the work of these three theorists demonstrates that although none of them reproduces the politics of Kant's critique as explicitly as Habermas, the Kantian theoretical perpetual peace in which the critic is caught between the possibility and impossibility of judgement is still implicit in their work. In Arendt's case, her adoption of the Kantian concept of reflective judgement is in tension with her dislocation of the realm of politics from the realm of philosophy. The result is that as a critic Arendt remains poised between the authoritative legislation of judgement and its irrelevance in the domain of the *vita activa*. Foucault's use of Kant as an exemplary critic results in a more subtle recalling of the politics of Kant's critique. The Foucauldian critic encapsulates the tension between the acceptance of limitation and the possibility of transcendence. However, because Foucault rejects the idea of universal conditions of critique, the multiple roles of the Kantian critic become expressed as the orientation of the critic towards a perpetual striving to overcome limitation. In Lyotard's case, the politics of his theorizing clearly follow the paradoxical possibilities of Kant's. The critical nightwatchman is judge, warrior, warmonger and peacemaker in turn, and in each of these roles the critic's authority shifts between being grounded in and oriented by an unknowable law and the impossibility of transcendental legitimation.

It is clear from both the examination of Kant's work and that of the succeeding theorists that critique is never a simple matter. It is neither the straightforward application of universal laws nor the unproblematic exercise of a capacity for judgement. What is crucial to critical theorizing in the Kantian sense is the way it involves constant grappling with its own limitations. However, having said this, it is clearly not the case that the critical work of Kant, Habermas, Arendt, Foucault and Lyotard is necessarily either understood or used according to the reading that I have given. Kant's characterization of his critique of reason as a paving of the way for metaphysics suggests that critique has resolved the problem of the legitimate authority of reason rather than putting it into perpetual question. Of the other four theorists, only Foucault consistently contests a reading of his critical theorizing as having established the authority of critique; although, as has been demonstrated, the instability of all of the possible grounds of the critic's authority is implicit in the work of the other three critics as well. The ambition of Kant's critique lays it open to being read as if it held the key to judgement. The problem with this is that in the Kantian critic's struggles to ground judgement, several different keys are suggested. This results, as was noted in Chapter 2, in the possibility of opposing interpretations of Kant, depending on which mode of grounding the critic's authority is selected, and therefore in the separation of the terms of the theoretical perpetual peace which are held together in Kant's thought. The ways in which Habermas, Arendt, Foucault and Lyotard themselves read Kant's critique selectively in the formation of their own critical discourse itself encourages one-sided interpretations of their critical practice. The tensions between the possibility and impossibility of authoritative critique become mapped onto oppositional readings of the four post-Kantian critics, so that we appear to be returned to the battles of reason which critique was intended to overcome. What I have in mind in particular here is the way in which, in contemporary social and political theory, a mode of critique with which Habermas and Arendt are identified (see the discussion of Linklater in this chapter and of Benhabib in Chapter 8) is opposed to a mode of critique with which Foucault and Lyotard are identified (see the discussion of Ashley and Walker in this chapter and of Hekman in Chapter 8). In this way of reading the different aspects of the legacy of Kant's critical thought, the tensions between them come to be set up as exclusive oppositions; legislative critique is set against strategic or aesthetic critique. One of the tendencies accompanying this division of Kant's heirs into opposing camps is that, however subtle the characterization of the favoured critical theory may be, the characterization of the 'enemy' is often highly uncritical, in the Kantian sense that it is couched in terms of the precritical vocabulary of either dogmatism or scepticism.

In the following sections of this chapter I will be examining the way in which attempts to articulate a critical theory of international politics in recent years have been developed in relation to the Kantian legacy identified above in all its ambiguity and complexity.

It will be argued that the critical theories of international relations display the same logic of legislation and limitation that marks Kantian critical theory and the post-Kantian theorists I have discussed. This is manifested in both the difficulties each theory has in identifying the ground of its critique; and in the ever-present danger of treating this difficulty as resolved and thereby risking a return to the precritical theoretical possibilities that critical theory is designed to overcome.

WRESTLING WITH SHADOWS

The first step in matters of pure reason, marking its infancy, is *dogmatic*. The second step is *sceptical*; and indicates that experience has rendered our judgment wiser and more circumspect.

(A: 761; B: 789)

The above quotation is Kant's comment on the development of the history of reason from dogmatic rationalism to empiricist scepticism. He goes on to argue that the battle between these two parties is properly only transcended by a third step, that of critique. In the context of the theory of international relations, a similar pattern is reflected. A dogmatic idealism in which the idea of world government is posited as the end of history is opposed by a sceptical realism in which anarchic relations between states are posited as an eternal verity. Critical theories of international relations emerge as the third step which transcends the orthodoxy of the idealism/realism opposition.[1] The realist perspective on international relations began to dominate international relations theory after 1945, following the collapse of the idealistic hopes for international community that held sway in the inter-war period, and has overshadowed all theorizing in international relations ever since. Realism sees the international realm as amoral and anarchic, occupied by self-interested sovereign states which are driven by the logic of desire for power and security, like Hobbesian individuals. The idealist perspective on the contrary looks to the international realm as the eventual site of a cosmopolitan kingdom of ends, a moral world order of peace and co-operation. Realism is distinguished by its static conception of international relations; states may change but the essential logic of their interaction remains the same. Idealism, on the contrary, thinks in terms of change and identifies history with progress.[2] On the surface, the two standpoints appear mutually exclusive and contradictory, but as critics of contemporary international relations theory have pointed out, their relation is much more like that of two sides of the same coin (Walker, 1993: 22–23). Realism is premised on the recognition of international politics as amoral; idealism on the insight that it is not, but ought to be, moral. The realist is the judge raising the contingent to the status of an absolute, the idealist is the judge applying an absolute standard to contingency; but there is agreement that the realms of 'is' and 'ought', theory and practice, politics and morality do not meet outside of the theorists' judgement.

Both realism and idealism are premised on Kant's presumption of the split between morality and politics. According to Kant, morality necessarily excludes politics, yet has no way forward other than through politics. Within the sovereign state, legality provides a facsimile of morality which relies on the absolute authority of the law standing in for pure practical reason. However, the resort of law is not possible in the same way within the international context. This seems to leave the critical philosopher no options other than the acceptance of a politics of the unsocial sociability of humanity as the end of history or the interpolation of the philosopher's judgement to read politics as if it were progress towards the unifying legislation of a kingdom of ends. These are two of the options enshrined in Kant's concept of perpetual peace. Thus realism and idealism are logically tied together by the same fundamental conception of the terms of international political theory and of the nature of international politics.[3] It is dissatisfaction with these terms and the way in which they constrain thinking about the international realm that has led to the emergence of critical voices within the theory of international relations. These theories, starting from the weaknesses of the alternatives offered by realism and idealism, have gone on to offer new, critical ways of understanding world politics.

A crucial objection to realism is that the morality/politics divide has become mapped onto the distinction between the domestic politics of the sovereign state and international relations between states. Although, through law, moral progress may be possible within the domestic sphere, international relations are presumed to be amoral and unchanging. This classical realist claim was famously stated by Waltz in the founding text of neo-realism, *Man, The State and War*, and it continues to influence much of what counts as research into, and understanding of, the international arena. In effect, the very phrase 'international arena' gains its meaning from the realist definition of the international as that which is not within but between states, and as that which is essentially outside of either legality or morality. Critics of realism point out that the effect of this isolation of the international sphere has significant epistemic and normative implications. The realist theorist is effectively blind to questions about the nature of states and the relevance of the domestic to the international. According to realist tradition, the international is constituted by a system of states which relate to one another in a context of anarchy. The logic of state behaviour and interrelation is governed by pursuit of power, security and rational self-interest defined in Hobbesian terms. The way to understand the international is through the detailed examination of certain state agencies, governments, diplomats, the military, and so on. The nature of actual states and the existence of non-state actors (e.g. multinational corporations, non-governmental organizations, the European Union, international peace movements, individual agents, etc.) must, therefore, according to the realist tradition, either be essentially marginal to the understanding of the international or have to be read back into the vocabulary of inter-state relations. In terms of what can be known about the international, critics of realism claim that it can, at best, attain only a very partial grasp of the world we actually inhabit as opposed to the world as it is constructed by the distinctions between morality and politics, domestic and international. On the normative side, critics of realism point out that the effect of the isolation of the international as a realm of anarchy is to raise power politics to the level of an absolute end of history. In closing off the possibility of change, realists close off the possibility of criticism and disguise their own judgement as a simple reflection of the way things are.

Unlike the realist, the idealist assumes that both domestic and inter-state politics can be read in terms of the same moral standards. Just as the domestic sphere, through law, can move to the instantiation of reason in history so, it is asserted, can the international sphere. The most frequent criticism of the idealist is that there are no grounds for the identification of history with progress on which the idealist relies. Realists object to idealism in much the same terms as Kant sees scepticism responding to the dogmatic claims of speculation, in that they argue that the claims of idealism cannot be substantiated. It is claimed that idealists are thinking in a world of shadows which they themselves invent. This world has no relation to empirical reality, indeed it is premised on ignorance of that to which our experience bears witness, i.e. war, power and greedy self-interest.

Critics of realism are also unhappy with idealism because it imposes an abstract standard of judgement on history that cannot be grounded, in the end merely reversing the realists' account of the priority of politics over morality.

In the above discussion I have referred generically to 'critics' of realism and idealism without differentiating properly between the different critical responses to these alternative founding paradigms of the discipline of international relations. In fact, in the plethora of theoretical approaches and debates in international relations, one can distinguish between a more moderate and a more radical strain of critique. The former kind of critique seeks either to improve on realism to make it more scientifically defensible; or draws selectively on elements of realism and idealism to provide a concept of the international that more closely reflects the presence of non-state actors as well as states, co-operation as well as conflict in world politics.[4] The latter kind of critique offers a challenge to the way in which the boundaries between morality and politics are drawn in both realist and idealist theory. It is this latter kind of critique which seeks to put the theory of international relations on an entirely new footing in much the same way as Kant's Copernican revolution was intended to pave the way for a new metaphysics. There are two schools of radical criticism at the forefront of the re-thinking of traditional international relations theorizing: the school of critical theory; and the school of postmodernism.[5]

HISTORY AND PROGRESS

The point of International Relations theory is not simply to alter the way we look at the world, but to alter the world. It must offer more than mere description and an account of current affairs. It must also offer us a significant choice, and a critical analysis of the quality and direction of life.

(Hoffman, 1987: 244–245)

Within international relations theory, critical theory is premised on dissatisfaction with the choice between realism and idealism. Critical theory of international relations draws on the philosophical tradition going back to Kant but finds particular inspiration in the work of Habermas. Following Habermas's early work, critical theory homes in on the relation between theorist and the object of theory, and opens up the question of why the theorist relates to the object in the way in which he or she does and what purpose this relation serves. In exploring this question, critical theorists find realism implicated in the maintenance of a particular kind of power politics and the prevention of other ways of thinking about the world. According to the critical theorist, realism conceives the world in a way that serves the interests of those who benefit from the world as it is. In ruling out the possibility of both change and criticism, realism is not describing the world, but manipulating it. At the same time, critical theorists do not accept the introduction of abstract and absolute other-worldly standards by which to judge the world, which is characteristic of idealism. For the critical theorist, the idealist is fundamentally as a-historical as the realist in the assessment of world politics. Critical theory therefore sees itself as bringing back both history and the possibility of criticism into the understanding of international relations.

An example of a critical theorist of international relations is Andrew Linklater, who has produced two books which aim at the construction of a theory of international relations that progresses beyond the traditional accounts: *Men and Citizens in the Theory of International Relations* (1982) and *Beyond Realism and Marxism* (1990). In the first of these two books Linklater is trying to establish an international relations theory that will challenge the traditional morality/politics dichotomy. He rejects both the a-historical amoralism of the realist and the a-historical moralism of the idealist. The philosophical ground for a new theory is found through the exploration of the ideas of Kant, Hegel and Marx read through the medium of Habermas. This exploration becomes the basis for the construction of a philosophy of history, synthesizing Kant and Marx, in which history is read as the development of 'humanization' (Linklater, 1982: 184–201). This development consists in the way that the progress of humanity as a species overtakes the progress of humanity as citizens of states. Linklater argues that increasingly we experience and judge as 'men' in a global context rather than as citizens bounded by states. This account of history challenges what Linklater terms the three postulates of political life. These are the postulates of realism: that the state has absolute rights in itself; that the morality of interaction between states differs from the ethical considerations relevant to individual human interaction; and that co-operation between states is always motivated by concerns for interests (Linklater, 1982: 204). From Linklater's standpoint, his philosophy of history offers a starting point for the theorization of international politics that improves on realism by challenging the domestic/international dichotomy and by historicizing the international realm and opening it up to critical assessment. On the other hand, Linklater claims to improve on idealism by locating the standard of judgement of international politics within history rather than in an abstact and ungrounded moral law.

Linklater's second book presents an argument for the synthesis of realist and Marxist perspectives on international relations in a new critical theory which will transcend them both. In his first chapter, Linklater discusses the three traditional paradigms of international relations theory identified by Wight: realism, rationalism and revolutionism (idealism) (Linklater, 1990: 8). Linklater suggests that these three approaches can be understood as involving a dialectical development in which revolutionism (in this text, Linklater has Marxism in mind as the revolutionist/idealist theory) supplements what is lacking in realism and vice versa, with rationalism constituting a kind of middle way between them (Linklater, 1990: 10). In his conclusion, Linklater ascribes a key strength to each tradition which must be incorporated into critical theory. Realism's key strength is in its analysis of war and the role of war in historical development. Rationalism's key strength is in its analysis of the principles underlying the coexistence of independent political communities; and Marxism's key strength is in its analysis of production and its practical orientation (Linklater, 1990: 171). However, these three starting points have to be supplemented by a fourth, a reading of history as the universalization of moral principles, or what the earlier text refers to as a process of humanization (Linklater, 1990: 165–172). In both of Linklater's books, history is the key to a critical theory of international relations that escapes the consequences of the morality/politics split. As Linklater sees it, critical theory has to avoid both the reifying of international anarchy into an absolute, and the abstract moralism of a critique relying on the ought of the categorical imperative. A moral/idealistic critique is to be replaced by an immanent critique in terms of a philosophy of history. For this philosophy of history, Linklater relies on Habermas to supply a conception of human history as a process of moral development which is driven, not by pure practical reason, but by the capacity of 'more advanced normative standards' to overcome crises within social systems (Linklater, 1990: 25).

Linklater shares with Habermas the problem of grounding the relation he postulates between transcendental standards of judgement and historical development. In the article 'The Question of the Next Stage in International Relations Theory: A Critical-Theoretical Point of View', Linklater suggests that a critical theory of international relations, while it cannot provide an all-encompassing explanatory framework, may still be able to provide an overall orientation within which different theoretical developments can be placed. He argues for this by pointing to the answers critical theory can offer to what are identified as the crucial normative, sociological and praxeological questions which any theorist of world politics must address. In every case the contribution of critical theory relies on a reference back to Habermas. The crucial normative question for international relations theory, according to Linklater, concerns the legitimacy of the systems of inclusion and exclusion implicit in modern state relations.

> One answer is suggested in Habermas's claim that advanced moral codes are committed to granting every human being an equal right to participate in open dialogue about the configuration of society and politics. The crucial consequence that stems from this claim is that there are no valid grounds for excluding any human being from dialogue in advance. No system of exclusion passes this moral test unless its constitutive principles can command the consent of all, in particular those to be excluded from the social arrangement in question.
>
> (Linklater, 1992: 92)

As Linklater sees it, Habermas's communicative ethics grounds the moral universalism of critical international relations theory, which should therefore be oriented to a cosmopolitan ideal, though an ideal which can only be described in abstract terms. The crucial sociological question for international relations theory for Linklater follows on from the moral orientation provided by the cosmopolitan ideal. It is the question of whether and how communities which transcend the borders of the nation-state may develop. Here Habermas's notion of communicative evolution as a kind of Kohlbergian learning process is invoked by Linklater.

> Habermas's analysis of social learning sets out some of the fundamental ideas which can be incorporated within a sociology of logics of inclusion and exclusion in international relations. More specifically, it may be useful to ask if modes of

inclusion and exclusion are the result of the interplay between the sorts of learning processes which Habermas identifies.

(Linklater, 1992: 95)

Linklater suggests that social learning processes may be the key to linking the normative orientation of critical theory of international relations within cultural, sociological and historical movements in the global context. The abstract demand for moral universalization is supplemented by a reading of history in terms of that demand. The answer to the praxeological question confronting the critical international relations theorist follows directly from the first two answers.

A critical approach to foreign policy analysis can explore the ways in which the potential for internationalism which exists in most modern states can be realised in international conventions which enshrine the moral principles of an alternative world order.

(Linklater, 1992: 97)

For Linklater, it is the responsibility of the critical theorist of international relations to work to promote this alternative world order through the analysis of its possibility. Thus the commitment to reading history as progress becomes part of what makes this progress possible.

It is clear from Linklater's account of his work that his aim is to recover the capacity for a moral critique of the international realm without relying on abstract and ungrounded criteria. He wants to preserve the idea of universal standards without becoming a-historical or utopian in his analysis. It is therefore not surprising that Habermas provides the central resource for Linklater's critical theory, since both thinkers are alike in wanting not to abandon critique but to make it more 'righteous' in the way in which its claims are made. It is equally unsurprising to find that Linklater's effort to transcend the choice between realism and idealism, politics and morality remains haunted by the terms of that choice. Just as in Habermas's work the relation between transcendental and empirical is opaque and uneasy, so it is with Linklater. In the end, both thinkers end up reflecting Kant in their efforts to bridge the gap between speculation and scepticism that they have inherited. Transcendental grounds for judgement are postulated, but are incapable of adequate deduction. The ideals which follow from the test of pure practical reason are abstract and empty. Empirical and transcendental, real and ideal are thought together only through the exercise of the philosopher's judgement, which interprets history as movement towards a moral end and which itself is seen to assist the bringing about of that end. Linklater claims that his critical theory involves a utopianism which is constrained by the comprehension of actual historical processes. Yet we are given to understand that a proper comprehension of historical processes involves reading history as if it were progress. This is a return to the moment of the philosopher's judgement in Kant's philosophy of history, in which nature is made to serve the ends of reason, since reason cannot serve itself.

The tendency for critical theory of international relations to repeat the antinomies of Kantian critique has become the focus of critical responses to the work of theorists such as Linklater. Whilst neo-realist theorists might dismiss critical theory as a new incarnation of idealism which confirms the irrelevance of morality to politics, other critics who, like Linklater, are unhappy with the conceptions of international politics available within orthodox accounts, suggest that the problem with critical theory is that it remains too entrenched in the modernist problematic of which both realism and idealism are aspects. This latter group of critics, generically labelled postmodernists, seek a critical theory of the international realm which genuinely transcends the terms of Kantian critique, refusing the choice between the acceptance of anarchy (realism) and a moral end of history (idealism) which is implied in those terms; and which they would argue are still implied in the terms of critical theorists such as Linklater. Postmodernist theorists of international relations draw on a range of thinkers amongst whom both Lyotard and Foucault are prominent.[6]

THE DISSIDENT WORK OF THOUGHT

As with critical theories of international relations, the starting point of postmodernist theories of the international is a dissatisfaction with the terms provided for the understanding and judgement of the international realm by realism and idealism. According to two key exponents of a postmodern approach to understanding international politics, Richard Ashley and Robert Walker, there is a crisis in the discipline of international relations. This is evident in the way in which empirical and conceptual research into international politics continually problematizes the orthodox disciplinary boundaries. In the context of a global political economy and the increasing presence of non-state and trans-state actors in the international arena, the identification of international with inter-state is no longer sustainable. Thus, as a discipline, international relations finds its sovereign territory being undermined and confused. Moreover, postmodernist theorists of international relations deny both realist pretensions to objective, descriptive truth in the analysis of international politics and idealist pretensions to access to independent, universal moral standards. In a joint article, 'Reading Dissidence/Writing the Discipline: Crisis and the Question of Sovereignty in International Studies', Ashley and Walker try to explain the nature of their own dissident critique. They do this by drawing a contrast between the ways in which readings of dissident work by orthodox theorists (amongst which are included critical theorists) struggle unavailingly to speak from a sovereign position, whereas dissident writings

> do not presume to speak a sovereign voice, a voice beyond politics and beyond doubt, a voice of interpretation and judgment from which truth and power are thought to emanate as one.
>
> (Ashley and Walker, 1990: 368)

Ashley and Walker offer a highly politicized reading of traditional international relations theory. They argue that at no point has the concept of state sovereignty and the domestic/international distinction been a straightforward reflection of the realities of global politics. In practice, the nature and limits of state sovereignty are continually contested, differently interpreted and have different effects. Inter-state relations have never existed in isolation from both sub-state and trans-state forces. Yet these concepts have been the principal means by which, as a discipline, international relations has laid claim to its territory. By urging the uniqueness of the international realm, the twentieth-century study of international relations has marked itself off from domestic political science and political theory, from economics and sociology and, of course, from moral theory. Ashley and Walker present the tradition of international relations as a constant effort to impose a sovereign veto on what can and cannot count as a contribution to the discipline. In this sense it is suggested that the study of international relations reflects international reality, by reproducing the same unstable logics of inclusion and exclusion that characterize global political relations. As Walker claims in another context:

Theories of international relations are more interesting as aspects of contemporary world politics that need to be explained than as explanations of contemporary world politics.

(Walker, 1993: 6)

Ashley and Walker are emphatic that idealist theories of the international are as much part of a territorializing ethic as realist accounts. In both cases, it is argued, a claim to sovereignty is being made, whether it is the sovereign voice of international anarchy or of international moral law. Critical theory of international relations is seen as providing yet another example of international relations theory establishing a claim to legislate over a particular ground. Ashley and Walker argue that theorizing is possible either in a register of desire or in a register of freedom (Ashley and Walker, 1990: 379–80). The register of desire is the register of territorializing theory which seeks to affirm the boundaries of thought whether cognitively or normatively. The register of freedom is a celebratory register in which such boundaries are called into question rather than established. This latter mode of theorizing is essentially marginal; rather than settling disputes over boundaries, it emphasizes their instability in a way reminiscent of Lyotard's critical nightwatchman. From the standpoint of theories in the register of desire, the value of celebratory theorizing can only be construed in a negative fashion as undoing what genuine theory strives to accomplish. It is thus that Ashley and Walker would understand both mainstream and critical theory responses to their work. However, Ashley and Walker want to argue that it is possible to construe the work of thought in the register of freedom as a positive ethical orientation, particularly for those people who are marginalized by mainstream accounts of global relations and values, whether in theory or practice.

For this person, the practical site is one where paradoxes of space, time, and identity disturb and undo any attempt to live and act according to some semblance of sovereign territorial being. For this person, who must make her life but cannot make of it a triumph of religious desire, the problem might be posed thus: *How might one proceed in a register of freedom to explore and test institutional limitations in a way that sustains and expands the cultural spaces and resources enabling one to conduct one's labors of self-making in just this register of freedom, further exploring and testing limitations?*

(Ashley and Walker, 1990: 391)

As we saw above, Ashley and Walker draw parallels between the actualities of global political relations and the ways in which those relations have been theorized. However, whereas realist and idealist theories do not recognize the politics at work in their own conceptions of the world, postmodern theories of international relations are claimed to be based on this recognition. What this means is not that postmodern theories are in any sense outside of that politics but, on the contrary, that instead of being associated with the politics of sovereign states, they are identified with the politics of the marginal and the oppressed. The project of self-making in the register of freedom is therefore the project of postmodern theory of international relations as well as being ascribed to those living on the borderlines of domestic states and global structures. Let us go on to establish what this project entails.

It is evident that Ashley's and Walker's reading of the tradition of international relations theory and their account of their own alternative postmodern approach has strong affiliations with Foucault's critical discourse. In particular, postmodern theories of international relations seek to expose the power at work in traditional patterns of inclusion and exclusion within the discipline in a way that self-consciously reflects Foucault's account of disciplinary power in *Discipline and Punish*. What appear to be descriptive reflections of states of affairs, or alternatively what claim to be the introduction of independent standards of moral judgement, are revealed to be the practices and effects of power. As with Foucault's work, however, the practice of genealogy raises the question of its own status and the status of its claims. Do the genealogical critics of traditional accounts of international reality themselves become caught up in the territorializing practice that they are seeking to subvert? Like Foucault, indeed in the light of Foucault's work, Walker and Ashley are acutely conscious of the 'blackmail of the enlightenment', which, by forcing a choice either *for* or *against* reason, would return their theorizing to the options of realist cynicism and idealist hypothesizing which they are trying to transcend (Foucault, 1984b: 42). Two ways of sustaining their theorizing in the register of freedom are suggested by Ashley's and Walker's work. The first way appears to keep postmodern theories of international relations within the project of genealogy, confining the critic to an iconoclastic role in which sovereign authorities are continually subverted. The second way returns Ashley and Walker to the ethics of relation to self explored in Foucault's later work, and holds out the possibility of distinguishing freedom from power in the work of thought.

A good example of postmodern theorizing in international relations which I would argue remains confined within genealogy as a project of infinite subversion can be found in Ashley's article 'Untying the Sovereign State: A Double Reading of the Anarchy Problematique'. In this paper, utilizing deconstructive techniques drawn from a reading of Derrida as well as Foucauldian genealogy, Ashley sets about demonstrating the instability of the central conceptual assumptions of neo-realist theories of international politics.

> Thanks to the discourse's incorporation of the sovereign voices of nonstate actors, any attempt to depict the state as a sovereign identity in its own right is immediately revealed for what it is – one among any number of possible representations, all equally arbitrary and each writable through the manifestly political exclusion of others.
>
> (Ashley, 1988: 251)

Ashley analyses the tradition as making critique possible only through necessary limitation being posited against the contingent limitations of historicity; as against this, the dissident postmodern theorist calls all limits into question. Ashley recommends the international relations theorist automatically to invert traditional conceptual hierarchies in order to reveal their arbitrariness. He goes on to explain postmodern international relations theory as theorizing without a location, as theorizing from the borderlines, and as theorizing from the void or no place. To try to make clear the nature of this kind of critique, in another article on postmodern international relations theory, 'Living On Border Lines: Man, Poststructuralism and War' (Der Derian and Shapiro, 1989: 259–321), Ashley quotes from Foucault's essay 'What Is Enlightenment?':

> Criticism indeed consists of analysing and reflecting upon limits. But if the Kantian question was that of knowing what limits knowledge has to renounce transgressing, it seems to me that the critical question today has to be turned back into a positive one: in what is given to us as universal, necessary, obligatory, what place is occupied by what is singular, contingent, and the product of arbitrary constraints. The point, in brief, is to transform the critique conducted in the form of

necessary limitation into a practical critique that takes the form
of a possible transgression.

(Foucault, 1984b: 45; Der Derian and Shapiro, 1989: 283–284)

The kind of 'practical critique' that Ashley develops in his analysis
of the anarchy problematique is reminiscent of the kind of argument
found in Foucault's 'The Order of Discourse'. In this text, a principle
of reversibility provides the key to a critical discourse which reveals
the mechanisms by which discourse establishes and polices its limits.
As with the argument of Foucault's own text, Ashley's argument
insistently raises and evades the question of the status of his own
critical discourse. Unlike Foucault, however, in suggesting that his
own critical discourse is not located, Ashley appears to claim that his
own discourse simply escapes the need for validation. The calling
into question of limits, being grounded on the contingency of all
limits, is not seen as calling into question that question itself. Thus
Ashley's critical discourse threatens to develop into a celebration of
the arbitrariness of the theorist's representation of the object of
theorizing. Rather than taking us into a new criticism, this returns
the discipline of international relations to the realism/idealism
dichotomy, in which contingency as the mark of both history and
judgement gives an absolute freedom to the theorist to claim
anything whatsoever about the world.

As Ashley sees it, the charge that postmodern theory in international relations means that anything goes is one that derives from a
thinking which remains governed by the blackmail of the enlightenment referred to above. In 'Reading Dissidence/Writing the Discipline', both Ashley and Walker are very concerned to counter the
idea that they speak from some alternative point of authority from
which the truth can be known, but at the same time they claim that
their discourse is not simply a matter of arbitrary inversions. This
brings us to the second way of characterizing the practice of
postmodern international relations theorizing. The terms that Ashley
and Walker use to capture their meaning are terms such as: unstable,
paradoxical, borderline, marginal, female and deterritorial. What
they are trying to express is the idea of speaking not from a place
but from practices of inclusion and exclusion. In their account, the
practices of inclusion and exclusion in mainstream international
relations theory are identified directly with practices of inclusion and
exclusion in global political life. In a similar way, therefore, Ashley
and Walker associate their theoretical practice and its transgression

of traditional boundaries with a different kind of international politics. The result of this is that their theoretical practice itself exemplifies an ethical relation to self and legislates for both theory and practice by its example. Clearly the exemplary validity of the work of the postmodern international relations theorist echoes the Foucauldian conception of the role of the specific intellectual. The way in which this conception is employed in Ashley's and Walker's argument, however, is more reminiscent of Lyotard than Foucault. Theorizing in the register of freedom takes on the explicit status of a Kantian regulative idea as a standard of judgement. Ashley and Walker emerge as 'on the side' of new social movements, indigenous peoples, the poor, oppressed and marginalized of the world. In problematizing concepts such as 'state' and 'man' in traditional theory, Ashley and Walker are always also affirming a different vision in which both theoretical concepts and political realities are demonstrated to be constructed and therefore open to deconstruction. This reading of both theory and history is governed by a commitment to an ethic of freedom.

Just as Linklater has a problem in accounting for his identification of historical development with transcendental standards of judgement, so Ashley's and Walker's critique has a problem in accounting for its capacity to distinguish between theory and practice in a register of desire and theory and practice in a register of freedom. In adopting Habermas's theory as having resolved the question of the possibility of judgement, Linklater glosses over the ambiguities in Habermas's own theorizing and risks a lapse back into the idealist positing of transcendental moral legislation and the identification of the philosopher as the specialist interpreter of the moral law. By using Foucault's concept of critical ontology as if it were a Kantian regulative idea, Ashley and Walker run a similar theoretical risk of setting themselves up as if they held the key to progress.

Linklater, Ashley and Walker are all seriously and self-consciously struggling to get beyond the theoretical options of realism and idealism and to ground a new critical theory of international politics. It is significant, however, that Kant's fate in his critique of reason, in which the stand-off he identifies between speculation and scepticism continues to re-surface after he claims to have resolved it, is echoed in the attempts to think critically of these contemporary theorists. Critical theorists of international relations argue that postmodern theories return the discipline to the resources of strategy and anarchy central to realism. Postmodern theorists argue that critical theory returns the discipline to the dogmas of idealism. More importantly, within each of the critical perspectives there remain tensions between claims to have found the way to authorize critique and the impossibility of that authorization. The latter tension is particularly strong within postmodern theorizing, which is poised between radical scepticism and claims to occupy the moral high ground of freedom.

CONCLUSION

The repetition of the paradoxes of Kantian critique both within and between critical theories of international relations brings the question of how the critical theorist can remain critical to the surface. The idea of critique as it is formulated in Kant's work and in theorists using Kant's work is one which involves the critic in finding a way through or between unacceptable alternatives. The nature of these unacceptable alternatives is differently formulated. For Kant, they are the alternatives of speculation and empiricism. For Habermas, they are the alternatives of 'this historical injustice of general theories, on the one hand, and the standardlessness of mere historical understanding on the other' (Habermas, 1979: 205). For Arendt, they are the alternatives of the legislation of action by thought and the pure meaninglessness of action. For Foucault, they are the alternatives of legislating for others and theoretical and political passivity. For Lyotard, they are the alternatives of substantive prescription of the true and the good and the abandonment of the language game of prescription. For Linklater, Ashley and Walker, they are the alternatives of realism and idealism. Critique only remains critical in so far as it does not lapse back into the oppositions which it replaces, but it is not clear how remaining critical is possible. Every resolution to the question of the possibility of critique appears to threaten a return to the unacceptable alternatives with which it began, so that the same battles end up being fought again and again. This is exemplified in the way that the opposition between idealism and realism is reproduced in the opposition between 'critical' and 'postmodern' theorizations in international relations.

However, at the same time as threatening a lapse back into the polarizations that critique was intended to overcome, critical and postmodern theorizations of international relations also demonstrate how, within critique, precritical polarizations are suspended in dynamic tension between the ambition and limitation of theory. This suggests that the conception of critique as a tendency towards failure is accompanied by a more positive conception. According to this positive conception, critique is a consistent refusal either to fail or succeed. The positive implication of the kind of theorizing that Linklater, Ashley and Walker are trying to formulate is that critical theory *does* take the risk of laying claim to authority but that, in acknowledging the nature of this risk, that authority always remains open to subversion. The authority of the critic cannot be grounded either in historical location or transcendental law, or in the authority of other philosophical critics. The critic is always fundamentally unprotected. It is clear from my exposition of Linklater, Ashley and Walker, that it is the two latter theorists who come closest to self-consciously exhibiting this lack of protection in their theoretical practice. Ironically, the mode of theorizing most prone to reject Kant as an idealist, in fact faithfully reflects the complexities and ambiguities of Kantian critique.

8

FEMINIST CRITICAL THEORY

INTRODUCTION

In the previous chapter it was argued that the resources of Kantian critique, filtered through the work of Habermas, Lyotard and Foucault, have a double implication for attempts to formulate critical theories of international relations. One implication, in which the legislative ambition of critique is prioritized, results in a tendency to lapse back into the alternatives of realism and idealism which critique is intended to transcend. The other implication, in which the critic pursues the possibility of critique whilst continually putting his own authority into question, highlights the difficulty of being critical in the Kantian sense. This is not a matter of a crude repetition of Kantian dualisms but of the problems of thinking with an account of what critique means that remains Kantian in its inspiration. In this final chapter I will be focusing on another area of critical theorizing, within feminist theory. In an obvious way, feminist theory introduces something distinctive to the modes of critical thinking that I have been investigating. Here there appears to be a concrete reference point, i.e. woman, in relation to and in the interests of whom critique is being conducted. In this sense, feminist theory might be seen to be closer to Marx than to Kant in its critical antecedents. This is not to say that Habermas, Arendt, Foucault and Lyotard do not relate their theorizing to concrete conditions, but for all these theorists the possibility of critique as such is not consistently tied down to the identity of any one specific group or interest. However, the development of feminist theory both in the contexts of epistemology and moral and political theory offers interesting parallels with the theoretical strategies employed by the critical theorists cited above. Like the critics of international theory, feminist critical theorists both become engaged in the battles of reason that they seek to transcend and enmeshed in the difficulties of sustaining critique as 'the peace of a legal order'. The concrete reference point 'woman' as both the beginning and end of feminist theory has become the terrain of a debate about the nature of feminist critique. Recent feminist work on epistemology, moral and political theory has developed from an earlier stance, which focused on the ways in which 'woman' and gender constituted a hidden agenda in the history of western thought, to a more self-reflexive critique. Clearly, any feminist theory is 'critical' in the general sense that it is premised on challenging the oppression and marginalization of women in both theory and practice. However, in this chapter my concern is with feminist critical theory that is primarily concerned with the scope and legitimacy of its own claims. In this kind of critique, the status of the contribution that feminist theory can make to understanding and judging the world itself comes under review. It is in this kind of feminist critique that theorists have turned to the modes of critical thinking with which this book is concerned to help to make sense of their own project.

The context in which feminist theory has become more self-reflexive and increasingly concerned with the status of its own discourse is a complex one, driven by both theoretical and practical considerations. In practice, the political challenges to the dominant voices of the women's movement over the last twenty years from women who cannot identify with those voices has pushed feminist theory into taking differences between women more seriously, and radically undermined the sustainability of universal claims on behalf of all women.[1] Theoretically, the argument between different strands of second-wave feminism necessarily forced theorists to examine the presuppositions of their own critical discourse and its limitations.[2] An example of the way in which feminist theory both develops internally and interacts with other critical traditions can be found in the context of feminist epistemology. Sandra Harding has famously distinguished between feminist empiricism, feminist standpoint theory and feminist postmodernism as three distinctive feminist theories of knowledge (Harding, 1991: 105–137; 164–187). Although Harding's synopsis of developments within feminist epistemology is somewhat crude and schematic, it provides a useful starting point for the consideration of feminist theory as critique. Both feminist standpoint theory and feminist postmodernism are, like Kant's critique of theoretical reason, intended to transcend the limitations of previous ways of thinking about knowledge, precisely by recognizing how the possibility of knowledge is limited. The ways in which the standpoint theorists demarcate both how knowledge is possible and what can be known put the feminist 'knower' in a legislative role. Standpoint theory argues that knowledge claims must be legitimated in terms of an authoritative set of criteria, which are bound up with the way 'woman' is positioned within universal, gendered relations of power.[3] Feminist postmodernists deny that there are any universal conditions which legitimate knowledge claims and argue that all knowledge and meaning is discursively constructed. Instead, a proliferation of alternative discourses and a constant engagement with the limitations of all standpoints is encouraged; so that the critic takes on either the role of encouraging conflict or one of judgement oriented by the ideas of freedom and difference. The way in which the debate between standpoint and postmodernist feminism has been conducted has increasingly tended to be in terms of questioning the relation of feminist theory to the enlightenment and the degree of its alignment with Kant and Habermas on the one hand, Foucault and Lyotard on the other, with Arendt's work occupying an ambiguous ground between the poles of transcendent universalism and contextualized pluralism.[4] This tendency is also apparent in debates concerning the nature and status of feminist theory's ethical and political claims.[5]

In this chapter it will be argued that feminist critical theory, in the sense of self-reflexive critique outlined above, struggles with the question of what critique means in ways that are influenced by the resources of critical theorizing on which it draws. As with the critical theories of international relations discussed in the previous chapter, the difficulties of sustaining critique without lapsing into a vocabulary of either dogmatic universalism or anarchic particularism return insistently to the fore.

FEMINISM/POSTMODERNISM

In the reader *Feminism/Postmodernism* (Nicholson, 1990) different feminist theorists argue about whether feminist theory needs universal theoretical and ethical underpinnings if it is to be an effective critical discourse. Those theorists who argue that feminist theory needs some kind of universal ground for their judgements suggest that if this ground is abandoned, the idea of the significance of gendered oppression and of liberation for the oppressed will cease to make sense. Those theorists who link themselves with postmodern critics argue that in holding on to the idea of universal underpinnings for theory and practice, feminist theory would be committing the same error as other metanarrative theories, i.e. becoming a-historical in its analysis and thereby risking the imposition of new orthodoxies insensitive to the range and multiplicity of the meanings of gendered oppression and liberation for different women. What emerges is an oppositional construction of modernist versus postmodernist modes of feminist theorizing, with both claiming a different kind of ethical advantage. Modernist theories are seen to affirm universal moral values and goals; postmodernist theories are seen as subversive of authority and power in all its forms. As Nancy Fraser and Linda Nicholson put it, in this case identifying feminism with universalist perspectives:

> Postmodernists offer sophisticated and persuasive criticisms of foundationalism and essentialism, but their conceptions of social criticism tend to be anemic. Feminists offer robust conceptions of social criticism, but they tend to lapse into foundationalism and essentialism.

(Nicholson, 1990: 20)

At its crudest, the modern/postmodern opposition as it is construed in feminist theory resembles Kant's version of the stand-off between speculation and scepticism in his discussion of the discipline of pure reason. Strong universalist theories are identified with the unsustainable claims of dogma; and postmodernist theories with the abandonment of any grounds for judgement. The struggle to construct a feminist critical theory is oriented to finding a way between these crude alternatives. Critical feminist theories that align themselves with the 'modernist' side of the debate work at the task of establishing that universal or general criteria for judgement are possible without lapsing into dogma. Critical feminist theories that align themselves with the 'postmodernist' side of the debate work at the task of establishing that plural and flexible accounts of judgement are possible without lapsing into scepticism. An example of a feminist theorist of the former type is Seyla Benhabib, for whom the thought of both Habermas and Arendt provides resources for constructing a new kind of critical theorizing. An example of a feminist theorist of the latter type is Susan Hekman, for whom the work of Foucault constitutes a more promising way forward for feminist critique.

Benhabib is unusual amongst feminist theorists in that she places her work firmly within the post-Kantian German tradition and is self-consciously aware of the way that her theoretical options have been constructed within it. She is sensitive to the strength of the case against an abstract grounding of judgement in transcendent but unknowable laws, but resistant to Lyotardian pluralism, which, she argues, results in an 'anything goes' relativism which itself depoliticizes and dehistoricizes judgement.[6] In contrast to these alternatives, Benhabib puts forward a case for a Habermasian account of judgement modified by a reading of Arendt's incomplete doctrine of judgement. The nature of Benhabib's approach can be gauged from her discussion of the critical engagement between Habermas's discourse ethics and the feminist ethics of care; and in her assessment of the relations between feminism and postmodernism. In Benhabib's view, what Habermas's communicative ethics most importantly contributes to critical theory is the idea of universal criteria of normative validity which are grounded in procedures of rational argumentation. The danger of Habermas's approach is that it can be interpreted very abstractly and formalistically.

> Unless discourse ethics is interpreted as a participatory democratic process on the part of all those affected, concerned, or influenced by the adoption of a contested norm, it can only be viewed as one more universalizability theorem in the tradition of neo-Kantian ethics operating with the myth of a general interest transparent to all rational minds.
>
> (Benhabib, 1986: 315)

Because of the dangers of over-abstraction, Benhabib argues that the work of feminist ethical theorists such as Gilligan provides a useful corrective to Habermas's normative theory. The 'concrete other' of the ethics of care complements the 'generalized other' of the conditions of discursive validation (Benhabib, 1992: 170). However, it is essential that the particularity and contextuality of the 'concrete other' does not come to dominate ethical judgement, since this would undermine the possibility of critique and change. Benhabib uses the example of the ethic of care and solidarity inherent in the mafia to demonstrate the pitfalls of both communitarian and feminist ethical theories which refuse the idea of external critical standards in morality or politics (Benhabib, 1992: 187). Benhabib wants to preserve the idea of minimal criteria which will establish the parameters of what can count as legitimate in moral and political discourse. She argues, however, that such universalist conditions mean very little unless the general principles are supplemented by the exercise

171

of a kind of judgement that does not involve the subsumption of particular instances under general rules or procedures. Just as both Kant and Habermas turn to aesthetic judgement to bring the abstract and the concrete together, so Benhabib turns to Arendt to mediate between an ethic of justice and an ethic of care.

> Arendt's incomplete doctrine of judgement, by weakening the opposition between contextual judgement and a universalist morality, could help us see through some false fronts in contemporary moral and political theory.
>
> (Benhabib, 1992: 124)

As Benhabib understands it, Arendt's view of political judgement can also be applied to moral judgement and essentially involves the idea of an 'enlarged mentality' through which judgement can acquire general validity without becoming a-historical and de-contextual. This kind of judgement entails a commitment to judging from the other's point of view, or thinking from the other's standpoint; with the other defined not in the formal rational terms of transcendental pragmatics but as concrete participants in public dialogue.

> If we reject Kantian a priorism, and his assumption that as moral selves we are all somehow identical . . . then I want to suggest we must think of such enlarged thought as an actual or simulated dialogue. To *think from the perspective of everyone else* is to know *how to listen* to what the other is saying, or when the voices of others are absent, to imagine oneself a conversation with the other as my dialogue partner.
>
> (Benhabib, 1992: 137)

The problem that remains for Benhabib's version of critical theory is to explain how the imaginary or actual dialogues to which she refers really do bridge the gap between transcendental and empirical, abstract and concrete, which she traces in Habermas's as well as Kant's thought. Arendt's concept of judgement provides the key for Benhabib's resolution of the dichotomies of critique. However, as was argued in Chapter 4, Arendt's appropriation of Kant's concept of aesthetic judgement in fact repeats the critical theorist's choice between reading the identity of empirical and transcendental into history or accepting the arbitrariness of judgement. Arendt does not and cannot explain the nature of judgement or under what circumstances it acquires general validity, except by reference to an orientation of reason itself dictated by the moral law – the ideal of a kingdom of ends. In neglecting the distinction between Kant's empirical and transcendental accounts of judgement, Arendt treats judgement as an inexplicable synthesis that will bypass the question of the ground of her own verdicts on history and the question of the grounding of law in political life. In drawing on Arendt to invoke the *enlarged mentality* which will make multiple conversations possible, therefore, Benhabib takes us back to the problem of the nature of that *enlarged mentality* and the terms of Kant's critique from which it emerges.

In her synthesis of Habermas's discourse ethics and Arendt's concept of judgement, Benhabib argues that she has found a way of rescuing modernist pretensions to critique without falling into the trap of positing unknowable, transcendental grounds for that critique. She goes on to attempt to demonstrate that feminist critics who embrace strong versions of postmodernist theory cannot sustain their critique without lapsing into confusion and abandoning both feminism and meaningful critique. In her article 'Feminism and the Question of Postmodernism' (see Benhabib, 1992: 203–233), Benhabib suggests three specific ways in which postmodernist claims undermine feminist critique and one general problem with postmodernist rejections of utopian thinking (Benhabib, 1992: 229). She uses Lyotard's *The Postmodern Condition* as the archetypal postmodernist manifesto.

The three ways in which postmodernist theses undermine feminism are as follows. First, by challenging the notion of autonomous subjectivity, postmodernists make nonsense of the concept of emancipation as the possibility of women authoring their own existence. Second, by denying the possibility of reading history in terms of grand narrative, postmodernists prevent women from reappropriating their history in the name of an emancipated future. Third, by denying the possibility of transcendent criteria for criticism of social and political reality, postmodernists either abandon critique altogether or restrict it to local, situated, immanent critique which is incapable of the radical social criticism needed to uncover gendered relations of power. Stated in this way, Benhabib's critical theory sounds much more crudely opposed to what she interprets as postmodern theory than, as she admits, is actually the case. The impression given by Benhabib's argument tends towards a caricature of her own theoretical position as repeating the lawgiving role so prominent in Kant's first two critiques. In fact, Benhabib does not assume either a view of the subject as a rational autonomous being, a view of history as progress or an Archimedean point for legitimate critique. Her views of the subject, history and critique itself are all formulated through reference to a combination of *interactive universalism*, *enlarged mentality* and *regulative ideals*; all of which unsettle the possibility of the legislative authority of critique. Moreover, even in Benhabib's objection to the postmodern turn away from utopian thinking, the charge against Lyotard (i.e. that he wrongly identifies utopianism as such with the rationalistic utopias of the enlightenment) is expressed in terms that invoke Lyotard's own language in his account of the game of the just.

> The end of these rationalistic visions of social engineering cannot dry up the sources of utopia in humanity. As the longing for the *wholly other* . . . for that which is not yet, such utopian moral thinking is a practical-moral imperative.
>
> (Benhabib, 1992: 229)

Although Benhabib's explicit critical aim is to move beyond the dualisms of abstract/concrete, universal/particular, autonomy/solidarity, in demonstrating the strength of her own theoretical approach she brings us back to the tensions of that vocabulary and to the difficulty of mediating those tensions. This does not reflect the triumph of Habermas over Lyotard, rather it reflects the persistence of an account of critique which remains within Kantian terms, as an attempt to think through and beyond mutually exclusive oppositions. Benhabib's interactive universalism, when defended against other kinds of critical theory, identifies itself principally as the capacity to imagine the regulative ideals which orient judgement. In the latter claim, Benhabib is explicitly following Arendt, Foucault and Lyotard as well as Kant and Habermas in invoking an aesthetic apprehension of otherness as a way of making judgement possible given the unknowability of the law. For Benhabib to set her own mode of theorizing *against* postmodernism is to risk the reduction of that theorizing and of that of her opponent back into the crude fight between speculation and scepticism; and to underestimate the extent to which her vocabulary is already shared by the 'enemy'.

In contrast to Benhabib's location of feminist critical theory in relation to Habermas and Arendt and her rejection of any strong postmodernist position, Hekman offers an argument going in what appears to be the opposite direction.

> Feminism and postmodernism are the only contemporary theories that present a truly radical critique of the Enlightenment

legacy of modernism. No other approaches on the contemporary intellectual scene offer a means of displacing and transforming the masculinist epistemology of modernity. This fact alone creates a bond between the two approaches.

(Hekman, 1990: 189)

Hekman rejects in turn three attempts to authorize a feminist critical theory (epistemological and normative) on the grounds that they all fall back into modernist, and therefore masculinist, errors. These three attempts are summarized as androgyny, feminist epistemology (standpoint) and Habermasian critical theory (Hekman, 1990: 158–163). The first comes close to Harding's version of feminist empiricism, in that it involves the idea that a proper grounding for theory can only be found when the privileging of masculinist qualities is corrected. In essence the androgyny theorists are arguing for the possibility, if not of a neutral, then at least of a balanced perspective from which to judge. Hekman objects to these theorists on both practical and theoretical grounds: practically, because she cannot see how such a balance is to be obtained within an unequal context of gender relations; theoretically, because she argues that androgyny does nothing to overcome the modernist dualisms in which masculine/feminine, reason/nature, abstract/concrete are completely distinguished from one another; and the former are privileged over the latter. Hekman's objection to feminist standpoint epistemology is that it reverses rather than displaces the polarities of traditional epistemology. It therefore does not resolve the problem of validating the privileged ground of judgement and merely substitutes one arbitrary authority for another. In the case of Habermas's critical theory, although Hekman acknowledges that he has a more nuanced relation to enlightenment thought than the two previous modes of critique, she argues that he remains firmly within a modernist paradigm. In particular, Hekman argues that Habermas remains wedded to a normative theory and a reading of history that asserts, without being able to substantiate, the victory of reason over nature and an abstract conception of emancipation as freedom beyond power.

In the postmodern era feminists cannot oppose the discourses of male domination by appealing to a metanarrative of universal justice and freedom. They can be opposed, however, by formulating a feminist discourse that displaces and explodes the repressive discourses of patriarchal society. Foucault's position, and that of postmodernism more generally, supplies a means of formulating such a discourse and articulating a feminist political practice.

(Hekman, 1990: 187–188)

For Hekman, Foucault represents a genuine possibility of moving beyond modernism/masculinism. She argues that Foucault's conception of power/knowledge and of regimes of truth offers the possibility of making sense of oppression and emancipation without commitment to enlightenment metanarratives and without the sceptical abandonment of judgement. She suggests that there are three aspects to the project of feminist critique which can be identified with Foucault's critical practice: critical ontology; exploring the limits of discourses; and formulating feminist discourse (Hekman, 1990: 187).[7] On Hekman's account, critical ontology refers to the process of investigating how the feminine has come to be constituted and valued in the way that it has. Here the technique of reversal and revaluation, by making strange the common-sense construction of masculine/feminine hierarchies opens up the examination of the limits of those common-sense constructions. In exploring the exclusions and ambiguities of dominant discourse, the material is found for a different construction of the limits of discourse, 'a feminist discourse that constitutes the feminine, masculine and sexuality in a different way' (Hekman, 1990: 187). This new discourse does not have an absolute status but one grounded in context and is itself open to displacement. For Hekman, a Foucauldian feminist critical theory is one which both 'displaces and explodes' patriarchal discourse and involves the positive construction of new identities. In this sense, Hekman's appropriation of Foucault takes us back both to his archaeology and genealogy and to his ethics and raises the question of the relation between freedom and power in the relation to self. Hekman dismisses feminist critics of Foucault who argue that he provides no ways of distinguishing between oppression and resistance, and gives two responses to such critics. The first is that there is a kind of general imperative to disrupt any and every regime of truth/power which claims a universal hegemony – practical or theoretical. This is an assertion of the priority of difference over identity, the requirement always to practise the principle of reversal as celebrated in Foucault's 'The Order of Discourse'. The second is to refer to the centrality of historical location, so that the recognition of oppression is identified as historically and socially specific (Hekman, 1990: 182–183). What Hekman does not address, however, is the relation between the universal critical imperative to disrupt and problematize accepted answers to the question 'Who are we?', and the specificity of what that imperative means in any given instance. It is this relation which Foucault struggles with in his ethics and in his use of the example of the Kantian judge to explain the nature of his critical practice. The possibility of authoritative critique is not resolved through the bringing together of an orientation towards freedom with specific historical contexts, rather it is consistently problematized. Foucauldian critique both rejects and depends on an idea of freedom distinguishable from power; freedom conceived as both the possibility for refusal which is a precondition of power and as the capacity to make oneself a work of art. A feminist theory that assumes Foucault has rescued the possibility of critique without legislative or universalist pretensions neglects the sense in which an idea of self-legislation anchors the work of the critical ontologist. The two ways in which Hekman responds to Foucault's critics separate out the universal and particular dimensions which are in tension within Foucault's conception of the work of the specific intellectual. What Hekman does not do is to explain how the presence of both of these threads indicates the overcoming of enlightenment dualisms in Foucault's thought. In practice, Hekman differentiates the Foucauldian approach to feminist critical theory and defends it against the alternatives by characterizing 'enlightenment metanarratives' as simplistic, dualistic grand theory and skating over the ways in which Foucault's critique remains located in 'the Enlightenment's call to critique' (Hekman, 1990: 183). Just as Benhabib does not explain the bringing together of universal and particular in her concept of *enlarged mentality*, so Hekman glosses over the relationship between the self-constituting freedom of critique and its specificity and locatedness. In doing this, Hekman presents the possibility of being critical in the Foucauldian sense as easier than it actually is, and encourages a reading of Foucault as an authority in a way which his discourse always both permits and refuses.

The feminist critics fight out the battle for legitimacy by subverting the grounds of each other's authority. Benhabib confronts postmodernism with its incapacity for judgement; Hekman confronts Habermas with the unsustainability of his transcendental claims. More interestingly, in the rich accounts each theorist gives of the authority of her own critique, the shadow of the crude battle between dogmatism and scepticism still falls. Neither the Arendtian judge nor the Foucauldian specific intellectual transcends, in the sense of resolving, the question of the possibility of critique. Within the work of both Arendt and Foucault and the feminist critics making use of that work, the dynamics of the Kantian theoretical perpetual peace continue to be at work. The critics shift constantly between different ways of establishing the authority of critique – from transcendent law to reflective judgement to an aesthetic idea of self-legislation – and the equally constant undermining of that authority.

FEMINIST CRITIQUE AND INTERNATIONAL POLITICS

The kind of discussion in which both Benhabib and Hekman engage as to the status of feminist critical theory is part of the context of recent attempts to formulate a feminist theory of international relations. As a project in feminist political theory, feminist international relations theory demonstrates very clearly the kinds of options available for the framing of a critical theory in relation both to an orthodox tradition of thought and to established alternatives to that orthodoxy. It is noticeable that feminist theoretical writings on international politics have been from the beginning embroiled in the task of validating their contribution in the face of demands from mainstream theories and from critical theories. Thus feminist writings on international relations have been dismissed as irrelevant because women have nothing to do with 'the state and its power as a unit of analysis'; they have been warned against 'fragmenting epistemology' by critical theorists; and they have been warned against slipping into claims of a privileged access to knowledge or morality by postmodernists (Hutchings, 1994: 149). Feminist critique of international relations finds itself contested from a variety of directions, both external and internal. Its credentials are under scrutiny by neo-realists, critical theorists and postmodernists. However, at the same time as having to account for its legitimacy to these external judges, feminist international theory is also self-reflexively examining its own credentials; assessing the choices between Benhabib and Hekman as well as between Linklater and Ashley.

For theorists working with an orthodox account of the international realm, the possibility of a feminist account of international relations is puzzling. It is assumed that the international realm and the concepts through which it can be understood are essentially ungendered and that the identity of the theorist is irrelevant to the project of theorizing. The realm of high politics, of law, war, diplomacy and foreign policy is sharply distinguished from the low politics of the private realm, the economy and civil society. The former has a logic of its own, the search for security in the context of anarchy, a logic which does not characterize domestic politics in the same way. In a similar way, the neutral, disinterested scientist of international relations must be distinguished from the partiality of the feminist theorizing from the women's point of view, a point of view traditionally located in the private sphere. This location of feminist theory and of women's lives as outside of international relations proper is reflected in the way in which feminist input into related disciplines, such as development studies, has been much stronger and is much better established than any feminist work in international relations as such.[8] The gendered significance of social and economic global policy making can be accepted, whereas the gendered significance of war and peacemaking cannot. At the heart of the feminist critique of orthodox international relations theory, which is a relatively recent development, is a challenge both to the traditional conception of the international realm and of the relation of the theorist to the object of theory. The first challenge extends the work done by feminist theorists in relation to theories of the domestic state by demonstrating the untenability of the private/public/international demarcation that has marked the understanding of political life in the modern period. The gendered mutual constitution of the public and private realms within the state is argued to be reflected in a gendered mutual constitution of national and international realms. Rather than inter-state relations being governed by a self-contained logic dictated by an anarchic international context, feminist theorists argue that inter-state relations are governed by a complex of economic, social, legal and political relations which are structured in ways that confirm women in positions of subordination and are, in turn, kept in place by that subordination (Enloe, 1989; Grant and Newland, 1991; Tickner, 1992). Like the critical theorists and postmodernists, in challenging the traditional concept of the international realm, feminist critics are also engaged in challenging the traditional concept of the relation of theorist to the object of theory. Feminist critics in international relations again build on feminist critiques of domestic political theory, arguing that concepts and theories which see themselves as neutral and disinterested are in fact sovereign constructions serving specific interests. It is claimed that concepts such as 'power', 'security', 'self-interest' and 'rationality', which are the mainstay of neo-realist theory, in practice reflect and enforce patriarchal values and priorities (Tickner, 1988). However, the indictment of established theory and the re-thinking it involves of the relation of the theorists to their object also pushes the feminist theorists to account for their own critical practice.

It is clear from the above, brief account of feminist objections to traditional assumptions in the theorizing of international relations that they have much in common with the critical approaches discussed in the previous chapter. Indeed, with regard to the challenge to the traditional conception of the international realm, feminists seem to be saying much the same thing as critical theorists and postmodernists. That is to say, they are challenging the distinction between domestic and international politics, denying that states are the only international actors and insisting on the importance of social and economic relations to the international sphere. In re-thinking the relation between the theorist and the object of theory, feminist critics are also following both critical theorists and postmodernists. However, it is at this point that the nature of the feminist critique becomes contested by the other critical approaches. It is the concept of *gender* and its theoretical significance that provides the focus for this contest. The question that worries the critical and postmodernist theorists is the question of what it means to claim that gender is not just an aspect of international political reality which has been neglected but that it affects the way in which that reality is to be understood. Critical theorists are concerned that to understand gender in this way may suggest the reduction of all knowledge to perspective and thus detract from the possibility of critique as judgement in relation to objective standards. Postmodernist theorists are concerned that to understand gender in this way is to suggest gender as the key to knowledge and thus to perpetuate a sovereign politics in theory.

The question of the theoretical significance of gender does not only worry critical theorists and postmodernists, it is continually being raised by feminist international relations theorists themselves. Broadly speaking, there are three different conceptions at work of the theoretical significance of gender in feminist international relations theory. The first and most common conception of gender and its role in critique is characteristic of the work of theorists such as Ann Tickner. Tickner's project in the theory of international relations is clear from the title of one of her articles: 'Hans Morgenthau's Principles of Political Realism: A Feminist Reformulation'. In this article, Tickner takes Morgenthau's principles and the concepts embedded in them and discusses the way in which they have been problematized by feminist theorists. In particular, Tickner challenges Morgenthau's concepts of power and the political, which she argues are foundational for international relations theory. As Tickner sees it, Morgenthau's concept of power as the capacity to control others is a reflection of masculine experience. It therefore neglects alternative senses of power which reflect feminine experience, the concept of power as 'power with' or 'empowerment'. Similarly, Tickner argues that the traditional assumption of the autonomy of the political from ethical and economic spheres in international relations rests on male identification with the public sphere, which itself rests on the masculinist distinction between private and public. Women's experience leads to a recognition of the political within the supposedly private sphere and therefore undermines the masculinist conception of the public/private divide and what follows from it. Throughout her argument Tickner is not proposing that her feminist reformulation of Morgenthau is the basis of a new international relations theory. Instead, Tickner claims that the feminist critique is a step on the way to a new universal science of the international in which both feminist and masculinist elements would be incorporated (Tickner, 1988: 437).

For Tickner it is clear that the theoretical significance of gender is that it provides an experientially grounded perspective which complements that of traditional approaches to the understanding of the international realm. The suggestion is that, when the two perspectives, masculinist and feminist, are given equal importance, then a universal ground for knowledge will have been attained. Tickner's view is strongly reminiscent of the androgyny argument within feminist epistemology with which Hekman takes issue. There are two sets of problems raised by this argument: first, it relies on fixed dualities between supposedly masculine and feminine viewpoints; this seems in essence to affirm the categorizations of orthodox theory rather than to overturn them, and it also raises the problem of how two such opposed perspectives are able to provide a mutual ground for knowledge; second, each of the perspectives is tied to the experienced identity of male and female under certain social, political and economic conditions, and it is unclear on what basis they are accorded their epistemological privilege. Tickner seems in danger either of asserting a fixed, essentialist base for these identities or of dissolving her fully human science into a generalized perspectivism, the alternatives of theoretical dogma or theoretical anarchy which threaten a return to the theoretical options of realism and idealism. It is in an effort to avoid these two alternatives that the second and third formulations of the theoretical significance of gender for international relations have been articulated.

The second view of the critical significance of gender for international theory is of the kind formulated by Sarah Brown in her article 'Feminism, International Theory, and International Relations of Gender Inequality'. Brown is suspicious of Tickner's viewpoint largely because she argues it tends towards the naturalization of gender as a category. Brown rejects any approach to social scientific understanding that grounds itself in a feminine/feminist principle as opposed to a masculine/maculinist one. Brown argues that both feminine and masculine identities are constructions and that to retain the concept of gender as difference is to confirm those constructions rather than to challenge them. A genuinely feminist social science, according to Brown, is one committed to the eradication of gender as an inequality of power.

> The conception of a feminist critical theory of international relations is fundamentally a political act of commitment to understanding the world from the position of the socially subjugated.
>
> (Brown, 1988: 172)

Brown's idea of a feminist critical theory is not reliant on an experiential grounding in the same way as Tickner's masculine and feminine viewpoints are. Instead, Brown invokes a combination of realist epistemology and Habermasian critical theory. From realism (drawing on Baskhar), Brown adopts the view that the true understanding of international reality must transcend appearances to identify the deep structures of international organization. From Habermas, Brown adopts the concept of emancipation or ideal equality as a standard by which to judge global reality which is implicit in historical development. Brown therefore incorporates feminist critical theory of the international into a broader critical theory which relies on transcendental normative standards for the orientation of knowledge. The theoretical significance of gender is not, therefore, in that it directly unlocks the gates of understanding but in that it manifests the presence of structured relations of inequality. Gender does not so much ground a critical theory of international relations as demonstrate the necessity for such a theory. If Tickner's approach to feminist theory raises problems about the epistemological privilege to be accorded to gendered identities, then Brown's also raises similar problems about the status of her own critical discourse. Her account relies on the plausibility of distinctions between appearance/reality and subjugation/emancipation that authorize some judgements of international relations and invalidate others. Like Linklater, Brown takes Habermas's claim as to the transcendental standards of judgement implicit in the logic of historical development, as having resolved the problem of the authority of critique. The result is that critique threatens to lapse into the dogmatic assertion of a key to authoritative judgement and to revert to being a version of idealism.

The third account of the theoretical significance of gender attempts to avoid the subsumption of feminist theory under a universal critical theory, whilst at the same time also avoiding the assertion of a single feminine/feminist perspective as the ground for a critique of traditional understandings of the international sphere. This third approach is represented in V. Spike Peterson's writings. It is a view influenced by encounters with postmodernist theorists both inside and outside the context of international relations, but also by an awareness of the significance of differences and power relations between women in the context of global politics and economics. According to this viewpoint, the idea of a single feminine gendered identity as a basis for either understanding or practice simply does not make sense. Moreover, the claim to such an identity both masks and confirms global hierarchies of power. At the same time, it is asserted that gender is a *lens* through which a deeper and less partial understanding of the international sphere can be attained.

> Feminism and postpositivism are similar in their critiques of dominating ideologies, objectivist metaphysics, and the constitution of body/power/knowledge. But our critical and transformational commitments also move us to situate knowledge claims in order to *become answerable for what we learn how to see.*
>
> (Peterson, 1992a: 58)[9]

In contrast to Tickner and Brown, Peterson abandons the idea of a general location for critique and links her critical position to that of the Foucauldian specific intellectual. However, as a feminist critic, she implies a level and kind of ethical commitment which is not necessarily characteristic of postmodernist approaches in general.

> Post-positivism keeps feminists attentive to the dangers of essentializing and totalizing practices, while feminists extend

post-positivism by exposing the gendered foundations of objectivism and by insisting on politically relevant critique.

(Peterson, 1992b: 204–205)

Given that Peterson does not see the theoretical significance of gender as only meaning paying attention to the position of women in the international sphere, it is evident that she regards the concept of gender as in some sense enhancing the kind of work pioneered by Ashley and Walker. It is not clear, however, in what way gender does make a difference. As gender is the mark of particular traditional patterns of inclusion and exclusion in international politics and the ways it has been conceptualized, then feminist post-positivist international theory can certainly offer an opportunity to theorize from the margins and transgress established boundaries of theory and practice, operating the principle of reversal in the Foucauldian sense. This cannot, however, signify the privileging of gender as a ground of judgement except as one basis for the unsettling and displacement of sovereign assumptions. Yet Peterson seems to want to claim more than this for the feminist post-positivist approach. Even as the possibility of a transcendental validation for feminist analysis is rejected it is reasserted in the claim to know the *political relevance* of critique. The pluralist conversation between feminist and postmodernist perspectives becomes shadowed by a regulative ideal of a future beyond oppression which must orient and anchor the judgement of the feminist theorist on behalf of the emancipation of women.

All feminist theorizations of international politics have two critical dimensions: they involve the critique of the way that global relations enforce and are enforced by the systematic subordination of different women in different ways; they also involve the critique of alternative ways of theorizing world politics. Involved in both dimensions is the reconceptualization of the international realm in richer and more complex terms and an ethical commitment to exposing and enhancing the position of women throughout the world. However, both dimensions also involve the question of how this critical theoretical work is possible. In order to legitimize the theoretical contribution that feminist critics have to make, the feminist international relations theorists become engaged in a struggle to establish what it means to be critical. Both the context of the discipline of international relations itself and of the development of feminist theorizing in general tend to construct both the problem of authorizing critique, and possible solutions to that problem, in terms that repeat the problematic politics of Kantian critique.

CONCLUSION

Postmodern feminism is emerging as a position of negotiation between standpoint feminism, with its conviction that real women exist and lean toward practical-moral imperatives, and feminist postmodernist skepticisms.

(Sylvester, 1994: 12)

The work of Sylvester, a feminist international relations theorist, is typical of a range of contemporary feminist theory which refuses, or seeks to find a way through, the choice between universalist dogma and particularist scepticism; and yet at the same time incorporates a tendency to define theoretical positions in terms of that choice. The language of that critical mediation remains uneasily placed between the vocabulary of transcendental legislation and a kind of critical free-for-all. Like the critical theories of international relations discussed in the previous chapter, feminist critical theories utilize conceptions of critique which, as I have argued in this book, are marked by their Kantian roots. The result of this is that critique is continually frustrated by its own impossibility as the critic seeks to ground and orient judgement. At the beginning of this chapter, I suggested that the implications of this paradoxical logic are twofold. On the one hand, there is a tendency for critique to lapse back into the terms that it is its purpose to transcend. On the other hand, this logic implies the refusal of critique either to fail or succeed in its aims. What emerges from the analysis of feminist critical theory in this chapter is that it is struggling to establish *how* the choice between dogmatism and scepticism is to be positively refused. As with the critical theories of international relations, neither historical location, transcendental law nor the invocation of other philosophical authorities can succeed in grounding and protecting critique. This is something of which both Benhabib and Hekman are self-consciously aware, even as their accounts of their own and others' critical practices threaten to return us to the precritical battles of reason.

CONCLUSION

In this conclusion I will be looking back at the politics of critique explored in this text, both negatively and positively conceived. These negative and positive conceptions suggest the kinds of theorizing that must be avoided on the one hand, and embraced on the other, if critical theories are to remain critical. These conceptions also suggest what implications critical political theorizing has for the under-standing and judgement of political actualities. It has not been my purpose in this text, nor is it my purpose in this conclusion, to argue *for* the idea of critical political theory. Instead, what I am attempting to do is to draw out the possibilities inherent in a mode of theorizing which I trace back to Kant. My account of what a critical political theorizing that sustains itself as critical must involve is one specific to the Kantian mode of critique which I have been exploring. According to my account, such theorizing ends, as it begins, in paradox.

Kantian critique begins, according to his own account, in his dissatisfaction with the unsustainable claims of rationalism and the scepticism of empiricism. The premise of critique is that reason is neither all-powerful nor powerless, but that it is limited. The critique of reason is the process through which the proper limits, and therefore the legitimate legislation, of reason can be determined. The paradox of critique is that it is reason that passes judgement on itself, so that Kantian reason is split from the beginning between the work of the critic and the object of critique. The assumption of the limitation of reason and its power to judge itself sets up a complex structure of antinomies between phenomena and noumena, theore-tical and practical, understanding and reason, nature and morality. Much of the work of the critic involves the striving to connect and synthesize the diremptions instituted by his or her own critical practice. However, the legislation of critical reason proves impossible to ground; and the application of the laws of reason in theory and practice is frustrated by the dichotomies on which critique is founded. In the critiques of theoretical and practical reason, the critic's lawgiving work is perpetually undermined. The legislation of theoretical reason is uncomfortably poised between the inaccessible thing-in-itself and the incomprehensible ideas and ideals of reason. The legislation of practical reason is inherently beyond understanding and also eternally divided from the natural impulses which it is intended to govern but can never overcome. Thus the critic's judgement appears all powerful on the one hand and irrelevant on the other. The critique of judgement appears to offer a way of mediating between the diremptions of critical reason. However, the reflective judgement of taste does not resolve the tensions of critique so much as reproduce them. The authority of the judgement of taste to command universal assent to a particular judgement is mysteriously located both in empirical history and in the supersensible realm. The feeling of pleasure or displeasure that accompanies the judgement of taste symbolizes the bridging of the gap between empirical and transcendental realms, and in doing so provides the critical philosopher with hope, but it does not heal the breaches of reason.

The vocabulary in which Kant describes the practice of critique is a political one. The critic is legislating to put an end to the wars of reason, but his judgement is haunted by the internal conflicts to which reason is perpetually prone. The politics of critique shift between those of foundational legislation and civil war, a politics which is reflected in judgement which mediates between the two. This politics is again repeated in Kant's explicitly political philosophy, which combines theories of right, history and judgement in an effort to bridge the gap between empirical motivation and the moral law, but fails in each of its attempts.

The politics of Kantian critique are most starkly reproduced in contemporary critical social and political theory in Habermas's work. In pursuing the project of the critical validation of reason in theory and practice, Habermas follows Kant in finding himself poised between the simultaneous possibility and impossibility of reason's legislation. In the sphere of ethical and political philosophy Habermas repeats Kant's struggles to overcome the gap between real and ideal in a theory of right, a theory of history and through the invocation of judgement. The political philosophy that results lurches between optimism and despair. The hopes riding on the evolution of the lifeworld and the contribution of the autonomous public sphere rest on the capacity of legality to realize morality (itself a paradoxical proposition) and on the philosopher's capacity to distinguish between the logic and dynamics of development.

Arendt's political philosophy of judgement is designed to avoid the legislation of reason in theory and practice. However, her recourse to Kant's critique of judgement to orient political theory and practice raises the ghost of both Kant's politics of critique and his critique of politics. The political philosophy that results puts legislative power back into the hands of the philosopher. The judgement of right and progress becomes the prerogative of the world spectator, whose privilege it is both to define what counts as political action and to endorse or condemn revolution. Arendt's heroic, agonistic conception of political action is shadowed by the authoritative, though inscrutable, verdict of the onlooker.

Foucault, the critical theorist without a theory, unlike Arendt, consistently refuses to ground his critical judgement either anthropologically or transcendentally. The result is a conception of critical practice in terms of strategy and aesthetics. For Foucault, critique is not the judgement of actuality against transcendental standards, but the challenging and overturning of the limits of existence. The politics of critique inherent in Foucault's work are manifested in the tension between the specificity of critique and its orientation towards an idea of self-legislation. The legislative ambition of critique returns as an aesthetic ideal which both governs and cannot govern the practice of critique.

Lyotard's political thought, like that of Foucault and Arendt, seeks to avoid the legislative role in which the philosopher prescribes an ideal end of history and judges empirical realities in terms of it. For Lyotard, however, the commitment against universal legislation in theory and practice itself acquires transcendental power. In identifying the game of the just with the regulation of Kantian ideas of reason, Lyotard rewrites the categorical imperative as an absolute respect for otherness. The unknowability of the other parallels the unknowability of the moral law in Kant's work and has the same implication in that the philosopher is caught between the necessity and impossibility of realizing the ideas of reason within the world. The result is a political philosophy in which the prioritization of difference and conflict is complemented by the authority of the philosophical judge to adjudicate and exacerbate the differend.

The politics of critique is characterized by a constant equivocation between different ways of establishing the critic's authority and the impossibility of grounding that authority. It is difficult to capture the dynamism of this equivocation between the possibility and impossibility of critique, because it is normally identified with either critique's success or its failure. It is the understanding of critique (both Kantian critique and the critiques of the later theorists) as having either succeeded or failed that dominates debates about the possibility of critical theorizing in international relations and feminist theory. In these contexts, theoretical arguments at times appear to be driven by the goal of demonstrating that what pretends to be critical in fact disguises either a colonizing dogmatism or a passive scepticism. At the same time, the debates of international relations and feminist theorists also depend on the recognition that critique *must* refuse the precritical alternatives that it is seeking to replace and therefore they (these debates) focus attention on how this refusal is possible.

What does it mean to understand the politics of critique as a consistent refusal either to succeed or fail? Negatively, it means that the politics of critique are neither authoritarian nor permissive and that none of the critical discourses considered in this text should be treated as either authoritative or useless. This negative implication confirms both the futility and danger of reducing critique to its precritical alternatives. Characterizing the critical other as a modernist dogmatist or a postmodernist sceptic merely returns the critic to a tedious and unwinnable war. At the same time, it encourages critics to identify their own critical practice as having overcome the difficulties of critique rather than preserving its tensions, thus risking precritical fates once again.

When critique is understood as a practice which can neither succeed nor fail, how can this be articulated in terms of what critique is, as opposed to what it is not? A crucial characteristic of Kantian critical theorizing is the range of roles that the critic plays in the quest to ground the authority of critique and the ways in which each of these roles proves unsatisfactory. This implies that critical theorizing cannot be permanently identified with any specific role (e.g. those of legislator, strategist or judge) and that a key element of genuine critique is its riskiness in attempting the impossible. The fundamentally unprotected position of the critic results in a lack of constraint on the roles that the critic can play coupled with constant exposure to having those roles undermined and transformed. A critical theorization of politics will only remain critical if it retains this characteristic. This implies that when the complex dynamics of the politics of critique are fully appreciated, the critique of politics which follows will combine prescriptive ambition with vulnerability. In other words, critical political theorists will pursue what lies beyond the given limits of the object of critique, whilst recognizing their incapacity to transcend those limits. Habermas, Arendt, Foucault and Lyotard are all striving to practise this kind of critique.

Kant's explicit political philosophy provides the best guide as to how critical theorizations of politics are likely to cash out in substantive claims about political actualities. What Kant's political philosophy demonstrates is a radical openness, both in terms of the philosopher's relation to politics and in terms of its specific prescriptions. The philosopher prescribes the grounding of law in both common agreement and the person of a sovereign legislator; and puts faith both in war and in law to bring about a moral end of history. These paradoxes indicate the ease with which 'the peace of a legal order' can slip into authoritarian or anarchic political alternatives, but they also indicate that critique is never specifically tied to one set of political prescriptions or another. The substantive claims of a critical political theory, therefore, can never be given in advance, whether through empirical or transcendental determination.

If critique is not about specific prescriptions, then Foucault is true to the spirit of critique when he claims that it is a matter of philosophical attitude rather than the articulation of a theory. There is a sense, however, in which this attitude itself constitutes the primary political claim of critique. It is not what the critics have to say about politics, but what they have to say about their own practice that becomes the political prescription of critical political theorizing. Kant, Habermas, Arendt, Foucault and Lyotard do not share the same conception either of politics or of what might count as political progress. Indeed, the very concept of 'political progress' is problematic for the latter three thinkers, implying as it does a substantive vision of an end of history. In spite of these differences, however, the idea of critique as exemplary politics haunts the work of all of these thinkers. The practice of the critic captures an impossible mediation between what is conditioned and what is conditioning – in other words, the critic moves on either side of the limits of reason (or history, judgement, existence, discourse). This capacity of the critic represents the political ideal which is inherent in critique, the ideal of a judgement which is self-validating and a practice which is self-legislating.

The distinctions which critique preserves and on which it is premised are problematized within the practice of critique itself, but critique does not provide the resources through which this problematization can be understood. It is not possible to understand how reason can be self-judging when its incapacity has already been declared. Neither is it possible to understand how the critic works at the limit, when the limit is constitutive of what the critic does. The political ideal which is instantiated in the practice of the critic therefore returns us to the paradoxes of the politics of critique. It is an ideal asserted with an authority which cannot be grounded and represents perpetual striving rather than possible achievement.

NOTES

INTRODUCTION

1 For an overview of Kant's place in current debates in liberal political thought and, in particular, the utilization of Kant in debates between liberals and communitarians, see Beiner and Booth (eds) (1993). The most famous liberal appropriation of Kant's thought is that of Rawls in *A Theory of Justice* (1971); in this text Rawls uses Kant to help to authorize a conception of justice. This is in marked contrast to the critical theorists I will be considering whose thought is premised on Kant's failure as an authority.

2 Throughout this text, I use the terms 'modern', 'modernist', 'postmodern' and 'postmodernist' as they are used in the literature I am considering as a way to characterize modes of theorizing rather than to refer to historical eras or substantive ethical and political claims. I am aware that a great deal of work which can be labelled 'modernist' or 'postmodernist' in social and political theory is not primarily concerned with the ways in which theoretical practice is accounted for. However, because the key concern of this book is with modes of critical theorizing, I am considering 'modernist' and 'postmodernist' arguments only in this context.

3 Arendt's work is used by different theorists in different ways, so that she is sometimes identified with modernist and sometimes with postmodernist modes of theorizing. Benhabib's reading of Arendt, which links her with Habermas, is discussed in Chapter 8, pp. 170–174. A reading that links Arendt to postmodern political theorizing can be found in Honig, 'Towards an Agonistic Feminism: Hannah Arendt and the Politics of Identity' (Butler and Scott (eds), 1992: 215–235; see also Honig, 1988; 1991). A useful discussion of Arendt's thought in the context of my particular concerns in this book is Ingram's 'The Postmodern Kantianism of Arendt and Lyotard' (1988). Ingram argues that Arendt's concept of judgement remains essentially modernist as does her reading of Kant.

4 I am not arguing for a kind of theoretical determinism here, but I would argue that any conception of politics is theoretically mediated, hence the possibility of debate over the nature and meaning of 'politics' and the 'political', as Held points out in *Political Theory Today* (Held (ed.), 1991: 5).

5 There is an exception to this in my discussion of O'Neill's work in Chapter 1, pp. 28–33.

6 Clearly there is a whole range of philosophical antecedents of the theorists I am discussing, and it would be possible to give an account of the critical practice of these theorists without prioritizing their relation to Kant. The figure of Marx could be argued to be more central for Habermasian critique than the figure of Kant, and the same claim could be made for Nietzsche and Foucauldian critique. The extent to which foregrounding the significance of Kantian critique is illuminating of the critical practice of Habermas, Arendt, Foucault and Lyotard can only be assessed in the light of an attempt to do so, and this is what this book attempts. It is a contribution to debate not a resolution of it.

7 Kant was politically engaged in contesting counter-enlightenment developments within Prussia, particularly in relation to censorship laws (see Gregor's discussion in her Introduction to *The Conflict of the Faculties*, 1979: vii–xxxiv; and Reiss's Introduction to Kant's *Political Writings*, 1991: 3–15). Many of Kant's lesser political writings were journal articles intended to contribute directly to political debate. For the political context of the work of Habermas, Arendt, Foucault and Lyotard, see Dews (ed.) (1986), Young-Bruehl (1982), Kritzman in Foucault (1988: ix–xxv) and Readings in Lyotard (1993c: xiii–xxvi) respectively.

8 My reading of Kant is very much influenced by Hegel's response to Kant's work in his philosophy of right and by Rose's argument as to the significance of Kant's critical philosophy in relation both to the characteristics of contemporary ethical life and the resources of social theory (see Rose, 1981; 1984). It is not my concern here to demonstrate the links between Kantian philosophy and particular legal and political conditions, but the argument for a deep link between the two is persuasively made by Rose and also by Caygill (1989); the latter's work is discussed in Chapter 1, pp. 33–36. In the context of this book a proper examination of the relation between critical theorizing in the work of Habermas, Arendt, Foucault and Lyotard and the economic, social and political context of post-war Europe and the United States was not possible. However, in many ways, the tracing of the Kantian legacy in the work of these thinkers cries out for such an examination, because it might answer the question as to why Kant's work remains so central for contemporary social theory, both mainstream and critical.

9 Arendt's and Lyotard's accounts of the political significance of the *Critique of Judgment* are discussed in Chapters 4 and 6 respectively. Another recent argument for the political importance of the third critique can be found in J. Bernstein's *The Fate of Art* (1992). In this book, Bernstein argues that Kant's conception of aesthetic judgement retains within it the recollection of community which has been lost in the political experience of modernity.

10 As with any reading, my reading of Habermas, Arendt, Foucault and Lyotard takes certain liberties with these thinkers. I refer to all of the thinkers as 'critics', 'critical' and engaging in 'critique', though this is not necessarily the language that they themselves use, particularly in the case of Arendt. I justify this common reference through a demonstration of

the relation of each critic's philosophical practice to Kant's critical philosophy. My analysis of all of the thinkers follows a similar pattern. By and large, I follow a chronologically organized trajectory within each thinker's work. Through the exposition of selected texts and arguments, I exhibit the ways in which the critics use Kant and reflect the tensions and ambiguities of Kant's critical thought. I do not give comprehensive consideration to each thinker's *oeuvre*, but I do treat their work holistically and in terms of continuous development (a way of reading which goes against the grain of Lyotard's work in particular). My concerns in this text are quite narrow and specific. However, because I see the 'radical impossibility' of Kantian critique as so important to all of the thinkers whom I consider, I would claim that the liberties I take in my reading do not fundamentally distort the spirit of their (Habermas's, Arendt's, Foucault's and Lyotard's) work.

Because of the range of material covered in this book, a full engagement with the extensive secondary literature available on each of the principal theorists was not possible. I have therefore concentrated on presenting my own reading of the primary texts, rather than attempting to respond to commentators and critics directly. References to secondary literature are confined to sources which help to situate or illuminate my own argument and to texts in which the key debates surrounding the theorists I am considering are most clearly dealt with. I have also not paid systematic attention to the references within the work of Habermas, Arendt, Foucault and Lyotard to each other, except in the context of Habermas's *The Philosophical Discourse of Modernity* in Chapter 3. The main reason for this is that (apart from Habermas) the thinkers' comments on each other's work are not, in general, focused on the nature of critical practice which is my theme.

1 PHILOSOPHY AS CRITIQUE

1 References to the *Critique of Pure Reason* follow the custom of giving the pagination of the *Akademie* edition (Vols III and IV) of the first and second editions as A and B respectively; these are also to be found in the Kemp-Smith translation. Other references to Kant will give the *Akademie* volume number and page, followed by the page number for the translation being used (with the exception of *Religion Within the Limits of Reason Alone*, where only the translation is cited). The bibliography gives details of the translations along with the relevant *Akademie* volume number. As regards the work of the other theorists I consider, I have made use of translated texts only, except in cases where no translation was available; details of all texts used are given in the bibliography.

2 Straightforward introductory expositions of these arguments can be found in Körner (1977) and Scruton (1982).

3 Although Kant underplays the significance of teleological judgement in explaining the principle peculiar to the faculty of judgement, the concept of 'purposiveness' which is central to teleological judgement is also crucial to aesthetic judgement, and both exhibit the mysterious power of self-

legislation which distinguishes determinate from reflective judgement. The teleological aspect of aesthetic judgement, its 'purposiveness without purpose' comes to the fore in Kant's account of historical and political judgement discussed in Chapter 2, pp. 51–55.

4 O'Neill is not using the idea of 'constructivist' Kantianism in the same way as Rawls, though Rawls is certainly a thinker with whom she is in dialogue (O'Neill, 1989: 206–218; Rawls, 1980).

2 KANT'S CRITICAL POLITICS

1 Arendt decisively dismisses the idea that Kant's political writings constitute a fourth critique (Arendt, 1982: 7). However, the work of Arendt herself, as well as that of Shell, Saner and O'Neill cited in the previous chapter, testifies to the interconnection between Kant's critiques of theoretical reason, practical reason and judgement, and his explicitly political work.

2 Most of Kant's minor political writings have been collected in the Reiss edition of Kant's *Political Writings* (1991). References to translations of the following essays all refer to that edition:
'Idea for a Universal History with a Cosmopolitan Purpose' (VIII)
'On the Common Saying: "This May Be True in Theory, But It Does Not Apply in Practice"' (VIII)
'Perpetual Peace: A Philosophical Sketch' (VIII)
'An Answer to the Question: "What Is Enlightenment?"' (VIII)
'Conjectures on the Beginning of Human History' (VIII)

3 The contrast between Shell's and Saner's accounts of Kant's politics, referred to in Chapter 1, exemplifies the range of the interpretations of Kant's political thought that are possible. Differences between interpretations of commentators are often traceable to whether they are relying more on Kant's theory of right or on the writings on history and judgement. Useful collections of current scholarship on Kant's political thought can be found in Beiner and Booth (eds) (1993); and Williams (ed.) (1992). Booth (1986) and Yovel (1980) focus on Kant's philosophy of history; Yovel's book gives a particularly useful account of Kant's philosophy of history as an important dimension of the critical philosophy as a whole; Murphy (1970) focuses on Kant's theory of right; and Riley (1983) and Williams (1983) both provide good comprehensive overviews of Kant's political thought.

3 HABERMAS AND THE POSSIBILITY OF CRITICAL THEORY

1 Habermas's work has inspired a large amount of debate, and he has frequently responded directly to his critics; see Thompson and Held (eds) (1982); R. Bernstein (ed.) (1985); Honneth and Joas (eds) (1991); Calhoun (ed.) (1992). An account of Habermas as a polemicist can be found in Holub (1991). For specific critical discussion of *Knowledge and Human Interests* and Habermas's response, see McCarthy (1978: 53–135); Keat

(1981: 66–132); Ottmann, 'Cognitive Interests and Self-Reflection' in Thompson and Held (eds) (1982: 79–87); Habermas's 'A Reply to My Critics', also in Thompson and Held (eds) (1982: 219–283).

2 For Habermas's own account of this development in his thought, see his 'A Reply to My Critics' in Thompson and Held (eds) (1982: 232–238); White gives a succinct account of the shift from knowledge-constitutive interests to universal pragmatics (White, 1988: 27–28).

3 Communicative rationality is the correlate of communicative action in the same way as means/end calculative rationality is the correlate of strategic action.

4 *The Theory of Communicative Action* is the main focus of discussion in the special issue of *New German Critique* (1985: 12, 35); and of Honneth and Joas (1991). Analysis of the extent to which Habermas has accommodated his theory too closely to systems theory can be found in McCarthy, 'Complexity and Democracy or the Seducements of Systems Theory' and Misgeld, 'Critical Hermeneutics vs. Neoparsonianism', both of which appear in *New German Critique* (1985: 12, 35).

5 It is not the case that Habermas agrees with Kohlberg in all particulars; see his discussion in Habermas (1990a: 119–133).

6 Habermas's concept of the public sphere can be traced back to his early work on the structural transformation of the public sphere in the seventeenth and eighteenth centuries (Habermas, 1989; Calhoun (ed.), 1992). The concept of the 'autonomous public sphere' has a specific role in Habermas's mature theory of societal rationalization, because it constitutes a means of counteracting the colonization of lifeworld by system. Autonomous public spheres include cultural and social movements and pressure groups; they are essentially spheres of political activity that are not part of the formal legal and political structure.

7 Habermas uses the term 'philosophy of consciousness' to refer to a post-Cartesian paradigm of subjectivity, which he argues has dominated modern philosophy. According to this paradigm, the subject is defined as sovereign knower in separation from the object of knowledge, and philosophy becomes the task of bridging the gap between the two.

4 ARENDT AND THE POLITICAL PHILOSOPHY OF JUDGEMENT

1 I am indebted to Christine Battersby for pointing out this parallel; it illustrates very clearly how, even when Arendt is not making explicit reference to Kant, the assumptions with which she is working are fundamentally Kantian.

2 I go on to explore this shift towards a political philosophy of judgement on pp. 92–100. Commentators differ on the extent to which Arendt does successfully bridge the gap between the *vita activa* and the *vita contemplativa* in her work on judgement. According to Beiner, the tension between the two is never resolved and is reflected in the difference between Arendt's earlier conception of judgement as located in the realm of action and her later removal of judgement into the realm of contemplation. Beiner

argues that Arendt only resolves the tensions in her account of judgement by withdrawing judgement into the abstract, disinterested ground of Kant's aesthetic judgement of taste and thereby impoverishing her own account of judgement (Beiner, 'Hannah Arendt On Judging' in Arendt, 1982: 139–140). For Young-Bruehl, on the other hand, the later work on judgement confirms the essential identity of the realm of action and of judgement, thereby undercutting a crude distinction between the *vita activa* and *vita contemplativa*. Young-Bruehl therefore rejects the mapping of the distinction between action and contemplation onto a distinction between transcendental and empirical worlds (Young-Bruehl, 1989: 46). My own view would be that in using Kant to underwrite the later work on judgement, Arendt is using the *vita activa/vita contemplativa* distinction in a way that increasingly reflects a transcendental/empirical distinction, as the discussion on pp. 90–101 will illustrate.

3 Material for all three volumes was delivered in the form of lectures, but Arendt had not completed any of the volumes for publication when she died, and had only just begun on a full version of the manuscript for judging. Enough material was available to make a fairly comprehensive version of the first two volumes posthumously publishable. However, Arendt's views on judgement can only be gleaned from fragmentary remarks in various essays and from a series of lectures on Kant's political philosophy posthumously edited by Beiner (see McCarthy in Arendt, 1978a: 217–230; and Beiner in Arendt, 1982: vii–viii).

4 Useful accounts of Arendt's problematic appropriation of Kant and the selective nature of her reading are given by Dostal (1984); and Riley, 'Hannah Arendt On Kant's Political Philosophy' in Williams (ed.) (1992: 305–323). Beiner's 'Hannah Arendt On Judging' offers an extremely thorough commentary on Arendt's use of Kant's concept of judgement and the problems that are involved in it (Beiner in Arendt, 1982: 131–141). Although, as all the commentators make clear, Arendt is using Kant for her own purposes and therefore reading him both selectively and inventively, I follow Beiner in arguing that the use of Kant confirms the reproduction of Kantian diremptions in Arendt's work. Partly because her reading is so selective, Arendt overlooks Kant's own difficulties in grounding the aesthetic judgement of taste, and therefore her work takes on a philosophical authority which at other points in her work she is trying to subvert.

5 FOUCAULT'S CRITICAL ATTITUDE

1 The charge that Foucault either needs or is concealing a theory of truth or a theory of justice in his work is frequently made (Cousins and Hussain, 1984: 265; Habermas in Couzens-Hoy (ed.), 1986: 103–108; McCarthy, 1990; McNay, 1992: 117). Other commentators are much more sympathetic to Foucault's systematic avoidance of universalist theory (Rajchman, 1985: 2; Carroll, 1987: 129; Bernauer, 1990: 120). The argument I put forward in this chapter is more in keeping with the latter critics than the former. However, I will be suggesting on pp. 121–122,

that although Foucault does not have or need a universal theory of truth and justice, his late work does invoke a general orientation towards self-legislation that plays a role similar to aesthetic ideas in Kant and which regulates critical practice.

2 It is important to note that, in his late work, Foucault characterized his critical discourse as encompassing archaeology, genealogy and ethics (Foucault, 1984b: 46). However, my chronological treatment is not simply a matter of analytic convenience; as will be demonstrated, there are substantive shifts between the critical discourse of Foucault's early work on the episteme, his genealogy of power relations, and his characterization of 'critical ontology' as ethical in his later work.

3 Hacking points out that *The Order of Things* arose out of Foucault's attempt to write an introduction for his translation of Kant's *Anthropology From a Pragmatic Point of View* (Hacking in Couzens-Hoy (ed.), 1986: 238; see also Hacking in the same volume: 32–33). *The Order of Things* is certainly the text in which Foucault engages with Kant most explicitly and systematically (Cousins and Hussain, 1984: 8; Bernauer, 1990: 45).

4 In Foucault's essay on Bataille, 'A Preface to Transgression', the idea of the experience of limit as a sublime encounter is made very clear (Foucault, 1977b: 29–52). For a discussion of the essay, see Rose (1984: 203–207); for a discussion of Foucault and the modernist sublime, see Rajchman (1985: 9–42).

5 This shift is one from archaeological to genealogical critique, though Foucault continues to see a place for archaeology in his critical practice (see Note 2 above). For a discussion of Foucault's distinctions between archaeology, genealogy and ethics, see Davidson in Couzens-Hoy (ed.) (1986: 221–233). I am less concerned with the problem of terminology in Foucault than with the way in which between *The Order of Things* and 'The Order of Discourse' there is a substantial change in Foucault's account of his own critical practice.

6 In Foucault's own work, apart from *Discipline and Punish* and *The History of Sexuality Volume I*, the best source for his reflections on the concept of power at work in these texts is the collection of texts in *Power/Knowledge* (1980b). An extensive secondary literature has emerged dealing with the complexity and slipperiness of Foucault's concept of power; see Dreyfus and Rabinow (1982: 126–207); Couzens-Hoy (ed.) (1986: 51–102); Armstrong (trans.) (1992: 159–211).

7 I am referring here to the kinds of thinking on power that emerge in 'The Subject and Power' (Dreyfus and Rabinow, 1982: 208–226); 'On Power' (Foucault, 1988: 96–109); and 'The Ethic of Care for the Self as a Practice of Freedom' (Foucault, 1991b).

8 This is not to suggest that the analysis of the ethical relation to self in the ancient world is not highly relevant to the concept of ethics in modernity that Foucault is developing in his later work, as the following discussion illustrates.

9 The idea of Foucault's critical ontology as exemplary critique is elaborated in Owen (1994: 210–213); and is also suggested by Rajchman (1985: 2; 107).

6 LYOTARD: PHRASING THE POLITICAL

1 For an overview of the trajectory of Lyotard's political thought, see Readings in Lyotard (1993c: xiii–xxvi); a more thorough analysis is available in Readings (1991: 86–139).

2 Lyotard's terminology and the way in which it changes is rather bewildering. This list of shifts in Lyotard's work refers to *Discours/Figure* (1971); *Libidinal Economy* (first published in 1974; translation, 1993a); *The Postmodern Condition: A Report on Knowledge* (first published 1979; translation, 1984); and *The Differend: Phrases in Dispute* (first published in total, 1983; translation, 1988a). I do not deal with *Discours/Figure* in my discussion of Lyotard's work (discussions are available in Bennington, 1988 and Readings, 1991); however, the other three texts and the vocabularies which Lyotard uses in them are at the centre of discussions on pp. 126–129, 129–135 and 135–140 of this chapter respectively. Readings offers a useful glossary of some of Lyotard's terms (Readings, 1991: xxx–xxxiv); however, as Readings points out, Lyotard's writing resists precise definitions and can only really be understood in context. In the following discussion Lyotard's terms are located within the argument of the specific texts with which I am concerned.

3 The concept of paralogical thinking refers directly to Kant's discussion of the paralogisms of pure reason (A: 338–367; B: 396–432). According to Kant's conception, a 'transcendental paralogism is one in which there is a transcendental ground, constraining us to draw a formally invalid conclusion' (A: 341; B: 399). Paralogisms, therefore, are peculiar inventions of reason, which are necessitated by the ambition of reason to ground the categories of the understanding in something substantive. It is the idea of paralogisms as invention that is central to Lyotard's use of the term 'paralogical'.

4 Lyotard offers a thorough account of the distinctions that he draws between judgements of the beautiful and the sublime in *Lessons on the Analytic of the Sublime* (Lyotard, 1994: 50–76). For an excellent essay on Lyotard's account of judgement in relation to Kant and Levinas, see Beardsworth, 'On the Critical "Post": Lyotard's Agitated Judgement' in Benjamin (ed.) (1992: 43–80).

5 In Lyotard's *L'Enthousiasme: La Critique Kantienne de L'Histoire*, the deep link he perceives between critical philosophy and politics and how this is tied up with aesthetic judgement is explored. It is in this text that Lyotard examines Kant's political writings most closely (Lyotard, 1986: 15–44; 45; 75).

6 This is my translation of the original, which reads:

> Cependant le pathos enthousiaste dans son déchaînement épisodique conserve une validité esthétique, il est un signe énergétique, un tenseur du *Wunsch*. L'infini de l'Idée tire à soi toutes les autres capacités, c'est-à-dire toutes les autres facultés, et produit un *Affekt 'du genre vigoureux'* [ibid.], caractéristique du sublime.
>
> (Lyotard, 1986: 64)

7 This is my translation of the original, which reads:

En écrivant la *Conjecture*, le juge critique prononce un verdict somme toute favorable sur la prétention élevée par le roman à phraser l'historico-politique. La condition dernière de cette faveur est qu'il sera un roman de culture, un *Bildungsroman*, au sens critique de la culture de la volonté, celle de son héros et celle de son lecteur.

(Lyotard, 1986: 103–104)

7 THE CRITIQUE OF INTERNATIONAL POLITICS

1 This is an oversimplification of the theoretical history of international relations as a social science, but it reflects the ways in which critical theorists tend to read the history of the discipline (see Linklater, 1982 and 1990; Walker, 1993). In a well-known article, 'Why Is There No International Theory?', Martin Wight sets up the alternative perspectives in international relations in terms of a polarity between realism and idealism (which he terms 'revolutionism'), with a *via media* between the two labelled 'rationalism' (Butterfield and Wight (eds), 1966: 17–34). The series of debates in international relations theory over the last thirty years has continued to be oriented in relation to Wight's polarization; for useful discussion of these theoretical developments, see Sylvester (1994: 68–168); also see Linklater (1990: 8). A re-thinking of the idealism/realism polarization in international relations theory is given by Griffiths (1992: 15–34).

2 The classical inspiration for idealist theorizing in international relations has tended to come from a reading of Kant's vision of perpetual peace as a moral end of history; or from appropriations of Hegel and Marx in terms of a reading of history as progress (Linklater, 1982: 97–120; 139–161). Realists, on the other hand, derive their inspiration from Machiavelli and Hobbes in their account of the eternal verities of international politics (see Tickner's summary of Morgenthau's principles of political realism, Tickner, 1988: 430–431).

3 Hurrell draws attention to the fundamental ambiguity of Kant's conception of perpetual peace and the ways in which Kant can be read as both an idealist and a realist (Hurrell, 1990: 204). I argue that this ambiguity is a necessary implication of Kant's simultaneous separation and identification of morality and politics in Chapter 2; see also Hutchings (1992).

4 Neo-realism in the work of Waltz represents the former alternative (Waltz, 1959; 1979). The latter alternative is exemplified by developments such as regime theory in Keohane's work (Keohane, 1984; 1989). An excellent example of criticisms of realism (both in its classical formulation in Morgenthau's work and Waltz's systematic structural neo-realism) which do not fundamentally challenge realism's epistemological and normative presumptions is Keohane (ed.) (1986).

5 In the context of international relations, the terms 'critical theory' and 'postmodernism' are used to refer to theorists relating their work to the Frankfurt School (particularly Habermas), on the one hand, and to primarily French post-structuralist and psychoanalytic theorists (including Derrida, Lacan, Kristeva, Lyotard and Foucault), on the other. In

practice, this terminology is not consistently employed within the discipline, although these are the terms which are most frequently used. Sometimes the terms 'critical theory' or 'post-positivism' are used to refer to both kinds of theorizing (although the latter term is more often identified with postmodernism, as in Peterson's work) and the term post-structuralist is also used loosely as roughly equivalent to postmodernism as a mode of theorizing (see Hoffman, 1987; Ashley, 1988; Peterson, 1992a). Within this chapter, the work of Linklater is used to exemplify 'critical theory' and the work of Ashley and Walker is used to exemplify 'postmodernism'; in both cases, the reference is to a kind of theoretical practice.

6 As noted above, this range of thinkers includes Derrida, Lacan and Kristeva as well as Lyotard and Foucault. According to my reading of the work of Ashley and Walker, however, Foucault is the most important reference point, although Ashley, in particular, also owes an important debt to Derrida in the ways in which he reads the traditional categories of international relations theory (see Ashley, 1988).

8 FEMINIST CRITICAL THEORY

1 Elizabeth Spelman provides a useful overview of the problems of exclusion in second-wave feminist thought (Spelman, 1988). One of the most famous contributions to the re-thinking of the concept of woman in the light of radical differences in female identity comes from hooks (1982); see also Mohanty, Russo and Torres (eds), (1991).

2 Rosemary Tong provides an introductory account of the different theoretical strands of feminism and their interrelation (Tong, 1989).

3 My interpretation of standpoint epistemology here is based on Hartsock's version in 'The Feminist Standpoint: Developing the Ground for Specifically Feminist Historical Materialism' (Harding and Hintikka (eds), 1983: 283–310). Harding gives a variety of possible versions of standpoint epistemology (Harding, 1991: 119–137). However, Hartsock's seems to me to be the clearest articulation of the idea of a feminist standpoint as a ground for knowledge that is currently available, and the one that is most clearly distinguishable from both 'feminist empiricism' and 'feminist postmodernism'.

4 It has already been noted how Arendt's work is utilized by different theorists in different ways (see Introduction, Note 3).

5 This tendency in feminist ethical and political theory is evident in a variety of recent collections of feminist debates, e.g. Benhabib and Cornell (eds) (1987); Nicholson (ed.) (1990); Barrett and Phillips (eds) (1992); Butler and Scott (eds) (1992). This is not to say that Kant is the principal reference point for work in feminist ethics and politics, but that Kant is clearly aligned, in these feminist debates, with enlightenment thought in terms of the ways in which his moral and political claims are grounded (see Flax, 'The End of Innocence' in Butler and Scott (eds), 1992: 447–448; 461: n. 5).

6 As is clear from the following discussion, Benhabib does not do justice to the strong ethic of commitment to the game of the just that underlies Lyotard's playful, pluralistic account of postmodernism.

7 According to the reading of Foucault given in Chapter 5, pp. 119–122, the concept of critical ontology would encompass all three of the elements which Hekman distinguishes.

8 This is evident from the articles by Moser, Newland and Goetz respectively in the reader *Gender and International Relations* (Grant and Newland (eds), 1991: 83–157).

9 Peterson has in mind Haraways's conception of situated knowledge here (Haraway, 1988: 583).

SELECT BIBLIOGRAPHY

The amount of secondary literature available on the material covered in this text is vast. I have chosen, therefore, to include only items directly referenced in the text or items consulted in the process of writing the text which were particularly relevant and useful for my purposes.

Aladjem, T. K. (1991) 'The Philosopher's Prism: Foucault, Feminism and Critique', *Political Theory*, 19, 2: 277–291.

Allison, H.E. (1983) *Kant's Transcendental Idealism: An Interpretation and Defence*, New Haven: Yale University Press.

Altridge, D., Bennington, G. and Young, R. (eds) (1987) *Poststructuralism and the Question of History*, Cambridge: Cambridge University Press.

Arendt, H. (1958) *The Human Condition*, Chicago: Chicago University Press.

—— (1961) *Between Past and Future: Six Exercises in Political Thought*, London: Faber and Faber.

—— (1965) *Eichmann in Jerusalem*, New York: Viking Press.

—— (1971) 'Thinking and Moral Considerations', *Social Research*, 38, 3: 417–446.

—— (1973) *On Revolution*, Harmondsworth: Penguin.

—— (1978a and b) *The Life of the Mind Volumes I and II*, M. McCarthy (ed.), London: Secker and Warburg.

—— (1982) *Lectures on Kant's Political Philosophy*, R. Beiner (ed.), Chicago: Chicago University Press.

—— (1986) *The Origins of Totalitarianism*, London: André Deutsch.

Armstrong, T. (trans.) (1992) *Michel Foucault, Philosopher*, Hemel Hempstead: Harvester Wheatsheaf.

Ashley, R. K. (1988) 'Untying the Sovereign State: A Double Reading of the Anarchy Problematique', *Millennium*, 17, 2: 227–262.

Ashley, R. K. and Walker, R. B. J. (1990) 'Reading Dissidence/Writing the Discipline: Crisis and the Question of Sovereignty in International Studies', *International Studies Quarterly*, 34: 367–416.

Barrett, M. and Phillips, A. (eds) (1992) *Destabilizing Theory: Contemporary Feminist Debates*, Cambridge: Polity Press.

Beiner, R. (1983) *Political Judgment*, London: Methuen.

Beiner, R. and Booth, R. J. (eds) (1993) *Kant and Political Philosophy: The Contemporary Legacy*, New Haven and London: Yale University Press.

Benhabib, S. (1986) *Critique, Norm and Utopia: A Study of the Foundations of Critical Theory*, New York: Columbia University Press.

—— (1990) 'Hannah Arendt and the Redemptive Power of Narrative', *Social Research*, 57, 1: 167–196.

—— (1992) *Situating the Self: Gender, Community and Postmodernism in Contemporary Ethics*, Cambridge: Polity Press.

Benhabib, S. and Cornell, D. (eds) (1987) *Feminism As Critique*, Cambridge: Polity Press.

Benhabib, S. and Dallmayr, F. (eds) (1990) *The Communicative Ethics Controversy*, Cambridge, MA: MIT Press.

Benjamin, A. (ed.) (1992) *Judging Lyotard*, London: Routledge.

Bennington, G. (1988) *Lyotard: Writing the Event*, Manchester: Manchester University Press.

Bernauer, J. (1990) *Michel Foucault's Force of Flight: Towards An Ethics for Thought*, New Jersey: Humanities Press International.

Bernstein, J. M. (1992) *The Fate of Art: Aesthetic Alienation from Kant to Derrida and Adorno*, Cambridge: Polity Press.

Bernstein, R. J. (ed.) (1985) *Habermas and Modernity*, Cambridge: Polity Press.

—— (1986) *Philosophical Profiles*, Cambridge: Polity Press.

—— (1988) 'Fred Dallmayr's Critique of Habermas', *Political Theory*, 16, 4: 580–593.

Booth, W. J. (1986) *Interpreting the World: Kant's Philosophy of History and Politics*, Toronto: University of Toronto Press.

Boyne, R. (1990) *Foucault and Derrida: The Other Side of Reason*, London: Unwin Hyman.

Brown, S. (1988) 'Feminism, International Theory, and International Relations of Gender Inequality', *Millenium*, 17, 3: 461–475.

Butler, J. and Scott, J. W. (eds) (1992) *Feminists Theorize the Political*, London: Routledge.

Butterfield, H. and Wight, M. (eds) (1966) *Essays in the Theory of International Relations*, Cambridge, MA: Harvard University Press.

Calhoun, C. (ed.) (1992) *Habermas and the Public Sphere*, Cambridge, MA: MIT Press.

Canovan, M. (1977) *The Political Thought of Hannah Arendt*, London: Methuen.

—— (1983) 'A Case of Distorted Communication: A Note on Habermas and Arendt', *Political Theory*, 11, 1: 105–116.

—— (1992) *Hannah Arendt: A Re-Interpretation of Her Political Thought*, Cambridge: Cambridge University Press.

Carroll, D. (1987) *Paraesthetics: Foucault. Lyotard. Derrida*, London: Methuen.

Cassirer, E. (1981) *Kant's Life and Thought*, New Haven: Yale University Press.

Caygill, H. (1988) 'Postmodernism and Judgement', *Economy and Society*, 17, 1: 1–20.

—— (1989) *Art of Judgement*, Oxford: Blackwell.

Cook, D. (1990) 'Remapping Modernity', *British Journal of Aesthetics*, 30, 1: 35–45.

Cousins, M. and Hussain, A. (1984) *Michel Foucault*, London: Macmillan.

Couzens-Hoy, D. (ed.) (1986) *Foucault: A Critical Reader*, Oxford: Blackwell.

Dallmayr, F. (1988) 'Habermas and Rationality', *Political Theory*, 16, 4: 553–579.

Deleuze, G. (1983) *Nietzsche and Philosophy*, London: Athlone.

Delue, S. M. (1985) 'Kant's Politics as the Expression of the Need for his Aesthetics', *Political Theory*, 13, 3: 409–429.

Der Derian, J. and Shapiro, M. (eds) (1989) *International/Intertextual Relations: Postmodern Readings of World Politics*, Lexington, MA: Lexington Books.

Dews, P. (ed.) (1986) *Habermas: Autonomy and Solidarity*, London: Verso.

—— (1993) 'Agreeing What's Right', *London Review of Books*, 13 June 1993: 26–27.

Dolar, M. (1991) 'The Legacy of the Enlightenment: Foucault and Lacan', *New Formations*, 14: 43–56.

Dostal, R. J. (1984) 'Judging Human Action: Arendt's Appropriation of Kant', *Review of Metaphysics*, 37: 725–755.

Dreyfus, H. and Rabinow, P. (1982) *Michel Foucault: Beyond Structuralism and Hermeneutics*, Brighton: Harvester.

Drolet, M. (1994) 'The Wild and the Sublime: Lyotard's Post-Modern Politics', *Political Studies*, XLII: 259–273.

Dumm, T. L. (1988) 'The Politics of Post-Modern Aesthetics: Habermas Contra Foucault', *Political Theory*, 16, 2: 209–228.

Enloe, C. (1989) *Bananas, Beaches and Bases*, London: Pandora.

Feher, F. (1989) 'Practical Reason in the Revolution: Kant's Dialogue with the French Revolution', *Social Research*, 56, 1: 161–185.

Foucault, M. (1970) *The Order of Things*, London: Tavistock.

—— (1972) *The Archaeology of Knowledge*, London: Tavistock.

—— (1976) *The History of Sexuality Volume I: An Introduction*, Harmondsworth: Penguin.

—— (1977a) *Discipline and Punish*, Harmondsworth: Penguin.

—— (1977b) *Language, Counter-Memory, Practice*, D. F. Bouchard (ed.), Oxford: Blackwell.

—— (1980a) 'The Order of Discourse', in *Untying the Text: A Post-Structuralist Reader*, R. Young (ed.), London: Routledge, 48–78.

—— (1980b) *Power/Knowledge*, C. Gordon (ed.), Brighton: Harvester.

—— (1984a) *Anthropologie du point de vue pragmatique*, Paris: Vrin.

—— (1984b) *The Foucault Reader*, P. Rabinow (ed.), Harmondsworth: Penguin.

—— (1985) *The History of Sexuality Volume II: The Use of Pleasure*, Harmondsworth: Penguin.

—— (1986) *The History of Sexuality Volume III: The Care of the Self*, Harmondsworth: Penguin.

—— (1988) *Michel Foucault: Politics, Philosophy, Culture*, L. D. Kritzman (ed.), London: Routledge.

—— (1991a) *Remarks On Marx*, New York: Semiotext.

—— (1991b) 'The Ethic of Care for the Self as a Practice of Freedom', in J. Bernauer and D. Rasmussen (eds) *The Final Foucault*, Cambridge, MA: MIT Press; 1–20.

Fraser, N. (1989) *Unruly Practices: Power, Discourse and Gender in Contemporary Social Theory*, Cambridge: Polity Press.

Gane, M. (ed.) (1986) *Towards a Critique of Foucault*, London: Routledge and Kegan Paul.

Gerresheim, E. (1974) *Immanuel Kant 1724/1974: Kant as a Political Thinker*, Bonn-Bad Godesberg: Inter-Nationes.

Gordon, C. (1986) 'Question, Ethos, Event: Foucault and Kant On Enlightenment', *Economy and Society*, 15, 1: 71–87.

Grant, R. and Newland, K. (eds) (1991) *Gender and International Relations*, Milton Keynes: Open University Press.

Griffiths, M. (1992) *Realism, Idealism and International Politics*, London: Routledge.

Habermas, J. (1971) *Knowledge and Human Interests*, Boston: Beacon Press.

—— (1973) *Theory and Practice*, Boston: Beacon Press.

—— (1979) *Communication and the Evolution of Society*, Boston: Beacon Press.

—— (1984) *The Theory of Communicative Action Volume I*, Boston: Beacon Press.

—— (1987a) *The Theory of Communicative Action Volume II*, Boston: Beacon Press.

—— (1987b) *The Philosophical Discourse of Modernity*, Cambridge: Polity Press.

—— (1989) *The Structural Transformation of the Public Sphere*, Cambridge, MA: MIT Press.

—— (1990a) *Moral Consciousness and Communicative Action*, Cambridge: Polity Press.

—— (1990b) 'Morality, Society and Ethics: An Interview with Torben Hviid Nielsen', *Acta Sociologica*, 33, 2: 93–114.

—— (1992a) *Faktizität und Geltung: Beiträge zur Diskurstheorie des Rechts und des demokratischen Rechtsstaats*, Frankfurt: Suhrkamp.

—— (1992b) 'Conclusion and Response', in C. Calhoun (ed.) (1992).

—— (1992c) *Postmetaphysical Thinking*, Cambridge, MA: MIT Press.

Hansen, P. (1993) *Hannah Arendt: Politics, History and Citizenship*, Cambridge: Polity Press.

Haraway, D. (1988) 'Situated Knowledges: The Science Question in Feminism and the Privilege of Partial Perspective', *Feminist Studies*, 14, 3: 575–599.

Harding, S. (1991) *Whose Science? Whose Knowledge? Thinking From Women's Lives*, Milton Keynes: Open University Press.

Harding, S. and Hintikka, M. (eds) (1983) *Discovering Reality: Feminist Perspectives on Epistemology, Metaphysics and Philosophy of Science*, Dordrecht: D. Reidel.

Hekman, S. J. (1990) *Gender and Knowledge: Elements of a Postmodern Feminism*, Cambridge: Polity Press.

Held, D. (ed.) (1991) *Political Theory Today*, Cambridge: Polity Press.

Hiley, D. R. (1985) 'Foucault and the Question of Enlightenment', *Philosophy and Social Criticism*, 11: 63–83.

Hill, M. A. (ed.) (1979) *Hannah Arendt: The Recovery of the Public World*, New York: St Martin's Press.

Hillis Miller, J. (1987) *The Ethics of Reading*, New York: Columbia University Press.

Hoffman, M. (1987) 'Critical Theory and the Inter-Paradigm Debate', *Millenium*, 16, 2: 231–249.

Hohendahl, P. U. (1986) 'Habermas' Philosophical Discourse of Modernity', *Telos*, 69: 49–65.

Holub, R. (1991) *Jürgen Habermas: Critic in the Public Sphere*, London: Routledge.

Honig, B. (1988) 'Arendt, Identity and Difference', *Political Theory*, 16, 1: 77–98.

Honig, B (1991) 'Declarations of Independence: Arendt and Derrida on the Problem of Founding a Republic', *American Political Science Review*, 85, 1: 97–113.

Honneth, A. and Joas, H. (eds) (1991) *Communicative Action: Essays on Habermas's 'The Theory of Communicative Action'*, Cambridge: Polity Press.

hooks, b. (1982) *Ain't I a Woman? Black Women and Feminism*, London: Pluto Press.

Hurrell, A. (1990) 'Kant and the Kantian Paradigm in International Relations', *Review of International Studies*, 16: 183–205.

Hutchings, K. J. (1992) 'The Possibility of Judgement: Moralizing and Theorizing in International Relations', *Review of International Studies*, 18: 51–62.

—— (1994) 'The Personal is International: Feminist Epistemology and the Case of International Relations', in *Knowing the Difference: Feminist Perspectives in Epistemology*, London: Routledge; 149–163.

Ingram, D. (1987) *Habermas and the Dialectic of Reason*, New Haven: Yale University Press.

—— (1988) 'The Postmodern Kantianism of Arendt and Lyotard', *Review of Metaphysics*, 42: 51–77.

—— (1991) 'Habermas on Aesthetics and Rationality: Completing the Project of the Enlightenment', *New German Critique*, 18, 53: 67–103.

Isenberg, B. (1991) 'Habermas on Foucault: Critical Remarks', *Acta Sociologica*, 34: 299–308.

Jacobetti, S. (1988) 'Hannah Arendt and the Will', *Political Theory*, 16, 1: 77–98.

Kant, I. (1902–) *Kants gesammelte Schriften*, Berlin: Königlich Preussische Akademie der Wissenschaften.

—— (1956) *Critique of Practical Reason*, trans. L. White Beck, New York: Macmillan. (V)

—— (1960) *Religion Within the Limits of Reason Alone*, trans. T. M. Greene and H. H. Hudson, New York: Harper and Row. (VI)

—— (1974) *Anthropology From a Pragmatic Point of View*, trans. M. J. Gregor, The Hague: Nijhoff. (VII)

—— (1979) *The Conflict of the Faculties*, trans. M. J. Gregor, New York: Arabis Books. (VII)

—— (1981) *Grounding for the Metaphysics of Morals*, trans. J. W. Ellington, Indianapolis: Hackett. (IV)

—— (1983) *Critique of Pure Reason*, trans. N. Kemp-Smith, London: Macmillan. (III and IV)

—— (1987) *Critique of Judgment*, trans. W. S. Pluhar, Indianapolis: Hackett. (V)

—— (1991) *The Metaphysics of Morals*, trans. M. J. Gregor, Cambridge: Cambridge University Press. (VI)

—— (1991) *Political Writings*, trans. N. B. Nisbet, H. Reiss (ed.), Cambridge: Cambridge University Press.

Kaplan, G. T. and Kessler, C. (eds) (1989) *Hannah Arendt: Thinking, Judging, Freedom*, Sydney: Allen and Unwin.

Kateb, G. (1984) *Hannah Arendt: Politics, Conscience, Evil*, Oxford: Martin Robertson.

Keat, R. (1981) *The Politics of Social Theory*, Oxford: Blackwell.

Keohane, R. (1984) *After Hegemony: Co-operation and Discord in the World Political Economy*, Princeton: Princeton University Press.

—— (1989) *International Institutions and State Power*, Boulder, CO: Westview Press.

—— (ed.) (1986) *Neorealism and Its Critics*, New York: Columbia University Press.

Kohn, J. (1990) 'Thinking/Acting', *Social Research*, 57, 1: 105–134.

Körner, S. (1977) *Kant*, Harmondsworth: Penguin.

Kortian, G. (1980) *Metacritique: The Philosophical Arguments of Jürgen Habermas*, Cambridge: Cambridge University Press.

Lapid, Y. (1989) 'The Third Debate: On the Prospects of International Theory in a Post-Positivist Era', *International Studies Quarterly*, 33, 3: 235–254.

Laursen, J. C. (1986) 'The Subversive Kant', *Political Theory*, 14, 4: 584–603.

Linklater, A. (1982) *Men and Citizens in the Theory of International Relations*, London: Macmillan.

—— (1990) *Beyond Realism and Marxism: Critical Theory and International Relations*, London: Macmillan.

—— (1992) 'The Question of the Next Stage in International Relations Theory', *Millennium*, 21, 1: 77–100.

Lyotard, J-F. (1971) *Discours/Figure*, Paris: Klincksieck.

—— (1984) *The Postmodern Condition: A Report on Knowledge*, Manchester: Manchester University Press.

—— (1986) *L'Enthousiasme: La Critique Kantienne de L'Histoire*, Paris: Éditions Galilée.

—— (1988a) *The Differend: Phrases in Dispute*, Manchester: Manchester University Press.

—— (1988b) *Peregrinations: Law, Form, Event*, New York: Columbia University Press.

—— (1989) *The Lyotard Reader*, A. Benjamin (ed.), Oxford: Blackwell.

—— (1991) *The Inhuman: Reflections on Time*, Cambridge: Polity Press.

—— (1992) *The Postmodern Explained to Children*, London: Turnaround.

—— (1993a) *Libidinal Economy*, London: Athlone.

—— (1993b) *Towards the Postmodern*, R. Harvey and M. S. Roberts (eds), New Jersey and London: Humanities Press.

—— (1993c) *Political Writings*, B. Readings (ed.), London: UCL Press.

—— (1994) *Lessons on the Analytic of the Sublime*, Stanford: Stanford University Press.

Lyotard, J-F. and Thébaud, J-L. (1985) *Just Gaming*, Manchester: Manchester University Press.

McCarthy, T. (1978) *The Critical Theory of Jürgen Habermas*, Cambridge, MA: MIT Press.

—— (1990) 'The Critique of Impure Reason: Foucault and the Frankfurt School', *Political Theory*, 18, 3: 437–469.

McGraw, B. R. (1992) 'Jean-François Lyotard's Postmodernism: Feminism, History and the Question of Justice', *Women's Studies*, 20: 259–272.

McNay, L. (1992) *Foucault and Feminism*, Cambridge: Polity Press.

Martin, B. (1982) 'Feminism, Criticism and Foucault', *New German Critique*, 9, 27: 3–30.

Mohanty, C. T., Russo, A. and Torres, L. (eds) (1991) *Third World Women and the Politics of Feminism*, Bloomington and Indianapolis: Indiana University Press.

Murphy, J. G. (1970) *Kant: The Philosophy of Right*, London: Macmillan.

New German Critique (1985), 12, 35.

Nicholson, L. (ed.) (1990) *Feminism/Postmodernism*, London: Routledge.

Nikolinakos, D. D. (1990) 'Foucault's Ethical Quandary', *Telos*, 83: 123–140.

Norris, C. (1993) *The Truth About Postmodernism*, Oxford: Blackwell.

O'Neill, O. (1989) *Constructions of Reason*, Cambridge: Cambridge University Press.

Owen, D. (1994) *Maturity and Modernity: Nietzsche, Weber, Foucault and the Ambivalence of Reason*, London: Routledge.

Parekh, B. (1981) *Hannah Arendt and the Search for a New Political Philosophy*, London: Macmillan.

Patton, P. (1989) 'Taylor and Foucault on Power and Freedom', *Political Studies*, 37, 2: 260–281.

Pefanis, J. (1991) *Heterology and the Postmodern: Bataille, Baudrillard, Lyotard*, Durham, NC, and London: Duke University Press.

Peterson, V. S. (1992a) 'Security and Sovereign States: What is at Stake in Taking Feminism Seriously?', in V. S. Peterson (ed.) *Gendered States: Feminist (Re)Visions of International Relations Theory*, Boulder, CO: Lynne Reiner: 31–64.

—— (1992b) 'Transgressing Boundaries: Knowledge, Gender and International Relations', *Millennium*, 21, 2: 183–206.

Philp, M. (1983) 'Foucault on Power. A Problem in Radical Translation?', *Political Theory*, 11, 1: 29–52.

Pippin, R. (1982) *Kant's Theory of Form: An Essay on the Critique of Pure Reason*, New Haven: Yale University Press.

—— (1985) 'On the Moral Foundations of Kant's *Rechtslehre*', in R. Kennington (ed.) *The Philosophy of Immanuel Kant*, Washington, DC: Catholic University of America Press.

Rajchman, J. (1985) *Michel Foucault: The Freedom of Philosophy*, New York: Columbia University Press.

—— (1986) 'Ethics After Foucault', *Social Text*, 13/14: 165–183.

—— (1988) 'Habermas' Complaint', *New German Critique*, 15, 45: 163–191.

—— (1991) *Truth and Eros: Foucault, Lacan and the Question of Ethics*, London: Routledge.

Rasmussen, D. M. (1990) *Reading Habermas*, Oxford: Blackwell.

Rawls, J. (1971) *A Theory Of Justice*, Oxford: Oxford University Press.

—— (1980) 'Kantian Constructivism in Moral Theory', *Journal of Philosophy*, 77: 515–572.

Readings, B. (1991) *Introducing Lyotard: Art and Politics*, London: Routledge.

Riley, P. (1983) *Kant's Political Philosophy*, Totowa, NJ: Rowman and Littlefield.

—— (1986) 'The "Elements" of Kant's Practical Philosophy', *Political Theory*, 14, 4: 552–583.

Roderick, R. (1986) *Habermas and the Foundations of Critical Theory*, London: Macmillan.

Rose, G. (1981) *Hegel Contra Sociology*, London: Athlone.

—— (1984) *Dialectic of Nihilism: Post-Structuralism and Law*, Oxford: Blackwell.

Rose, G. (1992) *The Broken Middle: Out of Our Ancient Society*, Oxford: Blackwell.

Rosenau, J. N. (ed.) (1993) *Global Voices: Dialogues in International Relations*, Boulder, CO: Westview Press.

Roy, R., Walker, R. B. J. and Ashley, R. K. (1988) 'Dialogue: Towards a Critical Social Theory of International Politics – Ramashray Roy, R. B. J. Walker and Richard K. Ashley', *Alternatives*, XIII: 77–102.

Saner, H. (1973) *Kant's Political Theory: Its Origins and Development*, Chicago: Chicago University Press.

Sawicki, J. (1991) *Disciplining Foucault*, London: Routledge.

Scruton, R. (1982) *Kant*, Oxford: Oxford University Press.

Shell, S. M. (1980) *The Rights of Reason: A Study of Kant's Philosophy and Politics*, Toronto: Toronto University Press.

Spelman, E. (1988) *Inessential Woman*, London: The Women's Press.

Steuerman, E. (1989) 'Habermas vs Lyotard: Modernity vs Postmodernity', *New Formations*, 7: 51–66.

Strawson, P. F. (1966) *The Bounds of Sense: An Essay on Kant's Critique of Pure Reason*, London: Methuen.

Sylvester, C. (1994) *Feminist Theory and International Relations in a Postmodern Era*, Cambridge: Cambridge University Press.

Taylor, C. (1984) 'Foucault on Freedom and Truth', *Political Theory*, 12, 2: 152–183.

Thompson, J. B. and Held, D. (eds) (1982) *Habermas: Critical Debates*, London: Macmillan.

Tickner, A. (1988) 'Hans Morgenthau's Principles of Political Realism: A Feminist Reformulation', *Millennium*, 17, 3: 429–440.

—— (1992) *Gender in International Relations: Feminist Perspectives on Achieving Global Security*, New York: Columbia University Press.

Tong, R. (1989) *Feminist Thought: A Comprehensive Introduction*, Boulder, CO: Westview Press.

Walker, R. B. J. (1988) *One World, Many Worlds: Struggles for a Just World Peace*, Boulder, CO: Lynne Reiner.

—— (1993) *Inside/Outside: International Relations as Political Theory*, Cambridge: Cambridge University Press.

Waltz, K. N. (1959) *Man, the State and War*, New York: Columbia University Press.

—— (1979) *Theory of International Politics*, Reading, MA and London: Addison-Wesley.

Watson, S. (1984) 'Jürgen Habermas and Jean-François Lyotard: Postmodernism and the Crisis of Rationality', *Philosophy and Social Criticism*, 10: 1–24.

White, S. K. (1988) *The Recent Work of Jürgen Habermas: Reason, Justice and Morality*, Cambridge: Cambridge University Press.

Williams, H. (1983) *Kant's Political Philosophy*, Oxford: Blackwell.

—— (ed.) (1992) *Essays on Kant's Political Philosophy*, Cardiff: Wales University Press.

Wolin, R. and Rajchman, J. (1990) 'On Misunderstanding Habermas: A Response to Rajchman' and 'Rejoinder to Richard Wolin', *New German Critique*, 17, 49: 139–161.

SELECT BIBLIOGRAPHY

Young-Bruehl, E. (1982) *Hannah Arendt: For the Love of the World*, New Haven: Yale University Press.

—— (1989) *Mind and the Body Politic*, London: Routledge.

Yovel, Y. (1980) *Kant and the Philosophy of History*, New Jersey: Princeton University Press.

INDEX